The
Price of
Terror

By Allan Gerson

The Kirkpatrick Mission:
Diplomacy Without Apology—America at the United Nations 1981–1985

Lawyers' Ethics: Contemporary Dilemmas (ed.)

Israel, the West Bank and International Law

By Jerry Adler

High Rise: How 1,000 Men and Women Worked Around the Clock
for Five Years and Lost $200 Million Building a Skyscraper

One bomb. One plane. 270 lives.
The History-Making Struggle
for Justice After Pan Am 103

The Price of Terror

Allan Gerson and Jerry Adler

HarperCollins*Publishers*

HarperCollins books may be purchased for educational, business, or sales promotional use. For information, please write: Special Markets Department, HarperCollins Publishers Inc., 10 East 53rd Street, New York, NY 10022.

Grateful acknowledgment is made to the Victims of Pan Am Flight 103, Inc., for permission to reproduce the jacket photographs, taken from *On Eagles' Wings* (edited by Georgia Nucci; copyright © 1990 by the Victims of Pan Am Flight 103, Inc.).

FIRST EDITION

Designed by Elliott Beard

Printed on acid-free paper

Library of Congress Cataloging-in-Publication Data is available upon request.

ISBN 0-06-019761-7

01 02 03 04 05 RRD 10 9 8 7 6 5 4 3 2 1

To the victims of Pan Am flight 103, and their families

Acknowledgments

A work of this nature is, of course, not possible without the collaboration and support of many individuals. But above all, we are grateful to the families of the victims of Pan Am 103, who taught us invaluable lessons in humanity, in perseverance in the face of unspeakable horror, and in how grief can be channeled into a lasting legacy. In particular we want to thank Victoria Cummock, Paul and Eleanor Hudson, Bruce Smith, Bob and Eileen Monetti, George and Judy Williams, Jane Schultz, and Peter and Suse Lowenstein.

We were also blessed with having a publisher, Jane Friedman, CEO of HarperCollins, who appreciated the importance of having this story told and encouraged the writing of this book. She immediately recognized that the families had begun a revolution, so that governments sponsoring terrorism could no longer hide behind the shield of sovereign immunity but would instead have to face the wrath of the families of the victims, accountable for their atrocities in a court of law. Jeff Stone, a visionary, shaped the story and secured publication. And two gifted editors, David Hirshey and Jeff Kellogg, brought to bear their talents in nurturing this work to fruition. We are immeasurably grateful to all of them.

On the legal side of this complicated story, we are especially indebted to Doug Rosenthal, Mark Zaid, and Frank Duggan of the plaintiffs' team for explaining the nuances and intricacies of the many legal maneuvers that were involved in the families' cause. Within the U.S. government, many officials gave unstintingly of their time in explaining the U.S. effort—on both the legal and political fronts, and the intersection of the two—to come to grips with the scourge of international terrorism. Some of them spoke on background, others on the record, and we prefer to thank them all collectively.

Writing this book was, of course, not without its difficult moments and roller-coaster ride of emotions. For keeping us relatively stable, and putting up with us during long periods of obsession, our families are owed a very special thanks, which we readily and gratefully acknowledge.

Contents

Preface

When we submitted the manuscript for this book, the awful events of September 11, 2001, were still in the future. Afterward, as we reread it, we couldn't help but be struck by the connections between the bombing of Pan Am flight 103 and the infamous attacks on the Pentagon and the World Trade Center. We never intended that our story of the Pan Am 103 families' long struggle for justice should serve as an object lesson in the face of another national tragedy. But surely it has something to teach us, after all, because the war against terrorism—or, more precisely, the terrorist war against America—did not begin on the morning of September 11, 2001.

At the time of the bombing of Pan Am flight 103 on December 21, 1988, it was the deadliest attack in history on American civilians. The site of the attack was, in effect, American territory—an American flagship carrier, a jumbo jet with 259 passengers and crew bound for New York's John F. Kennedy International Airport. Some would argue that the first major terror attack against America took place even earlier, in 1983, with the suicide truck-bombing of the U.S. Marine barracks in Lebanon, in which 241 soldiers on a peace-keeping mission died. No meaningful response, military or otherwise, followed. And in 1991, when the evidence of Libya's involvement in the attack on Pan Am flight 103 led to criminal indictments, again no military action was taken. Worldwide economic sanctions were imposed, but in 1999, after Libya surrendered for trial the two agents accused of having planted the bomb, the United States alone was left with the task of enforcing the sanctions.

With no prospect of a military response, and not much likelihood that a criminal investigation would reach the Libyan leaders who ordered the attack, the families of the Pan Am flight 103 victims were left to forge a remedy of their own: a civil cause of action in U.S. courts intended to make governments sponsoring or encouraging terrorism pay for their crimes.

In the aftermath of September 11, 2001, the American nation has been forced to consider things too-long ignored. It is reaffirming the truth that eternal vigilance is the price of liberty. It is also learning that lack of national will leads to disastrous results. Here, the story of the Pan Am flight 103 families' search for justice provides a road map to what could have been done, what was accomplished against great odds, and what remains to be done.

Allan Gerson and Jerry Adler
SEPTEMBER 2001

1

The Darkest Day

It happened on the darkest day of the year, December 21, 1988: a moonless, dank winter night in the town of Lockerbie, in southern Scotland. Overhead, a little more than a half hour into its flight from London to New York, a Boeing 747 had just leveled off at 31,000 feet, making a steady 500 miles an hour against a quartering wind from the west. The airplane carried 243 passengers, most of them Americans flying home for the holidays, and a crew of 16.

We know a lot about these people. The FBI investigated their families and friends, reporters profiled them, lawyers pored over their lives and entered the facts into evidence. A year later, a woman named Georgia Nucci, whose son was a passenger on that airplane, compiled their biographies and photographs into a memorial book with a midnight-blue cover. The faces in the book were mostly young. Even the business executives in first class were mostly in their thirties. The others were families on holiday, soldiers stationed overseas, college students returning from a Syracuse University semester-abroad program. They were looking forward to sleeping in their own beds again, seeing their parents and friends for Christmas.

There were more than a dozen young children on the airplane. LaWanda Thomas, twenty-one years old, an Air Force technician stationed in West Germany, was returning to her family in Michigan with her son, who was less than three months old. Om and Shanti Dixit, middle-aged husband and wife, were flying home to America after their son's wedding in India, with their pretty twenty-nine-year-old daughter and her two young children. They had flown first to Germany, where they caught the origination of this flight, which went from Frankfurt to London to New York and on to Detroit: Pan American 103.

The 747 was a gigantic object, improbably suspended nearly six miles off the ground by the insubstantial force of air flowing under its wings. At takeoff it had weighed a little over 700,000 pounds, about a third of which was jet fuel. The passengers weighed an estimated 40,000 pounds, together with their carry-on luggage. There was 66,452 pounds of luggage and freight in five compartments. Of that vast weight, an estimated twelve ounces, unknown to anyone on board, consisted of a Czech-made plastic explosive known as Semtex, hidden inside an inconspicuous brown Samsonite suitcase. Nearby an electronic timer was silently counting up the seconds. The men who had put the Semtex on the plane had been skillful and deliberate. They had molded it to fit inside the hollows of a Toshiba cassette player, packed the player in a suitcase and filled the suitcase with an assortment of seemingly innocent clothing—although, as it turned out, they could just as well have filled the suitcase with pink sticks of dynamite and written DEATH TO AMERICA on the inside lid, because no one ever looked inside.

It happened just past 7:00 P.M., as the timer closed a circuit that triggered a detonator embedded in the explosive. The Semtex instantaneously transformed itself into a ball of superheated gas. The suitcase had been loaded near the side wall of a baggage container, and the container was at the end of the row, so that when the bomb went off it was only twenty-five inches from the aluminum skin of the airplane. On the other side of the hull was the thin air of 31,000 feet. The blast tore a hole the size of a basketball in the fuselage. Shock waves raced along the curved hull; the floor buckled and the frame cracked at a point just forward of the wings. The front of the plane—the cockpit, first-class, and business-class cabins—was bent back to the right, and in separating, knocked off the number 3 engine, inboard on the right side. Within three seconds after the explosion, the airplane had broken open and begun spilling passengers into the air.

There are questions here perhaps better left unspoken. But the people who loved those passengers want to know how it felt at that very moment. Did the explosion cut off their oxygen and kill them at once? Did it render them unconscious? Or, falling through the black sky toward oblivion, were they aware of what was happening to them? At that instant the fates of several hundred unrelated people were suddenly joined, together with the families waiting and the people on the ground toward whose roofs 100 tons of explosive jet fuel was heading. What, exactly, were they feeling?

Cold, certainly; fifty-degree-below-zero cold, and darkness, and the 500-mile-an-hour wind of their momentum, strong enough to strip the shirts off their backs. Drink carts, luggage, and seats would have turned into projectiles, along with the babies, ripped from their mothers' laps. The cabin pressure, ordinarily kept at the equivalent of about 3,000 feet above sea level, would have instantly dropped to the level of the surrounding atmosphere, leaving them all gasping for oxygen.

And then they would have started to fall. It would have taken a surprisingly long time. A human body tossed into the air at 31,000 feet quickly reaches a velocity of around 250 feet per second, or 160 miles an hour, but as the density of the air increases at lower altitudes it actually slows, and hits the ground at around 120 miles an hour. Those who were tossed out of the plane right after the explosion probably took about three minutes to fall. "They most likely would have a tendency to start to tumble or rotate a little bit," an accident expert testified some years later, "but the natural inclination for the arms and legs to spread would cause them to terminate rotation and somewhat flatten out." Those who remained with the front part of the plane—the cockpit crew and most first-class passengers—fell in around two minutes. The rest of the plane continued flying, at a steepening angle of descent, down to around 19,000 feet, when it abruptly turned vertical and plummeted, breaking apart as it went. Early in that process, the wings broke off, along with a small section of the fuselage near the front of the coach cabin, and the people in that part of the plane fell the fastest. The wings, because of their shape and the weight of the engines and fuel tanks, hit the ground at more than 400 miles an hour, covering the distance in about 45 seconds. With hundreds of square miles of uninhabited fields all around, this piece chanced to land on a street of houses in Lockerbie, where eleven more people disappeared into the 150-foot-long crater it made.

As they fell, they were most likely still alive. All but a few of the bodies were recovered. Most of the autopsies showed fat embolisms in their lungs, evidence of a traumatic injury that was not immediately fatal. Experts interpret that to mean that in the first few seconds after the explosion, people were flung and knocked about in the cabin, banging their heads and limbs (coroners call this "flail injury"), but that most of them survived until they hit the ground. But this is conjecture, because the impact injuries were so terrible, so devastating, they masked anything that might have happened earlier.

Were they still conscious as they fell? Did they suffer all the way down, did they struggle, did they scream? Under test conditions in decompression chambers, in the thin air of 31,000 feet most people can maintain "useful consciousness" for less than a minute. Compounded by shock and trauma, by the breathtaking wind and cold, the lack of oxygen may have rendered them mercifully unconscious. But they were falling all that time, too, toward the warmer and more oxygen-rich atmosphere near the ground, which might have revived them on the way down.

This is not just of theoretical interest. Their suffering was a tort, a legal wrong for which compensation is due, and its precise degree and nature made a great deal of difference. Thus, among the uncountable hundreds of thousands of pages of documents generated by that singular event, there is the record of a two-day trial in Brooklyn, New York, in which a jury of ten citizens was asked to decide whether 259 strangers suffered as they fell 31,000 feet to their deaths. There were no family members present for this trial, as there had been for the months of trials that preceded it. For a day the jury heard experts, hired by the plaintiffs, argue that the passengers would have experienced the initial events as little more than a jolt, leaving them able to contemplate in full measure their impending doom. This was followed by a day in which opposing experts testified that the first seconds after the bomb exploded were a hellish chaos of lethal laptops hurtling through the cabin, of mind-numbing cold and hypoxia. And then in summation, the defense lawyer made the argument that the jury had a duty to console the surviving family members with something that would mean more to them than money. Coincidentally, something that wouldn't cost the insurance companies anything. "Your verdict should send a comforting message to the families," he announced. "It should tell them there is no evidence [their] loved ones suffered in this accident." As if a jury could do that! As if a grieving mother's mind could work backward from a jury verdict to infer the facts of her child's death!

But, in fact, that is just what the jury did. Or, to be accurate, they made this decision in one specific case that was under consideration, involving two passengers seated in row 4 of first class. In theory they could have tried this question again 250 times over; but the judge, Chief Judge Thomas Platt of the U.S. District Court for the Eastern District of New York, applied that finding to everyone on the airplane. Therefore, the courts have spoken. If you ask, did the babies suffer as they were torn from their mothers' arms, did husbands and wives reach for one another as they fell through the dark, did the fathers see their childrens' faces in the lights of the town below, the official legal answer is that they did not. Take from that what comfort you can.

As they fell from the plane, they fell out of their lives. In an instant they were transformed from living presences in the world—faces, voices, hands and bodies—to memories. Their children would grow up, and recollections of them would dim and waver. Their parents would grow old without them and, at the moment of their own deaths, cry out for them. People would have dreams of them, and even in their dreams, dread the pain of awakening to the world from which they had vanished. All that has gone on ever since, and will go until the last person who loved them is dead.

There is a woman, Suse Lowenstein, a very beautiful woman. She was born in Germany and came to America to pursue a career as an artist, and there she met and fell in love with an American Jew whose parents had been in a concentration camp. They married and had two handsome sons and a wonderful life together. Peter Lowenstein was a wealthy businessman who flew his own jet, a six-seat Gulfstream, and Suse spent her time making sculptures, free to work as she pleased and to sell only when she chose to. And on the darkest day of 1988 she was waiting for her husband to come home and drive with her to the airport, where they would meet their son Alexander, who was a senior at Syracuse University. Before he had left for London, he had modeled for a sculpture his mother was doing, and while she waited for Alexander to come home, she worked on this sculpture. And then a friend called.

"Is Alexi home yet?" the woman asked. Her voice sounded strange and her tone was urgent. But Suse was lost in thought about her sculpture.

"Not yet," she answered casually.

"What time is he coming home?"

Suse told her.

"What airline is he on?" the friend asked. That is how the mind works when contemplating disaster. It seeks to give fate every chance to prove it wrong. What airline? What flight number? So many possibilities.

Suse told her.

"My God!" the woman screamed. "Haven't you heard? It crashed in Scotland!"

And Suse screamed back at her: "How dare you! Don't you ever say such a terrible thing again!" And she slammed down the phone, and she immediately felt faint and doubled over, before forcing herself to get up and switch on the radio.

And now, twelve years later, you can see just how it feels when your child or your husband or sister has been killed in a plane crash. Not long after the bombing, Lowenstein began sculpting herself as she was when she heard the news, hunched on the floor, hugging her knees to her chest. She went to a meeting with other people whose relatives had been killed on Pan Am 103 and mentioned this to a woman she met there, who said she, too, would like to pose for a sculpture. The project grew into a piece Lowenstein called *Dark Elegy*. She put a notice about it in a newsletter for family members of the victims. One hundred people said they would pose for her, all of them women. The work required a unique intimacy between artist and subject. Most men would not have been comfortable with the process by which Suse talked the family members through their recollections, then photographed and modeled them in the nude. And the women could not have posed for someone who hadn't lived through that moment herself.

The work has grown to more than fifty figures. They are larger than life-size, with a rough, mottled, brown and rust-colored skin of epoxy applied over a triple thickness of chicken wire supported by a steel armature. Although they constitute one work, the individual figures don't relate to one another; each is within her own impenetrable bubble of grief and loss. Their faces are indistinct. They kneel, clutching at the air or cradling their heads; they are hunched over or stretched out flat, and their mouths are open to scream, or else hang in slack, mute horror. The piece has traveled to various places, including Syracuse University, where many of the victims were students, but as Suse added figures it became cumbersome to move. Now it occupies a large circle on the lawn of Lowenstein's own house, on the water, near the eastern tip of Long Island, not far from where Pan Am flight 103 would have made landfall on its way to John F. Kennedy International Airport. She can see it from her kitchen window. Someday, she hopes, it will have a permanent home, perhaps at the United Nations, where people from many countries can see it and ask themselves if there is anything in the world worth having at the cost of so much pain.

The people whose children died on Pan Am 103 tend to believe that no grief is as great as that of a parent whose child has been killed. You brought a child into the world, undertaking the sacred obligation to protect him—and you failed! How many times had you told yourself you would lay down your own life for her—and you never had the chance! Suse Lowenstein said something like this to a newspaper reporter one day.

Afterward she heard from a young woman whose husband of a few months had died on the plane. The woman was hurt by Lowenstein's remark; it was outrageous and unfair, she said, for Suse to imply a comparison to anyone else's suffering. Suse was hurt, because she knew and liked this woman, but all she had to go on was her own experience, which told her that she had suffered a wound greater than any other she could imagine. And as time passed the young woman married again, and she had a child, and after the child was born she wrote to Suse: Now at last I understand what you meant. You were right.

"It never goes away," says George Williams, a man now in his seventies, whose only child died in the bombing. "We wake up every morning and say, what are we doing here on Earth? People ask, will I ever have closure? And I say, yes, when they close the lid of my coffin."

Another woman was waiting for a man she loved to come home from London. Her name was Victoria Cummock, and she was waiting, along with her children, for her husband, John Cummock. She was a former fashion model, the granddaughter of a Peruvian aristocrat who had served as ambassador to the United States (but she was American through and through and had grown up in the blue-blooded bastion of Greenwich, Connecticut); she had been married to John Cummock for eight years in 1988, and they had three children, Christopher, Matthew, and Ashley. John Cummock, a lapsed Mormon from Utah, was a vice president of Bacardi, the beverage company. He had been working on an acquisition in London, flying there almost every week that month for a day or two of meetings. Then he would fly home to Coral Gables, Florida, arriving home after the children were asleep. On this trip he had left on Sunday and was scheduled to come home on Thursday, December 22. He had invited Vickie to join him, urging on her the delights of the Christmas windows in Harrod's, but she was busy at home. After her third child, Victoria had given up a career in advertising, where she'd been a vice president of J. Walter Thompson, to start her own interior design business from her house. On the 21st she was visiting a house that she was renovating when the news about Pan Am 103 came over the radio. "Oh, that's so sad, just four days before Christmas!" she exclaimed, and then spontaneously proposed a moment of silence to the workmen, who dutifully bowed their heads and stood at attention with their caps over their hearts.

That night she was wrapping presents in the dining room with her mother when her husband's boss appeared at the door.

"Eddie!" she exclaimed. "What are you doing here?"

"Has anyone called you?" he asked grimly.

"What do you mean, has someone called me? About John? John doesn't come home until tomorrow night."

Cummock's boss shook his head. John finished his meetings a day early and changed his ticket to Pan Am 103, he told her. He never checked back into his hotel.

"No, that's impossible," Cummock said evenly. Among the three people present, she was by far the calmest. "John always calls me every day. Well, he didn't call today, come to think of it. But I'm sure you're mistaken. Pan Am would have contacted me by now if he were on that plane."

They turned on the television and the screen erupted into pictures of fiercely burning wreckage and a telephone number to call for information. She dialed it for the next hour without getting through. Then she thought of calling her minister, whose wife was a flight attendant; perhaps he knew of a government number for information on airplane disasters. Ten minutes later the minister, ashen-faced, rang her bell.

"Oh, God," she said lightly. "Don't overreact."

At one o'clock in the morning she reached a Pan Am operator, who immediately started asking questions: her name, her children's names and ages, social security numbers. She now believes this information was used to build a dossier on her, for possible use in defending a future lawsuit. Emphatically, Pan Am's former lawyers deny that was their company's practice.

"I don't want to keep answering questions," Cummock said to the woman on the phone. "I just want to know: was my husband on the plane?"

Well, there was a different number for that information. Cummock dialed that number for three hours more.

"Can I have your name and age please?" the woman asked peremptorily.

"Look, I've been up all night," Cummock replied. "I keep being told to dial all these numbers and nobody tells me anything. I have three children who will be up in a few hours. They're going to know something's wrong, and I never lie to them. You've got five minutes to call back and tell me if John Cummock was a passenger on that plane or I'm going to call the media, I'm going to call my congressman, I'm going to call F. Lee Bailey."

Five minutes later a Pan Am spokesman called back and informed her that yes, there was a J. Cummock on the plane, and no, there were no survivors. So Victoria Cummock would not have been a very good subject for *Dark Elegy*; her sculpture would show a woman sitting at the telephone, taking notes. She spent the next two hours tracking down child psychologists, based on a list she had kept of practitioners who had come to talk at her children's preschool. She wanted advice on what to tell her children. Ashley was three at the time and the boys were four and six.

She didn't get to sleep at all on the night of the 21st, and by the next day, it seemed, all of Coral Gables knew about John Cummock.

"Everybody on the planet showed up at my house," she recalls. "The media all landed on my doorstep. Journalists were sneaking into the house through doors left open in the back; there were lawyers handing cards to people as they walked up the driveway to my house. The lawyer who wrote our wills showed up. He pulled me into the bedroom to talk. He wanted to sue Pan Am for $20 million. John was a brilliant young man with a terrific future . . . I'm looking at him and my mind is screaming NO. He starts talking about things that hadn't even dawned on me: Do you understand, you have three children you have to raise alone, they'll need tuition, they'll need mental health care . . . I mean, he was right about that, I can't tell you how much we spent for therapy, but part of me was still thinking, this isn't really happening, any minute John is going to show up at the front door and it'll all have been a big mistake.

"Finally I said, You have to leave.

"He said, Just tell me: do you know how your accounts were set up?

"I said: You have to leave! Now!

"He had a contract in his pocket for me to sign. I couldn't believe it. Man's inhumanity to man doesn't begin or end with people putting bombs on airplanes."

As was the practice then, the airline assigned a liaison to her, a "buddy." "A ticketing agent," Cummock says dismissively, "they were all volunteers, they took a four-hour course maybe ten years ago, and their first disaster was your disaster. She would call me twice a day and ask, how was I doing? I said, I just want to get John back"—meaning his body. "How do I get him back? Do I call the Lockerbie police? The FBI? The FAA?"

Cummock found a number for the State Department consular office responsible for dealing with American citizens killed or injured overseas. The line answered with a recording listing significant disasters from around the globe ("If you're calling about the earthquake in Armenia, press 1 . . ."), and eventually, after several more choices, transferred her to an operator whose first question was, "Was your husband injured?"

"He fell 31,000 feet from an airplane!" Cummock snapped back. "What do you think happened to him?"

After two weeks, her sister called her from Tortola; BBC radio had broadcast a list of the newly identified dead, and John's name was on it.

Cummock's minister flew to Lockerbie to bring John home with him. Three-fifths of the weight of Cummock's body was gone. He'd been gutted from the knees up by his tray table. But they put his navy blazer around what was left of his torso and stuffed it out, and he didn't look that bad when Victoria and her children saw him for the last time.

Other families were not as fortunate. Most of the bodies shipped back from Lockerbie to JFK arrived in sealed caskets in the animal-quarantine area of the airport. Families were told they had a "shipment," and after they found their way there the caskets were unceremoniously dumped at their feet by a forklift truck. The families were informed the remains were not suitable for viewing. This was a common practice in the airline industry, reflecting a belief that families who view the remains tend to hold out for larger judgments.

One set of parents did insist on viewing the remains of their daughter and discovered they'd been sent the wrong body.

Like most families, the Lowensteins buried Alexander's casket without opening it. "We didn't know any better," says Suse Lowenstein. "We were in shock, really. If I could undo time, I would go back and hold him one more time. And I envy the ones who did."

One man who took no particular notice of the crash of Pan Am 103, except as another tragedy in a world already full of them, was Allan Gerson. Gerson, one of the authors of this book, is also a character in it. Although he set in motion some of the key events of this story, it cannot be told through his eyes alone. The characters in this book mostly fall into one of two categories: they are the relatives of people who died in the bombing of Pan Am 103, or they are lawyers who, one way or another, found themselves caught up in the landslide of lawsuits and legislation that grew out of it. Gerson is a lawyer.

Actually that description doesn't entirely do him justice; his specialty was "public international law," a practice more esoteric even than the kind of international law that deals with multinational corporations and overseas investments. It deals with relations among states, treaty obligations, the definition of aggression, and the limits of legitimate self-defense. Many lay people aren't even aware it exists, and in his darker moments Gerson tended to doubt it himself. If (as students are taught from the first day of law school, in the famous formulation of Judge Learned Hand) the law is nothing more nor less than what the judge says it is, then in a dispute between nations, the law is whatever the parties choose to make of it—generally, with no judge, jury, or court to say otherwise.

Gerson was born in 1945, in the fabled city of Samarkand, in what was then the Moslem province of Uzbekistan, then a part of the Soviet Union. His parents had fled eastward out of Poland just ahead of the Germans; the Soviets, Hitler's allies at the time, welcomed them by deporting them to a labor camp in Siberia. They were freed in 1942 and made their way south, hoping to reach Palestine by way of Iran. But they never made it, and after the end of the war found themselves in Germany, in a displaced-persons camp run by the U.S. Army. Gerson was five and a half years old when his family finally reached New York, and he wasn't even Gerson then; the family entered the country with false identities.

He grew up in New York and went to New York University Law School and Yale, where he earned a doctorate in international law. After working for a few years handling appeals for the U.S. Department of Justice, in 1979 he joined a new unit called the Office of Special Investigations (OSI), set up to identify and deport Nazi collaborators who had come to the United States under false pretenses. He was the new office's first lawyer.

He was good at it, but as a prosecutor he never developed the requisite ruthlessness. The vast power even the lowliest government lawyer could wield over the lives of presumptively innocent citizens, which most prosecutors find exhilarating, troubled him instead. The deportation proceedings were tried largely as civil cases, with much lower standards of proof, and fewer safeguards for the defendant, than criminal proceedings. But the result was often a one-way ticket to face a firing squad in the Soviet Union. Gerson's controversial 1981 article in *Commentary*, "Beyond Nuremberg," expressed his concerns about his work in OSI.

In the summer of 1981 another opportunity came his way. Israel sent planes to bomb an Iraqi nuclear reactor that could have been used to make atomic weapons. From the office of Jeane Kirkpatrick, the new American ambassador to the UN, the call went out for an international lawyer to deal with the tricky legal work of explaining why the United States shouldn't join in condemning the Israeli attack as "aggression." Gerson became counsel to the U.S. mission and to Kirkpatrick. Kirkpatrick was one of Gerson's heroes: outspoken against tyranny, confrontational toward aggressors, tough-minded in defense of American interests. He fought alongside her all through the Falklands War (which played out in the United States as an epic struggle between Kirkpatrick and Secretary of State Alexander Haig over the fine-tuning of American neutrality between England and Argentina), the Soviet attack on Korean Air Lines flight 007, the military intervention in Grenada in 1983, and countless skirmishes between the Israelis and most of the rest of the world in the never-ending war over the phrasing of UN Security Council resolutions.

After Kirkpatrick left the U.S. Mission in 1985, Gerson was well-placed for another high-level job. He was encouraged to apply for the post of general counsel to the CIA, but he didn't want his fate tied to William Casey, who was clearly nearing the end of his career. Attorney General Ed Meese was seeking to create a new position in his office dealing with "international affairs," and that seemed like a better bet; Meese was as powerful and as close to the president as almost anyone in government. As deputy assistant attorney general for legal counsel and counselor for international affairs, he held a top security clearance and briefed Meese regularly on national security matters. It was a potentially powerful job, but, like many government posts, its real influence depended on having the political winds at his back.

Not long after he took up the post, he was visited in his office by a close friend and informal adviser to Meese named (as he chose to style himself) e robert wallach. Wallach was later to become a central figure in the now largely forgotten Wedtech scandal, involving a corrupt military contractor in the Bronx, New York. But in 1985 he was deeply involved in promoting, for reasons prosecutors later deemed suspicious, construction of a new oil pipeline through Iraq to Jordan's Red Sea port of Aqaba.

"Gerson," he announced solemnly, "I have an assignment for you that's the most important thing you'll ever do. You have the chance to make peace in the Middle East. It's all up to you."

Aware of Wallach's close relationship to Meese, Gerson overlooked the fact that Wallach had no official rank within the Justice Department. "I'm going to make peace in the Middle East?" he asked, incredulous. "What are you talking about?"

Wallach outlined the plan for the Baghdad-to-Aqaba pipeline. "It will open up the whole Middle East," he said confidently. "The Iraqis will ship their oil through it and they'll have to have peace with Israel."

"That's great, but what does it have to do with me?"

Wallach leaned forward and whispered confidentially, "Saddam is afraid the Israelis will blow up the pipeline. He wants a guarantee that if the pipeline is blown up, the United States will rebuild it."

"So where do I come in?"

"He wants a letter from the United States saying that if Israel blows up the pipeline, the U.S. will divert aid allocated to Israel to pay for rebuilding the pipeline. That way the Israelis won't even want to blow it up. Reagan met with Shimon Peres. Peres wants this, and Reagan wants it too."

"So I still don't get it: WHAT DOES THIS HAVE TO DO WITH ME?"

Wallach leaned back and smiled. "It's very simple. We need you to write a letter from the attorney general's office saying the president has the authority to reallocate foreign aid this way, and we need it by Sunday." This was late on a Thursday afternoon.

Gerson said he'd look into it. He wanted to be a team player. Perhaps, he thought, this was the way business was done in the Justice Department. Even if the idea struck him as faintly crackpot, he wouldn't have wanted to stand in the way of bringing peace to the Middle East. On the other hand, it seemed to him that once Congress allocates foreign aid and the bill is signed into law, the executive branch can't just decide to give it away to someone else. The more he studied the question, the more convinced he became of this. He drafted an opinion that said there was no legal way to do what Meese wanted, turned it in on Sunday morning, and that was the last Gerson heard about the great Baghdad-to-Aqaba pipeline.

That episode may have marked a turning point in his career as a deputy assistant attorney general. Gerson's skills are conceptual and creative rather than bureaucratic. It was during this period, with free time on his hands, that he became a serious amateur photographer, with a specialty in stark, almost abstract, desert landscapes. A year or two later he left government—permanently, although he didn't know it at the time—for a fellowship at the American Enterprise Institute, which in those years was a kind of shadow government of Reaganites whose particular shading of conservatism was out of favor with the Bush administration. He ran seminars, wrote papers on foreign policy, and started work on a book about his years at the United Nations. It was published in 1991 as *The Kirkpatrick Mission: Diplomacy Without Apology.*

Only he hadn't entirely heard the last of e robert wallach. One day in 1987 he got a call from a *New York Times* reporter named Jeff Gerth, who'd been digging around in Wallach's history and unearthed the dusty trail of the pipeline. Gerson said he could help fill him in, on two conditions: "You keep my name out of this, and you show me the story before it runs." And Gerth gave what Gerson took to be his word.

Two hours after Gerth departed, Gerson was called in for a chat by the independent counsel investigating Wallach's role in the Wedtech affair. A deputy prosecutor named Carol Bruce told him, "The *New York Times* is doing a story tomorrow. We know you're the source."

"I don't know what you're talking about," he said.

"Yes, you do," Bruce responded. "And we're going to subpoena all your records, all your files, all your notebooks, all your appointment books . . . and you."

"My God," he told her, "there's a lot of personal stuff in there. I write poetry in there. Can I look through it and give you what's relevant?"

"We'll decide what's relevant."

Gerson headed straight to the *Times* Washington bureau and marched up to Gerth in his cubicle.

"What did you do to me, you little prick?" he demanded.

And Gerth said, "Look, I didn't tell them anything. They figured it out for themselves. They're not stupid."

"Show me the story."

"I can't do that," Gerth replied.

"Who's your boss, you little shit?"

Gerth said William Safire was acting head of the *Times* bureau. That was a lucky break for Gerson. He knew Safire.

"Get me Safire on the phone or your head is going through the computer screen."

Finally Gerth showed Gerson a copy of the story he'd written for the next day's paper, and of course Gerson's name was all over it. So he stood over Gerth and made him rewrite it to take his name out of it, and he went home feeling a little better about the whole thing.

Except, of course, that he still had to face the grand jury. And Gerson would be there not as a prosecutor but as a witness, perhaps even a target, although his only role in the whole affair had been to try to stop it. That put the experience in a new light. The grand jurors weren't lawyers or government officials; they were fourteen ordinary citizens of Washington, and more than one seemed to be dozing off as the prosecutor droned on about complexities of the Baghdad-to-Aqaba pipeline deal. It occurred to him they were mostly waiting to be sent to lunch. And, he realized, all it takes is for the prosecutor to say, *Okay, people, you want to get home—indict Gerson, and you're free for the day.*

"And in that case, I'm toast."

A good lesson for a lawyer. Every lawyer should have an experience like that at least once in his or her professional career. Gerson, at least, walked away in one piece, and went back to holding conferences, writing scholarly articles and his book about the UN.

2

Pan Am's Shame

Even before anyone in Lockerbie knew what was about to hit them, the disaster was apparent to an air-traffic controller who saw the transponder signal from Pan Am 103 abruptly disappear at 31,000 feet, and the solid blip of the radar return shatter into lights that slowly separated and twinkled on his screen, he recalled, like Christmas-tree ornaments. Years later, relatives attending the trial of the two accused bombers would find this account far more chilling than the testimony of people on the ground, who heard a noise like a freight train filling the sky, who felt the earth shake with the impact and saw the thousand-foot-high fireball. Terror, they found, lay not in the pyrotechnics of the explosion but in the soothing banality of the radio exchanges with the cockpit crew, the awareness of the minutes ticking down to 7:02, the ominous silence and the pinprick of fear growing with each sweep of the radar trace.

In London and in Washington, criminal investigators were already packing bags that night for Scotland. A 747 doesn't just break apart in level flight and crash in pieces (or at least, that wasn't known to happen in 1988; the fuel-tank explosion of TWA 800 off Long Island was still seven years in the future). Beginning that very night, and for months afterward, a small army of searchers combed 850 square miles of rugged Scottish countryside, of forested hills and boggy lowlands stretching all the way to the North Sea, picking up anything, as one said, "that wasn't a rock and wasn't growing."

Twenty minutes later, and the plane might have blown up over the Atlantic and disappeared forever, along with any clues to the bombing. No one knows why bombers clever enough to have built and smuggled the bomb onto the plane couldn't have figured that part out. The usual explanation is that the plane, scheduled to depart at 6:00 P.M., was not actually airborne until 6:25. But Bruce Smith, a Pan Am pilot whose wife, Ingrid, was aboard flight 103 on her way to meet him in New York, describes that as a typical taxi delay; Pan Am 103 was essentially on time that night. Smith's own theory is that in setting the timer in Malta (where investigators believe the bomb was built and put aboard a flight to Frankfurt, connecting with Pan Am 103) the bombers forgot that local time was an hour earlier in London. That assumes, as nearly everyone does, that the bombers didn't want the wreckage to be found. A plane that disappeared over the ocean without a trace would have killed just as many Americans but would have left open the theoretical possibility that it had crashed on its own. Would that have served their purpose as well? No one ever claimed responsibility for the bombing, so we don't know.

From the beginning, investigators were looking for signs of a bomb, such as the distinctive "petaling" of metal around a blast hole. Within a few days, they had found evidence of a powerful localized explosion in one of the 747's luggage containers. Officials announced this finding on December 28. But it was what they'd been expecting all along.

More than a disaster, then, it was a crime. And more than a crime. Although FBI agents dutifully interviewed family members in search of jealous wives, greedy heirs, or disgruntled business partners, there was never any serious suggestion that ordinary criminal motives were behind the bombing. From the beginning the investigation proceeded on the assumption that the motive was political, the victims chosen at random for their misfortune to be flying on an American airliner. To put it another way, it was an attack on the United States of America, and for what the comparison may be worth, more Americans died aboard Pan Am 103 than the *Lusitania*.

And from that singular event effects rippled outward around the globe and forward in time, down to the present day. Other disasters, comparable in terms of loss of life, have receded into memory, but Lockerbie lives on, its legacy inscribed in laws, its victims commemorated in the sacred ground of Arlington National Cemetery. The nose cone of the 747 lying on its side in a Scottish field is an immediately recognizable icon of terrorism. The bombing cost billions of dollars in direct damages, insurance payments, and economic hardship. Pan Am was bankrupt and out of business within a few years, taking with it the jobs of more than 20,000 employees. The deaths shattered the lives of the victims' families, and many lost jobs and businesses in the years that followed; some, indeed, went bankrupt themselves, despite sharing in insurance settlements totaling more than $500 million.

The sinking of the *Lusitania* led to America's entry into the First World War; no military action resulted from the Lockerbie bombing, but in effect the families of the victims waged their own war. Paul Hudson, who helped found and lead the first association of family members, Victims of Pan Am 103, estimates that over the succeeding weeks 100,000 people attended funerals and memorial services for the victims. The relatives were, for the most part, educated middle-class people, with access to elected officials and three qualities the national media found irresistible: grief, articulateness, and proximity to New York City. Their lobbying efforts helped isolate Libya to the point that for most of the 1990s Tripoli was virtually the only capital city in the world you couldn't fly to; visitors had to travel there by ferry from Malta or take a dusty five-hour drive from Egypt. The roster of those who crossed the family members and paid the price is headed by Abraham Sofaer, a former federal judge who was legal adviser to the State Department in 1988. Sofaer, who had been widely regarded as a possible Supreme Court nominee, found his career sidetracked after a fatal misstep in the high-stakes legal battles that followed the bombing. The same episode cost Gerson a job with a prominent Washington law firm, but along the way he helped write a new chapter in international law. Thanks to events he set in motion, terrorists who might be undeterred by the threat of American military force now must weigh the possibility of retaliation by the world's largest contingent of lawyers. Ordinary American citizens have been empowered to hold terrorist states accountable—no less than tobacco and tire companies—by making them pay for killing innocent people in the course of doing business.

Anger provided the energy for these changes. A red torrent of anger flows through the story of Pan Am 103. Over the years people did despicable things out of anger. When a published report suggested, wrongly, that a young woman on the plane might have unintentionally carried the bomb in a gift from an Arab boyfriend, the father of another passenger telephoned her grief-stricken parents to denounce her. People undertook quixotic efforts, such as that of George Williams, who wrote an impassioned four-page letter to the pope in an effort to head off the resumption of diplomatic relations between the Vatican and Libya. Williams felt compelled to apologize to the pope— the pope!—for a letter that might seem "rude, disrespectful or antagonistic." Williams's only child and namesake, whom he called Geordie, was twenty-four in 1988—a strapping, handsome young man, an honor student in high school and college and a first lieutenant in the U.S. Army who was returning to his home in Maryland from West Germany aboard Pan Am 103. The army shipped his body back to the States, and an army coroner told Williams that under no circumstances should he open the casket. We now know that this was a mistake. No one ever regretted having viewed the body of a child or a spouse, but many who didn't have been sorry ever since. When our loved ones die horribly and violently, it is a measure of our love that we can look without flinching at their corpses, at their crushed and gutted bodies, and say, we love you still. In 1990 Williams went to Scotland for the Fatal Accident Inquiry and asked to see photographs of his son's body. This was against the rules of Scottish criminal procedure. The photographs were potential evidence in a criminal case, and Scottish law prohibited their release, no matter how unlikely that an eventual prosecution (a remote possibility itself at that point) would turn on the details of one particular death among hundreds. Williams persisted. The officials relented and sent the photographs to Williams's lawyer, who looked inside the envelope and told Williams: George, I can't let you see them. He sent them to Williams's doctor, but the doctor, too, refused to give them to Williams. Williams insisted. The doctor finally agreed to show Williams the pictures, but only at the hospital. Williams went to the hospital with his priest. He opened the envelope and saw that Geordie's face was gone. Williams recognized him "from the shape of his head, and his hair, and his legs. . . . He ran track and had fantastic thighs." He kept one picture of his son, and his priest burned the others. Williams, a decorated Korean War veteran, a blunt, forceful man who wears a Marine tie clasp, later calculated that he had cried every day for two years after Geordie died. He has stopped crying, but he has not gotten over being angry.

But who was there to get angry with? From the start, investigators had suspected that Pan Am 103 was blown up by agents acting under orders from one (or more) of three countries: Iran, Syria, or Libya. Early on, Iran and Syria, the patrons of a particularly violent group of Palestinian terrorists operating in the Mideast and Europe, were the main suspects. In October, police in Germany—where the first leg of Pan Am 103 had originated—had broken up a cell of this group, the Popular Front for the Liberation of Palestine–General Command (PFLP–GC). They had seized a large cache of weapons, including bombs hidden in radio-casette players and wired to barometric pressure–sensing detonators. Such a bomb can have only one purpose: to blow up an airliner in flight. If an American plane was the intended target, then Iran, one of the backers of the PFLP–GC, had a specific motive in 1988, beyond the perpetual Palestinian–Israeli conflict. In July, the USS *Vincennes* had mistaken an Iranian airliner for a hostile fighter and shot it down over the Persian Gulf, killing all 290 aboard, many of them religious pilgrims. Iran pointedly did not accept American assurances that the episode was a mistake. The Federal Aviation Administration specifically warned of the possibility of an attack on an American airline in two security bulletins in late 1988. If the Iranians were sending a message, an attack just before Christmas would seem like a good way to get their point across. But no proof was ever found, or in any case, produced in public, for this plausible theory. By 1990 attention had turned to Libya, and in November 1991 American and British prosecutors jointly indicted two suspected agents of Libya's intelligence service on charges including 270 counts of murder. Even then, though, the suspects were little more than unpronounceable names and opaque faces, specters in a remote and hostile country, seemingly forever beyond the reach of American or British justice. And so the anger turned to other parties, less directly culpable but closer at hand: to the airline, which was blamed for letting the bomb on the plane, and to the government of the United States, which appeared, in the days and weeks just after the bombing, indifferent to the fate of its citizens abroad.

From the beginning, there was a fundamental difference between family members and the government over the significance of the bombing. To the families it was obvious that an American citizen who was killed by terrorists aboard an American airline was different from one who drove his rental car into a tree on the A40. One was just a casualty; the other an unwitting martyr to his country. The example of the Beirut hostages, who were greeted as heroes on their return, was still fresh in the national memory, and the family members thought their sons and husbands deserved no less. Eleanor Hudson demanded a flag for her daughter Melina's coffin, reasoning that Melina had died because of her nationality. Many other relatives came independently to the same view, although it invites the question of how to regard the deaths of the seventy-one non-Americans (from twenty countries) on the plane, and the eleven who died on the ground. But the overwhelmed officials of the State Department's Bureau of Consular Affairs, which is responsible for legal matters arising between American citizens and foreign governments, had no precedent for these demands. "We were kind of taken aback by the requests for flags and drumrolls," said Michael Kraft, senior adviser in the State Department's Office of Counter-Terrorism. "These were private citizens, except for the ones in the military. We didn't do that for civilians." No officials were on hand to lend a touch of dignity when the remains of the victims were returned to American soil, at a cargo warehouse in an obscure corner of JFK.

The families looked for solace to the White House, but the Reagan administration, ordinarily quick to defend American interests, was oddly reticent about the attack. Partly this was an accident of the calendar. The bombing took place just before Christmas, with less than a month of Reagan's term remaining. In 1988 the Cold War was on its way to ending, and the administration had no appetite to take on new crusades. And as soon as George Bush took office, the bombing was something that happened on someone else's watch.

For almost a week, following a token expression of sympathy from spokesman Marlin Fitzwater, there was silence from the White House. That was in conspicuous contrast to the reaction following another attack on a civilian airliner, the 1983 Soviet shootdown of Korean Air Lines flight 007, which accidentally crossed into Soviet airspace on a flight from Anchorage to Seoul. Like the Pan Am 103 victims, the 269 passengers and crew aboard the Korean plane were sacrificed to make a political point—in one case, that even America's flagship carrier was not immune to attack from enemies of the United States; in the other, that Soviet airspace could not be violated with impunity. But the earlier episode involved a foreign country's flagship, and only around thirty-five Americans died (although one of them was a congressman from Georgia, Larry McDonald.) The Soviets probably intended a warning to South Korea and other Western allies, rather than a direct attack on America. Yet the KAL 007 episode was treated as a matter of the gravest national concern. President Reagan gave a speech from the Oval Office. Kirkpatrick was summoned back from vacation to the UN; in a speech largely written by Gerson she denounced the bombing to the Security Council as showing "the true face of Soviet perfidy"—the strongest language heard there from an American representative since the Cuban missile crisis of 1962.

Reagan did eventually take note of the Lockerbie bombing, promising on December 28 "to make every effort we can to find out who was guilty of this savage and tragic thing." But the context of his remarks (a statement issued to reporters as he prepared to fly to Palm Springs for a

New Year's holiday) suggested something less than a second Pearl Harbor. The *New York Times* relegated this statement to page 10, along with a less-than-ringing declaration from President-elect George Bush (en route to a fishing expedition in Alabama) of his administration's intent to "punish [the bombers] firmly, decisively . . . if you could ever find them."

The families' suspicions were inflamed as well by the now-infamous "Helsinki warning." And who could blame them? On December 5, 1988, a man speaking English with a thick Arabic accent telephoned the U.S. embassy in Finland to report a bomb threat against a U.S. airliner. Some of the details he provided—such as a mysterious Finnish woman who was supposed to smuggle the bomb aboard the plane on behalf of a Palestinian accomplice—do not correspond to the facts of the Pan Am bombing. The caller was known to Finnish authorities, and he had warned of several other bombings that had never taken place. Investigators have concluded that the man he named in the plot was actually guilty of nothing more than stealing the caller's girlfriend. But he specified Pan Am as the target. The bomb, he said, was going to be put aboard a plane in Frankfurt, Germany, which is where Pan Am 103 originated before its stop in London. The time frame for the attack was the next two weeks. Pan Am 103 blew up sixteen days later.

In other words, the Helsinki warning was almost certainly a hoax, but it was also essentially correct—adding up to an epistemological nightmare, even for people who were not half-mad with grief. It might never have come to light, except that in the time it took for the warning to be investigated and discounted, it had made a bureaucratic round-trip from the State Department to the Federal Aviation Administration and back to State, which transmitted it to various European embassies. On December 13 an "administrative notice" was posted in the American embassy in Moscow regarding the threat. It noted that the FAA "reports that the reliability of the information cannot be assessed at this point . . . In view of the lack of confirmation of this information, post leaves to the discretion of individual travelers any decisions on altering personal travel plans." Several thousand people, including most of the Americans in Moscow on official business, were believed to have seen it. That included a number of journalists, but under the guidelines at the time, no one put out a press release aimed at the public, and there were no stories in American newspapers in the days before December 21.

To many of the families this was proof that the government, in protecting its own, had shown cruel, if not actually criminal, indifference to the lives of their loved ones. That is true even of those who acknowledge that the warning probably was a hoax, or those who admit that many passengers probably wouldn't have paid much attention to the tentatively worded notice anyway. Rebooking a one-way ticket from London to New York just before Christmas can be difficult and expensive. Daniel and Susan Cohen, whose beautiful and high-spirited daughter, Theodora, died in the bombing, are famously confrontational and persistent critics of the government. For a dozen years their names on a call slip have struck fear into bureaucrats. In a book they wrote together last year, they say that if the warning had been publicized, they would have insisted on finding another flight for Theo. But, as they say, "Theo would probably have chosen to ignore it; most twenty-year-olds think they are immortal."

For years afterward, rumors circulated about mysterious figures who canceled reservations on Pan Am 103 at the last moment, presumably tipped off by some more authoritative source than a lovesick immigrant in Finland. An Army combat engineer named Chris Revell had been scheduled to return home with his wife aboard that flight, but he left a few days early instead. Chris Revell's father, Oliver "Buck" Revell, was the deputy director of the FBI; this was the kind of factoid that could give rise to no end of conspiracy theorizing. Some family members found it suspicious that the 747, with more than 400 seats, carried only 243 passengers at one of the busiest travel times of the year. Ominously, they reported that at various points in the weeks before December 21, students trying to book a seat on the flight were told it was sold out. A presidential commission would eventually analyze the booking history of Pan Am 103 and conclude that there were "no unusual patterns" of cancellations; the passenger load was consistent with comparable flights on other days and in prior years. At various times, though, certain classes of fares were sold out, which is why some students were unable to make reservations. The secret-warning scenarios are a subset of the Pan Am 103 conspiracy theories, overlapping (but logically inconsistent with) the belief that the bombers were targeting specific passengers with connections to American intelligence. In a book published in 1990, *The Fall of Pan Am 103,* the journalists Steven Emerson and Brian Duffy identified at least one CIA agent aboard the plane, two employees of the State Department's Bureau of Diplomatic Security, and a major in Army intelligence who had been on an extremely sensitive mission in Beirut, helping to locate the American hostages held captive there. The fact that *they* didn't know the plane would be bombed should dispel suspicions that other random travelers were tipped off in advance, but some people drew the opposite conclusion, that the plot to blow up the airplane was deeper and more sinister than anyone could have imagined.

Paul Hudson was in Lockerbie when he heard about the Helsinki warning for the first time. He'd been in the first group of Americans to arrive there, late on the afternoon of December 23—after politely but insistently fending off a phalanx of Pan Am officials who tried to keep him, first, in New York, and then in London. The journey ended with a circuitous bus trip from Edinburgh that appeared timed to deliver the relatives to Lockerbie under cover of darkness. "Every reporter in Europe was there," he says, "and they wanted to keep us away from the reporters." His only goal at that time was to identify his daughter Melina's body and bring her home to be buried—he had stopped off at the dentist on his way to the airport and collected Melina's dental records—but found himself distracted by what he was reading in the papers. A British tabloid carried a screamer about the Helsinki warning: WHY WEREN'T THEY TOLD? It gave him plenty to think about during the week it took for the authorities to come up with his daughter's body. Meanwhile more families were arriving.

"When I was in Lockerbie," Hudson says, "I passed around a sheet for family members to sign up for a newsletter, something that could tidy things up, maybe get answers to some questions and provide some mutual emotional support. Then it became something very different. The galvanizing thing was the non-response of our government, the total lack of communication with family members. That really enraged many people. The other thing was the lack of help in basic things like identifying bodies, collecting personal effects, and transporting bodies back to the United States. For a while it looked like it was going to take months. That upset a lot of people too."

And if Hudson, who was a lawyer and an expert in victims' rights, was having trouble getting things done in Lockerbie, it certainly wasn't any easier for Victoria Cummock, an interior designer in Coral Gables, Florida. "I assumed it was just me, because I was off down here in Florida," she says, "and everyone else was in New York or in Washington, they were getting the answers. Then I discovered no one knew anything, anywhere." The Consular Affairs office set up a working group to deal with the disaster, the largest mass death in peacetime of American citizens abroad. Fifteen to twenty consular-affairs officers manned a long rectangular table, fielding questions from both family members and the press, in what Michael Kraft described as a "frenzied, but not chaotic" operation. But their operations were hampered by the fact that, for two days after the crash, they were working from a passenger list supplied by Pan Am that had only surnames and first initials; the State Department later said that it lacked legal authority to demand a complete manifest from the airline, and no ranking government official took the obvious step of calling any of the company's top executives. When they finally obtained the list, "the Department began notifying Pan Am 103 next of kin by telephone," according to the official report of the investigative commission, "but stopped doing so after some who had been contacted by Pan Am objected to being contacted again . . ." On the other hand, the families that *didn't* get called by the State Department interpreted the silence as indifference. At least a few insisted they were never contacted, although the working group's records show they were. Authorities in Scotland were equally overwhelmed, and for the first week after the bombing the process of identifying and releasing the remains went agonizingly slowly. The Scottish police initially seemed determined to hold on to the bodies as evidence until the crime was solved. Bruce Smith, the Pan Am captain whose wife died aboard the plane, eventually turned to the London tabloids for assistance, and after a front-page story his wife's body was returned to him the next day; it helped, naturally, that his wife was English. For family members waiting back in the States, though, relying for information on a phone link to an overworked clerk in Washington, the delay was just one more bit of evidence that their government didn't care about them.

What they were finding out about Pan Am was even worse. Pan Am, for most of the postwar decades, was not just another airline but the de facto national airline of the United States and, therefore, a natural target for terrorists. In 1970 a Pan Am plane flying from Amsterdam to New York had been hijacked by two Palestinian gunmen and flown to Beirut and then Cairo; after ordering everyone off, the gunmen blew up the plane on the ground. Three years later, 30 people were killed when guerrillas attacked passengers boarding a Pan Am airliner in Rome. In the years since, Pan Am had mostly escaped the scattered attacks on airliners that took place around the globe, averaging about three a year. Not all of them were political, and most did not destroy an airliner in flight. The most serious was the June 23, 1985, bombing of an Air India 747 as it approached the Irish coast on a flight from Toronto to London; all 329 people aboard were killed. Until two hijacked 767s were flown into the World Trade Center in New York, this was the largest death toll of any act of air sabotage in history. Sikh separatists were blamed for the Air India attack. Around the same time, a radical Islamic group hijacked a TWA flight from Athens to Rome and held 39 Americans captive on the ground in Beirut for seventeen days. All were eventually freed except for a U.S. Navy diver named Robert Stethem, who was killed and hurled to the ground from the airplane.

The TWA hijacking, which played out endlessly in the American media, led to calls for tighter aviation security, some of which were incorporated into new FAA regulations. Pan Am met the challenge in its own way, with an advertising campaign. It took out full-page ads, signed by its chairman, C. Edward Acker, boasting of plans for "one of the most far-reaching security programs in our industry. A program that will screen passengers, employees, airport facilities, baggage and aircraft with unrelenting thoroughness." A new subsidiary, called Alert Management Systems, was formed to implement the program using "Pan Am's own highly-trained security experts and many of the most sophisticated screening devices in the world . . ." News shows covered the inauguration of the Alert program at JFK on June 12, 1986, with highly trained security experts patrolling the ticket counters with their crack bomb-sniffing dogs. Naturally such extraordinary safety came at a cost, and to pay for it Pan Am instituted a surcharge of $5 a ticket on flights to and from Europe—projected to raise a total of around $17 million a year.

But the whole idea was merely to reassure customers. It wasn't going to stop them any other way, unless the terrorists were scared of dogs. "One of the most far-reaching security programs in the industry" had been thrown together in a month, following a meeting of Chairman Acker, Chief Operating Officer Martin R. Shugrue, and a mid-level Pan Am executive named Fred Ford. At Pan Am's trial in 1992, Ford testified that Shugrue and Acker had expressed "very sincere concern over the declining load factors" on transatlantic flights—in other words, they weren't selling enough tickets. They blamed this on "the fear of safety, or lack of safety, and the fear of terrorism," and asked Ford to put together a program to "restore customer confidence." Since the summer travel season, which could make or break Pan Am's profits for the year, was about to start, they gave him five weeks to do it. They did not, however, give him the $17 million they expected to collect from the safety surcharge on tickets; that money went into the corporation's general revenues. Under the circumstances, the easiest thing to do was terminate Pan Am's contract with Wackenhut, which had been supplying security at their JFK Worldport, and rehire most of the same guards, magically transformed by new uniforms into Alert's "highly trained security experts." The bomb-sniffing dogs never turned up any bombs—not too surprising, since they were actually ordinary German shepherds leased from a Long Island kennel.

The company did invest in a study by one of the world's leading experts on airline security, the former chief of security for El Al, Isaac Yeffet. But when they received his report in September 1986, they didn't like what Yeffet's company, KPI Ltd., had found. "Pan Am is highly vulnerable to most forms of terrorist attack," KPI concluded. The airline offered "virtually no training program for the security staff, not even at the senior officer level." Counter and gate personnel frequently neglected to ask the required questions intended to select passengers for more intensive screening. "Pan Am is almost totally vulnerable to a midair explosion through explosive charges concealed in the cargo," KPI wrote. "It must be regarded as good fortune that, for the time being, no disastrous act of terrorism has struck the corporation." Senior managers, who buried the study, later testified that they thought Yeffet was trying to shake them down for a lucrative ongoing contract.

Meanwhile the new FAA security rules had taken effect, but Pan Am's "far-reaching" security program hadn't bothered to comply with them. FAA officials summoned Pan Am's European security executives to an unusual meeting in Brussels to discuss numerous lapses. One in particular stands out in retrospect, relating to baggage handling at designated high-risk airports, including both Heathrow (a natural target for the Irish Republican Army) and Frankfurt (the busiest airport in Europe, and a major transfer point for flights from Eastern Europe and the Mideast). The rule was intended to deal with the threat of a bomb smuggled onto an airplane in luggage. Terrorists had gone to a lot of trouble to put bombs onto planes, including romancing unsuspecting women passengers and giving them gifts to take on board; in the spring of 1986 El Al had narrowly averted a disaster at Heathrow when they discovered just such a bomb in the luggage of a young Irish woman. But the FAA recognized that the simplest method is to put a bomb in a checked suitcase, and then not show up for the flight.

The biggest risk was assumed to be from passengers transferring to American airlines from foreign carriers. In theory, American carriers were screening passengers at check-in to identify security risks. If you were, say, a young Arab man traveling alone on a Lebanese passport, you might be selected for additional security checks, including a baggage search. At the very least there would be a paper trail linking you to the flight, a counter agent who might remember your face. So, reasoned the FAA's security people, it was much more likely that the bomber would start his journey in another city, on another airline— perhaps from a country such as Syria or Libya, where American investigators would find cooperation on the ground fairly meager. He would check his bag through to New York, get off in Frankfurt (if he bothered getting on the plane in the first place), and disappear.

Accordingly, the FAA required that all baggage at high-risk airports be matched on the tarmac with a passenger who actually boarded the airplane. If the passenger didn't take his seat, the bag had to be located, taken off the plane if it had already been loaded, and either searched by hand or left behind. Everyone recognized that this would probably make the flight late, but even passengers in a hurry would agree that "better late than never" is a singularly apt expression when it comes to air travel.

Pan Am didn't like that rule. Delays caused by baggage matching in Frankfurt could throw off a whole day's schedule all the way to New York. By early 1988 management believed it had found a way around them. Pan Am purchased a number of additional X-ray machines, hired people to sit in front of them, and implemented a policy of X-raying all "interline" baggage at Frankfurt. That was meant to substitute for the match-and-search requirement laid out by the FAA. A March 1988 memo to security officials at London and Frankfurt from Pan Am's corporate head of security, Dan Sonensen, was read at the trial. It concluded: "In the event of a no-show interline passenger, and his bag is loaded in the belly, we go."

"And then there are four exclamation points," the lawyer noted.

The witness reading the memo corrected him. "Five."

There are at least two problems with this procedure. The most obvious one is that plastic explosives don't show up on X-ray machines, at least not the machines Pan Am was using at the time. The wiring and batteries that bombs require do show up, of course, but an X-ray operator could easily miss them inside something like a radio-cassette player. The less obvious problem is that under Pan Am's system, the few bags that deserve serious scrutiny (because the owners didn't board the plane) are mixed in with a much larger group from which the danger is comparatively slight—and the operator has no way to know which ones they are.

Nevertheless, Pan Am executives were to insist, before and during the trial, that their departure from the written regulations had been approved orally at a meeting with an FAA official. FAA officials denied that any such approval ever occurred, and no written record of it was ever produced. But many of the families of the victims found it more relevant that the FAA inspected Pan Am's Frankfurt operation two months before the bombing. Although the agency found "very substantial problems" in security, it seems, improbably enough, to have overlooked Pan Am's substitution of X rays for matching and searching baggage—which, according to the theory of the case developed by prosecutors, was precisely the loophole exploited by the bombers.

As these facts emerged in the weeks and months after December 21, 1988, it seemed increasingly to the families that it wasn't just a money-grubbing corporation that had let them down, but also their very own government, which had been looking the other way when its citizens' lives were at stake. And as the months turned into years, and the families' thoughts turned from grief to justice, the seed of suspicion thus planted was to grow into a conviction that the bombing of Pan Am 103—that cataclysm, that monstrosity, that dagger to the heart—was in the government's view just an international incident to be managed, one among many; a political problem, to be weighed in the context of competing interests; even, perhaps, an opportunity to be exploited. Like God himself, who had in his all-seeing wisdom permitted the deaths of their loved ones, the government pursued its own unfathomable purpose.

3

Investigation

After such a tragedy, people are advised to bury their dead and get on with their lives, but the Pan Am families found such advice impossible to follow. A few days after the bombing, the Pan Am contact person assigned to the Cohens called them at their home in Port Jervis, New York, offering help. Dan Cohen held out the receiver so she could hear Susan sobbing that her life was over. I can't help you with that, the woman said, and never called back. For months afterward Victoria Cummock would find herself glancing at a clock, noting the time, and then having to go to a window and look outside to see if it was morning or night. In dozens of houses, the door was shut on a child's bedroom at the top of the stairs, with the bed all made up and the clean clothes folded, and the door stayed shut, and nothing moved in the rooms but the shafts of sunlight sweeping the floor. Years after the bombing, when Eileen and Bob Monetti, of Cherry Hill, New Jersey, finally cleaned out the room that had belonged to their son, Rick, they saw, undisturbed, the fingerprint powder with which FBI technicians had lifted the latent prints that were transmitted to Scotland and used to identify his body.

Melina Hudson's body had been identified by a ring she had been wearing, and when he got it back, Paul Hudson had it strung on a chain that he still wears around his neck. She had a magnificent funeral in the Roman Catholic cathedral in Albany, New York. Her mother planned it as if it were a wedding, down to the videotaping. The bishop officiated, and the eulogy was delivered by the parish priest in Exeter, England, where Melina had been an exchange student. The priest had taken a liking to the pretty American teenager who came to church faithfully every week. "She introduced herself to him after Mass one Sunday," Eleanor Hudson said. "There were not many Catholics in the town. And she was someone you remembered if you met her." After burying his daughter, Paul Hudson thought he was ready to go back to his law practice and his real-estate business. But his mind was on a street in Scotland where Melina's body had fallen to earth. He spent a good deal of his time attending the funerals of other Lockerbie victims in central New York State and elsewhere. In mid-January there was a memorial service at Syracuse University, and Hudson went to that as well.

He was developing, also, a consuming interest in air safety, in Semtex and timers and luggage screening. He contacted the Aviation Consumer Action Project (ACAP), the Naderite organization concerned with air safety. As a lawyer, and as counsel to the New York State Crime Victims Compensation Board, Hudson was no innocent. Still, he was shocked at what he discovered about the system to which he had entrusted his daughter's life. "I had assumed there was a pretty good security system in place, and the terrorists had just found some clever way of getting around it. Most security systems aren't perfect, and if you work hard enough and you're dedicated enough you can defeat it. But ACAP opened my eyes. The security system at that time was pretty much a sham, something set up to convince the public that something was being done." He arranged for someone from ACAP to speak to the family members after the service at Syracuse, and he added the addresses of more relatives to the list he was accumulating in the file cabinet in his office.

In early January, Victoria Cummock was still trying to get her husband's body back from Scotland. Someone gave her the phone number of a South Florida congressman, and she called him, and for the first but by no means the last time she heard the magic phrase with which Washington officials can make the most importunate citizen disappear: "That's outside my district." He offered his condolences and with enormous relief redirected her to her own representative, Dante Fascell, who happened to be chairman of the House Committee on Foreign Affairs.

By the time she met with Fascell, John's body had been returned, but Cummock had no death certificate, none of his belongings, and a growing list of questions about how the disaster came to happen. Their meeting began on a note of epic misunderstanding. Cummock clung to her belief that within the great United States government there was an agency somewhere equipped and eager to help her, and all she needed was the right phone number to call, which this important and sympathetic man was surely able to supply. Fascell knew better, though. He had seen numerous tragedies go unremarked and unacknowledged, the victims bobbing helplessly in the waves as the ship of state sailed on imperturbably. So he offered what he could give and what he thought she needed, which was consolation. "Victoria," he said earnestly, "there are so many injustices in life, and I see so many of them here in my office. Don't let this consume your life. Go home, take care of your children and put your life back together. Who knows when, or if, we will have these answers?"

That was precisely the wrong thing to say to her. "Well, with all due respect, is anyone even asking the questions?" she erupted. "I mean, it's been TWO WEEKS already."

Fascell gave up on trying to console her. He told her that his committee had a hearing scheduled on February 9 to investigate security at foreign airports. He invited Cummock to testify, and when she said she couldn't possibly leave her children that soon, to submit a statement instead. She said she would do that.

"On December 21, 1988, Pan Am Flight 103 crashed in Lockerbie, Scotland, the result of a terrorist bomb," her statement began. "John Cummock, my husband, best friend and father of my three children was murdered along with 269 other people. This was the largest single act of terrorism against the United States in its history.

"Fifty-five days later, I am appalled that no United States government agency or official has even acknowledged, to the families, that this life-shattering event even occurred; what they plan to do about the murder of approximately 200 Americans; or even what they plan to do to protect American citizens in the future."

The letter ran to six pages, including four pages of her own "findings and conclusions" about the inadequacy of the State Department procedures for notifying families and the shameful state of airline security. The letter was entered into the record along with remarks by the secretary of transportation, the CIA's declassified analysis of the Foreign Airport Security Act, and submissions from the Airline Pilots Association and the Council of Europe on enhanced aviation security measures. Victoria Cummock had discovered her medium, and it was congressional testimony. She was analytical and articulate and spoke to politicians in language they understood, and she did it with the moral authority of a woman whose husband had been murdered. The Subcommittee on International Operations had scheduled hearings in early March on the budget for the State Department, which was seeking additional funding to offset the cost of dealing with the Pan Am 103 disaster. Fascell's office invited Vickie and another family member to give their versions of how State's Bureau of Consular Affairs was doing its job.

The invitation terrified her. It came just two months after her husband had been killed. Her children had been sleeping in her bed since the bombing and wouldn't let her out of their sight. Her friends had no confidence that she would remember what she was supposed to do when she got off the airplane. But she was committed to seeing this through. "It's not easy to go up there and talk about this," she told an interviewer from the *Miami Herald*. "I resent the fact that I have to be there. But when there's silence all around you, you feel, my God, how insignificant were these people?" She arranged to fly back the same day so as not to spend the night away from her children. Arriving in Washington on March 9, without a coat, she felt an unfamiliar sensation in the air, but she couldn't quite name or recognize it. Eventually it dawned on her: it was cold.

But her fragile emotional state only made her testimony more compelling. The subcommittee chairman, Mervyn Dymally of California, let the State Department testify first: the assistant secretary for consular affairs, accompanied by three other officials, thoroughly prepped with statistics about phone banks and person-hours, working groups and task forces. Then he called on Cummock, who came prepared with her own chronology of government contacts. It showed that the State Department took eight days from the crash to call her to ask if she'd heard from Pan Am; five weeks to write asking if she was the correct next of kin to receive John's body. That was long after he'd already been buried. Although the State Department had received the belongings of ninety-two Americans from the British police, they had not yet been returned to the families, she told the congressmen. Half in tears, she spouted all the questions that had been bubbling up in her for two months: Was there a bomb? Who was responsible? Why was it taking so long to get belongings, death certificates, autopsy reports? "I am not really familiar with procedures here," she said half-apologetically, although she was already getting a taste of the power that great tragedy can bestow on those it touches. As a rule, congressional hearings are less a Socratic search for the truth than a way to put on the record certain facts preselected by the members or their staffs to make a political point. In any case, it is the prerogative of the representatives to ask the questions. Cummock turned that process around. Pursuing her own agenda, she launched into a dissection of FAA policy regarding bomb threats. Only twenty-three "high-level" bomb threats had been recorded in Europe in 1988, she reminded the subcommittee—not so many that it would have disrupted air travel greatly if the rigorous "El Al procedures" for hand-searching luggage had been used on the affected flights.

This was, perhaps, more than the committee had bargained for. "Somehow all of that pales in front of your tragedy, does it not?" Rep. Larry Smith, a Democrat from Florida, interjected. "You are not interested in—"

His remarks end in one of the most eloquent dashes in the history of the *Congressional Record*. Victoria Cummock, a witness, cut him off. She surely was interested in the minutiae of airline security.

"And, basically, the bottom line was that, you know, it was too costly to do this," she went on. "And I really feel that for those twenty-three situations in all of Europe that is really not asking an awful lot."

When she was thanked for her testimony—a gentle reminder that other important national business was awaiting—she took it as a signal to launch into her closing remarks. "I have here over 400 letters requesting that mandatory uniform policies and procedures be enacted through the airline industry . . ." she began. Then, "For me at this point in my life to try to pick up the pieces and start investigating who is supposed to do what, and keep telephone logs, and keep data, and start forming support groups and everything else, I think that it is deplorable. And here we are with the best and most humane country in the world. I cannot believe that this is what it has been left to."

That was the first of more than a dozen congressional appearances—she's unsure of the exact number—Cummock was to make over the next decade. She was so excited by the experience that she went straight to a telephone, and then realized, with a shock, that the number she was about to dial was her husband's. Her demeanor that day set the tone for many of her subsequent public appearances: an earnest, ingenuous, plain-spoken citizen thrust unwillingly into the spotlight, driven only by a humble search for justice. Somehow, she had achieved a remarkable, Zen-like detachment toward the actual perpetrators of the bombing. Bruce Smith, the pilot whose wife was killed on Pan Am 103, once remarked that he would like to take the two suspects up to 31,000 feet and see how long it took *them* to hit the ground. The remark deeply disturbed Cummock, who considers Smith a friend and an ally. "I thought it was really sad that Bruce had all this anger," she mused. "I've been asking myself, what in God's name compelled you to do all this for eleven years? It wasn't anger. My motivations were to learn the Lockerbie lessons so that others don't have to die."

But those who have worked with her have also seen another side of Victoria Cummock: extraordinary energy, drive, self-discipline, tenacity, glamour, taste, and wealth. She can move easily in sophisticated circles and has spent the last several years in an exquisite restoration, for her family's use, of a colonnaded mansion that is one of the oldest houses in South Florida. One powerful senator courted her as a possible congressional candidate, and another tried to strike up a romance. Long before unwanted fame sought her out, she was a fashion model and a successful advertising executive with J. Walter Thompson in Miami; before that, she was the demure granddaughter of a Peruvian admiral who later became Peru's ambassador to the United States. Her father, the admiral's son, was a dashing naval attaché who married an American and raised seven daughters in Greenwich, Connecticut. Since 1988 Cummock has devoted herself to promoting aviation security and to counseling and consoling the victims and families of victims of mass disasters, particularly the 1996 crash of ValuJet flight 592 in the Florida Everglades only a few miles from her home, and the bombing in 1995 of the Murrah Federal Office Building in Oklahoma City. Her compensation for this work has been mostly in the form of photographs of her with Presidents Bush and Clinton, of plaques and mementos and letters of gratitude. But her efforts have not entirely endeared her to the other Pan Am 103 relatives, most of whom are neither famous nor wealthy and sometimes refer to her, behind her back, as the "grief junkie."

Beginning just days after the bombing, Cummock had begun trying to contact other family members. It was slow going with nothing to work from but newspaper lists of victims, consisting of just names and hometowns. When she heard about a memorial service at St. Patrick's Cathedral in New York City, she prepared an open letter to the other relatives, offering condolences and inviting them to call, and she had her father and sisters hand out copies on Fifth Avenue. She was looking for allies in her quest for information, but most of the people she spoke to were in no condition to help; as soon as she introduced herself they would burst into sobs. Paul Hudson was an exception. He kept her informed of what was happening up north. In February a number of relatives met at a restaurant in New Jersey and organized the original family group, Victims of Pan Am 103. The group was led, in those early months, by Hudson and Bert Ammerman, a New Jersey high school administrator. Ammerman had lost a brother on the flight, which set him apart from most of the other activists among the families, who were the parents or spouses of victims. Hudson and Ammerman were both among the first American family members to reach the crash site. They were an oddly matched pair: Hudson, soft-spoken, with thick glasses and a diffident manner; Ammerman, burly, ruddy, and blunt. They held a press conference at a New York hotel to demand an independent investigation of the actions of both Pan Am and the U.S. government. Hudson, who had expected a modest turnout, was astonished to see the room packed with dozens of cameras and uncountable hordes of reporters. "That," he says, "was when I realized this wasn't going to go away like most other air crashes."

But the episode also demonstrated the limitations of media attention without political muscle behind it. They had asked that future terrorist threats against airplanes be publicized, and the next day the new secretary of transportation, Samuel Skinner, held his own press conference to dismiss the idea. "If we shut down airlines every time there is a threat, we will allow terrorists to disrupt the economy, not only of this nation, but of the world," Skinner said. The families' questions and demands weren't going to be answered by a public relations spokesman or a television reporter. They wanted an investigation, and they wanted it to be authorized by Congress and equipped with subpoena powers, conditions that virtually assured the opposition of the Bush administration. The new group set April 3, 1989—103 days after the bombing— for a rally outside the White House, followed by a marathon lobbying session in Congress.

In mid-March Cummock finally received a letter from someone connected to the government. It was a solicitation for political contributions from Jeb Bush, not yet governor of Florida but a prominent businessman and Republican fund-raiser, and the son of the president. Cummock knew him, slightly, from functions at the private school where they both sent their children. She responded the next day with a four-page letter of her own, reminding him that "both my late husband John and I historically supported the Republican Party until he was murdered." She went on to describe the shabby treatment she had endured at the hands of the State Department, the inadequacies of the U.S. aviation-security procedures, and the lack of response from the White House. "My sense of patriotism, value and respect for the United States has been shattered," she wrote. "How can I instill in my three small children a love for this country, which has shown no value or respect for their father's life, or the lives of those who perished along with him?" Jeb and his wife, Columba, had recently returned from the scene of a catastrophic earthquake in Armenia. Vickie suggested that if he was going to do disaster work he could spare some time for the earthquake that had struck her family.

Bush called her the next day. "I'm terribly sorry about what happened to John," he told her. "But I'm not in office, my father is. All I can do is promise that your letter will be on his desk for him to read, and what he does with it will be up to him."

Did Cummock's letter somehow personalize the tragedy for the president? Or did the prospect of hundreds of grieving widows and parents protesting outside the White House concentrate his mind? In any case, the White House called to set up a meeting. Cummock asked for the meeting on April 3, the day of the Washington rally, and she said she would be accompanied by the leaders of the family association. She was not, she emphasized, interested in a photo opportunity. Of course not, she was assured. Her group would be allotted precisely twenty minutes.

Clearly, in agreeing to meet with the families, Bush did the decent thing under the circumstances. Even so, he was violating a basic rule of White House handlers: *never let people like that meet the president.* Democratically elected officials are activists by nature. They want to connect with people. Not many are gifted with Bill Clinton's uncanny ability to forge an emotional connection to ordinary people, irrespective of any intention to actually act on it. If a president says he will do something, he cannot later claim that he's been overruled. It is, therefore, one of the duties of the White House staff to absorb the laments of the nation's bereaved and promise to get back to them right away. "Part of our job was to keep the families out of the Oval Office," says Nick Rostow, a former general counsel to the National Security Council. "That was a lesson from the Tower Commission"—the embarrassing post-mortem on the Iran-Contra scandal that so tarnished the last years of the Reagan administration. The problems began when Reagan attended the funeral of Robert Stethem, the Navy diver who was killed in the TWA hijacking in Beirut. Reagan met with some of the Lebanon hostage families there and came back to the White House and said, *We've got to do something!* That led, by complicated paths, to the humiliating deal by which the hostages' freedom was purchased with American arms. Nobody wanted something like that to happen again.

And in the end, it didn't, but what did happen was tragic in its own way. Hudson and Ammerman walked out of the White House and announced to their supporters, gathered for a rally in nearby Lafayette Park, that the president was in favor of military action against the perpetrators of the bombing. This, of course, was just what many of them wanted to hear. According to Hudson's recollection, Bush brought the subject up himself, right at the outset of the meeting, and couched it as an expression of "my own view." It would be somewhat surprising if Bush, a lifelong politician and former CIA director, had said anything so unqualified. Perhaps, in expressing what he said was a personal view, the president was signaling that this wasn't a settled tenet of American policy. His language certainly implied that any action would depend on obtaining convincing proof of responsibility of a foreign government. But those were subtleties lost on many relatives. They cheered the news when they heard it, and went home comforted by the thought that the mighty power of the United States would be used to avenge the murders of their children, spouses, and parents. As of the summer of 2001, they were still waiting. In varying degrees, for many of the families, this is a betrayal that the United States of America will never live down.

The delegation had other issues to cover with the president. Before going in, with the twenty-minute deadline looming, Cummock had warned the others not to look at their watches, not to take anything to eat or drink, and at all costs not to stand until a Marine actually prodded them out of their chairs with a bayonet. Twenty minutes ticked by, forty minutes, and the president seemed in no hurry to end the meeting. In the end it ran to almost an hour. On the request for an independent panel, with its attendant potential to embarrass the Reagan-Bush administration, Bush was noncommittal. But he took a great interest in Vickie's trouble in getting information and help from the bureaucracy. He ordered the State Department to produce a chronology of their contacts with Cummock. Anyone who thinks the government is unresponsive or inefficient would be reassured to know how fast it can work when a request comes from the president. The six-page memo was on Bush's desk in time for him to send it on to Vickie the very same day. It showed that she was called on December 23, again on the twenty-ninth ("unfortunately, very little new information was available"), and then not until January 6 ("to advise her of the status of the return of her husband's personal effects . . ."). It was accompanied by one of the handwritten notes for which Bush was famous. "I was sickened when Jeb told me you had heard *nothing,*" Bush wrote. "Please tell me if the attached is accurate. We have a large and sometimes seemingly insensitive government, but I want to be sure that the attached contacts were as represented. I know today was not easy for you. Indeed I was choking up myself . . . My respects and best wishes. Vicki, I do care." And undoubtedly he did. But in official Washington the gap between action and caring, even the caring of a president, could be a gaping chasm, laced by a river of tears.

Now the families faced their first political battle, trying to win an independent investigation. They fanned out over the Capitol, and before the day was over they visited the office of every U.S. senator. The administration had not yet taken a public position on the question, but it didn't want the issue to get away from it, either. Skinner, the secretary of transportation, called another press conference to announce that the government would purchase up to 100 "thermal neutron analysis" machines to scan luggage for the presence of explosives. The machines were to be installed in more than thirty high-risk foreign and domestic airports, at a cost approaching $100 million. "We are not going to let cost get in the way of security," Skinner said bravely. More than seven years later, when TWA 800 blew up shortly after taking off from JFK—an explosion that eventually was determined to have been most likely accidental—the machines, which turned out not to work quite as well as advertised, had yet to be installed. As late as September 2001, when terrorists hijacked four airliners on the same day, Americans were reminded that the crucial job of screening passengers and luggage at most American airports was in the hands of people earning around six dollars an hour.

The bomb aboard Pan Am 103 was to bring down not just an airplane, but an airline. From the time Pan Am chairman Thomas G. Plaskett was told about a possible crash—approximately five minutes after the radar image of the plane over Scotland began breaking up—Pan Am had less than three years to live. The company was already in financial difficulties when Plaskett joined it from American Airlines in early 1988, although it made money in the third quarter of the year, the last one before the bombing. Jeff Kriendler, Pan Am's chief spokesman, later told reporters that even without the disaster of flight 103 the company's independent survival was doubtful and a merger with another airline was probably inevitable. But now Pan Am's fate was out of its control. Its defense against the silent accusations of 270 corpses lay in the hands of more than a dozen insurance companies, which had apportioned among themselves $750 million in liability coverage. They were led by a consortium managed by United States Aviation Underwriters (USAU), a subsidiary of the commercial insurance giant General Re. And USAU, for whatever reasons, declared war on the families.

The insurance companies claimed to have the law on their side. The law, in fact, was printed on the backs of the very tickets the passengers had held, in the fine print no one ever reads. Under the law in effect in 1988, if you flew from one country to another your rights to compensation in the event of a crash were limited by treaties and compacts and protocols going back to the very dawn of commercial aviation. The basic structure was set out by the Warsaw Convention of 1929, the result of four years' work by a distinguished international panel of jurists. In theory they were creating a uniform standard of compensation for the benefit of both airlines and passengers. In setting the actual amounts, though, the industry's interests weighed rather more heavily than the passengers', since—as the U.S. Second Circuit Court of Appeals noted years later in its decision *In re Air Disaster At Lockerbie*—most of the countries drafting the treaty either owned or heavily subsidized their own airlines. Compensation accordingly was fixed at 125,000 Poincaré francs, an impressive-sounding sum that at the time amounted to a few thousand dollars. In the Montreal Agreement of 1966, American airlines voluntarily upped this amount to $75,000, which was the figure still in effect in December 1988. At that, the families were fortunate the bomb had not, in fact, gone off a half hour later, when the plane would have been over the ocean. Crashes occurring more than ten miles from land fell under the Death on the High Seas Act, which under some interpretations would have limited compensation to the princely sum of $2,333.

To exceed the $75,000 limit on compensation, families would have to prove that the crash resulted from the airline's "willful misconduct," a curious phrase that made its way into the annals of American tort law. It meant more than just ordinary carelessness: plaintiffs would have to show that Pan Am acted in reckless disregard of the consequences of its actions and knew, or should have known, that it was running a potentially fatal risk. That's one reason aviation law is such a rarefied specialty. Trial lawyers accustomed to proving "negligence" by building owners who leave ice on the sidewalk, or even "gross negligence" by the manufacturers of toasters that electrocute their owners, would shrink from the challenge of proving that a crash was caused by the airline's "willful misconduct." And here they would have to prove it despite the fact that the plane was actually brought down by a bomb. Against the advice of its own general counsel, Robert Alpert—who was reading the hair-raising reports of incompetence coming from Pan Am's own investigators in Frankfurt—USAU took the position that they would fight any willful-misconduct claims.

Accordingly, on February 20, the family members finally heard directly from Pan Am, in the form of a three-page letter signed by Plaskett. The tone of the letter veered unpredictably from stilted to unctuous. Acknowledging that it had been "several weeks [nine, in fact] since the tragedy," Plaskett stopped short of apologizing for the company's silence but explained that he had "felt it necessary to refrain from communicating with you too soon and without sufficient information that might be informative to you . . . I did not want to intrude upon your privacy at a time when you were faced with handling so many personal details." The point of the letter was buried in the next-to-last paragraph, which advised the recipients "that the appropriate legal heirs of each passenger are entitled to certain compensation as provided by existing international treaties and agreements . . . A representative from Pan Am's insurers, United States Aviation Underwriters, will soon contact you in writing concerning the procedures to be followed." The essence of the offer, when it was officially tendered, was $100,000 right away, in exchange for giving up forever the right to collect more in a future lawsuit. That was more than they would have had to pay under the Warsaw Convention, but $100,000 sounds like much more than $75,000. In sum, Pan Am was valuing the lives of the 243 passengers at a total of $24.3 million—a little more than half of what Lloyd's of London, which had insured the hull of the aircraft for $40 million, would end up paying Pan Am for the destruction of the airplane.

There were legal minds at work on the other side as well. Lawyers had begun signing up clients within days of the crash. Within a week, aviation lawyer Stuart Speiser, with six clients already signed, announced that he was planning to sue not just Pan Am but the U.S. government. His theory was that the State Department had neglected to publicize the Helsinki warning, which might have kept some of the victims off the flight. Suing the United States had the procedural advantage that the Warsaw Convention limit would not apply. It did, however, present an interesting factual challenge, inasmuch as the Helsinki warning had been determined to be a hoax. Speiser brushed that issue aside, though, proclaiming: "I don't think we have to prove whether the threat had anything to do with the crash. It doesn't matter whose bomb it was."

He was wrong: it did matter whose bomb it was. But it would be years before anyone knew the answer to that question. Moreover, the legal obstacles to suing the United States are almost insurmountable. The plan to sue the government was quickly abandoned, leaving Pan Am and its security subsidiary, Alert, as the only likely defendants. This gave rise to much soul-searching in the small, elite circle of aviation tort lawyers. Negligence (or "trial") lawyers work on contingency fees, meaning they take a share of anything the plaintiffs collect— typically around a third, plus expenses. Unless and until they win a judgment at trial, or negotiate a settlement outside court, they're paying their own salaries and fronting expenses, which can run to well over a million dollars. Their profession requires an unsentimental calculation of the chances of success as well as of the value a jury is likely to put on a given victim's life. It is a point of pride for many of them to turn down many more cases than they accept. Some, like Michel Baumeister, of the firm of Baumeister & Samuels, won't accept a case unless they figure it to be worth at least seven figures. "In this case, you had the Warsaw Convention to deal with, first of all," said attorney Lee Kreindler, whose firm, Kreindler & Kreindler, eventually represented the largest number of families and who, as head of the plaintiffs' committee, effectively ran the lawsuit. "You had the problem that it was a bomb, which obviously the airline didn't put on the plane intentionally. Plus, you had all the evidence walled up by the criminal investigators. It looked like an almost impossible situation, but we took the cases anyway. Sometimes you just roll the dice and gamble."

Almost no one took up the insurance company on its $100,000 offer. As the law viewed it, the value of the life of a passenger on board flight 103 was not a fixed quantity. Indeed, it varied by a factor of nearly 200, depending on (among other variables) the age, family status, and earnings history of the decedent; the identity of the next of kin; the states either of them resided in; and the skill and chutzpah of the attorney pursuing the case. In almost every case, though, it was considered to be worth more than $100,000. The exceptions involved families who died together, leaving only distant relatives as next of kin. That particular brand of tragedy had only minor standing in the eyes of the law, and several of those cases were quickly and quietly settled at $100,000 per "seat," which is how the aviation insurance industry refers to victims. Most of the other cases became part of the lawsuit that Kreindler and his colleagues pursued over the next seven years. There was one other significant exception. That was the case of Ingrid Anita Smith, the wife of Bruce Smith, a lifelong Pan Am pilot, who stopped to ask himself, *Who really killed my wife?*

Smith himself was fifty-two years old in December 1988, and Ingrid was twenty years younger. She was English, and although she was frequently misidentified in newspaper stories as a stewardess, she was actually a chiropodist, employed by the National Health to soothe weary taxpayers' bunions in and around the town of Bray, twenty miles from Heathrow airport. They'd met five years earlier, in Majorca, in a bar—although Smith hastens to add in recounting this story that Ingrid had gone in there with her mother. In photographs, Ingrid is lovely, with a shy, sweet smile. Like almost everyone else touched by the Lockerbie disaster, Smith has given some thought to the emotional hierarchy of loss. He has four sons from his first marriage and, on reflection, he concludes that the death of a child would be worse than the death of a spouse. Bruce Smith would never have said, as Susan Cohen did after the bombing, that his life was over. All it cost him was the next twelve years, plus his job and every dollar he had.

He was waiting in New York for her on the afternoon of the 21st. They were to fly together to Washington, where he was scheduled for a Washington–Paris–Tel Aviv–Paris trip the next day, with a two-day layover, and she was going with him to spend Christmas in Israel. He was planning out their holiday when his son called him in his hotel room and told him to turn on the television. Smith went straight to Pan Am's operations center at JFK and asked to see the roster of names from the flight. Then he packed for England and got on a plane that same night and was at Heathrow early the next morning.

Almost as soon as the letter came with its offer of $100,000, Bruce made up his mind to take it. Pan Am was, by 1988, a money-losing airline with its glory years long behind it. Nevertheless, it inspired fantastic loyalty in its employees. Bruce Smith loved Pan Am. After it went out of business, he flew for a few years for Delta, which had taken over many of its routes. But he could never bring himself to feel a part of any other airline. Even today his business card identifies him as a Pan Am captain (retired). "I didn't blame Pan Am for putting the bomb on the airplane," he says, "and I think if anyone should understand that, I should. That could have been me flying that airplane. I didn't need the money and I didn't see the point in putting the airline out of business. My goal was to find out who did it and punish them if I could. I would have felt the same if it had been TWA that was bombed."

So Smith took the money, although not on the precise conditions that were offered. The insurance companies drew up a release that, as he read it, would have foreclosed him from suing not just Pan Am and Alert Security and Boeing and every other company or individual remotely responsible for building, maintaining, or operating the airplane, but anyone else on the planet, including, if they could be found, the terrorists who bombed it. Smith sent it back and said it was his intention to pursue his wife's murderers in any way possible, including in court. After he got that language changed, he tackled the "subrogation" clause, standard insurance-company language that in effect said: If you ever collect money from anyone else for this incident, you will kindly pay us back the money we just gave you. On the third go-round, Smith got that excised as well.

Smith didn't need money to compensate him for Ingrid's death. On the other hand, he thought it might be possible to put the money to a useful purpose. He drafted a letter and sent it to a list of the victims' relatives that he had obtained from Victoria Cummock. Smith contended that Pan Am was a victim of the bombing just as they were. The real culprits were the terrorists, and the obligation of the victims' relatives was to pursue justice against them, not the airline. He proposed establishing a reward for information leading to the capture of the bombers. He consulted law enforcement officials, who told him that international terrorists were disciplined and well funded; luring an informer would take millions. For symbolic purposes, he decided on $5 million, which was approximately the value of the bounty Iranian revolutionaries were offering for the death of the English novelist Salman Rushdie. (Rushdie earned his *fatwa*, a religious death sentence, for alleged blasphemies in his novel *Satanic Verses*, which was published earlier in 1988. In an odd and somber coincidence, the book opened with an airliner exploding in the sky over England.) Bruce offered to put up, personally, the entire amount of his settlement for Ingrid's death. While acknowledging that families who had lost breadwinners probably couldn't afford to settle for only $100,000, others perhaps could. If even half of the families of the university students aboard the plane pooled their money with his, the reward fund would be starting out with over $2 million.

The responses to Smith's proposal were telling. "The only thing I really accomplished with this idea," he says, "is I got Lee Kreindler mad at me. He thought I was taking money out of his pocket." In principle, of course, no one opposed punishing the terrorists. But they saw little hope of that happening, even if the bombers could be identified. "Let us take the 'best case' scenario," one man wrote back to Bruce. "What if you manage to raise $5 [million], and an informant comes forward. He is credible; the criminal is in Damascus, Syria or Libya, 'vital links of evidence' are established. What then?

"This is a case of state-sponsored terrorism. Ahmed Jibril is in a safehouse in Damascus, Syria, protected by Syrian Dictator Hafez Assad. . . . He will have to be forcibly removed, which implies sending U.S. troops into Syria. . . . [I]s the U.S. prepared to do this and possibly upset the delicate balance of power in the Middle East?"

Daniel Cohen was even more pointed in his reply:

" . . . I have no inside information, and I presume you don't either. But I have talked to people in Washington and in the media who are close to this case. They all insist that the U.S. government knows who did it, who paid for it, how they did it and why. It is not lack of knowledge, but lack of will that keeps the U.S. from striking back. . . .

"Pan Am would be very happy to have the families take their $100,000 and use it in the fruitless pursuit of some low-level international hit man. That would divert attention from their failure. And it would be a lot cheaper for them. I, for one, have no intention of letting them off the hook. I want to go to trial. It's not the money—it's the exposure I want. . . ."

Smith is a pilot, a tough and independent-minded breed; he was born in the West and raised in Alaska and studied international relations at Stanford University. It is a point of pride with him that he did his mourning for Ingrid without resort to grief counseling or psychotherapy. ("I don't believe in paying people to listen to me. Why should I need counseling? We knew what happened. We couldn't change it.") As far as he was concerned, he had identified a rational approach to a problem and was taking steps to implement it. But his rationalism blinded him at first to the emotional reality that as much as he loved Pan Am, the other family members despised it. They rejoiced when it went out of business, and they fought attempts to revive it, and they even fought a sentimental proposal to preserve its logo on the midtown Manhattan skyscraper that had been its headquarters. (Daniel Cohen in a letter to the editor of the *New York Times,* Feb. 29, 1992: "Does the Manhattan skyline really need this symbol of tragedy and failure? I don't think so." Bruce Smith, to the editor, in reply to Cohen's letter: "History did not begin on December 21, 1988. The people who were Pan Am, who served it well and led the development of civil aviation for over sixty years deserve to be remembered. Let the Pan Am Building and the logo stand as their memorial.") To this very day— long after the building was sold and renamed for its new owners— some family members will go out of their way to avoid walking on Park Avenue, from which it is impossible to avoid seeing the building, which has been renamed for its new owner, Met Life. In light of all that, it was an impossible task to convince any of the other relatives to forgo their lawsuits, especially by someone who was still wearing a Pan Am uniform. Smith got a letter from a woman whose twin sons had died on the plane:

My personal belief is that we will NEVER apprehend those responsible for this obscene act. In fact, there seems to be a real effort not to stall the investigation, as you said, but to downright prevent it. . . . My anger and rage is directed toward the governments responsible for allowing this to happen, and your employer, Pan Am.

Smith quickly realized he was not going to raise $5 million, or for that matter anything at all, in private donations from the family members. Even Cummock, who was more sympathetic than most, wasn't about to forgo a settlement that could run into eight figures. Bruce therefore turned his attention to the government. He discovered that a federal antiterrorism reward program actually existed, although payouts were capped at only $500,000. The program was administered by the State Department's antiterrorism office, which, when Bruce approached them about raising the payout, was not uninterested, but hamstrung by the fact that it was the middle of a budget cycle. Officials there suggested that nothing could be done until the next round of appropriations, almost a year off, a response that Bruce, whose wife had just been murdered, found irritatingly lacking in urgency. "I learned the Washington run-around," he says. "Listen, sympathize, send the poor guy on to someone else, and do nothing." Frank Duggan, a savvy Washington pol who would spend years working with the family members, calls this process "grin-fucking."

Over the next eighteen months Smith worked the halls of Congress and the State Department, and eventually, in a bill sponsored by Sen. Frank Murkowski of Alaska, got the payout raised all the way to $2 million. Then Smith approached Plaskett, the Pan Am chairman, and through him extracted a pledge of an additional $1 million from the industry trade group, the Air Transport Association. The Airline Pilots Association matched that sum. Both of those pledges had strings attached limiting the payouts to cases involving American civil aviation. But still, he had come a long way toward his goal; by mid-1990 the price was up to $4 million for information leading to the capture and arrest of the men who killed Ingrid Smith and 269 others.

And everyone else, of course, still got to sue Pan Am. As for Bruce

Smith, he ran through his $100,000 pretty quickly, staying in Washington for up to a week at a time, spending nearly $2,000 a month on transatlantic phone calls alone. He didn't realize it at the time, but he would eventually spend much more—hundreds of thousands of dollars, just about all the cash he had or could raise—on the cause of justice for Ingrid and the rest of those who died at Lockerbie. And he would end up more or less broke, and with his retirement fund gone, but, as he says: "What would you do if it were your wife?"

4

"National Will"?

You could hardly have found a more conventional, more upstanding group of citizens than the relatives of the Pan Am 103 victims: corporate executives, teachers, engineers, lawyers; a pilot, a sculptor, an interior designer. They were for the most part comfortable within their own worlds and accepting of government authority and institutions. The bomb transformed them into outsiders and skeptics, Ancient Mariners buttonholing reporters with horrifying tales of corporate greed and duplicity, government indifference and incompetence. Never again could they watch a campaign speech or a television commercial and complacently mutter "bullshit"; they had to shout it to the skies. Paul Hudson was a lawyer, a civil person, who knew how to get his point across without hurling accusations of mendacity. But how could he contain himself at a House subcommittee hearing, as the chairman cited testimony by a high State Department official that "if we have a specific and credible threat to civil aviation security which cannot be countered, we will strongly recommend to the air carrier that it cancel the threatened flight."

From his seat in the witness chair, Hudson propped himself up on his elbows and erupted: "Mr. Chairman, Mr. Chairman, Mr. Chairman!"

Taken aback, the chairman, James Oberstar of Minnesota, asked for a moment to finish his remarks. As soon as he was done, Hudson began a denunciation of the way the State Department had handled the Helsinki threat, which he obviously thought had been specific and credible enough to warrant action: "With all due respect, Mr. Chairman, to Ambassador McManaway [the State Department's ambassador at large for counter-terrorism] I for one cannot take his statements any longer at face value. . . . There is a position that has been conveyed that the [Helsinki] threat was a hoax. But when I asked the number two person at the FBI whether that person who committed this hoax had ever been arrested, or charged . . . the answer I was given is no, that person was never arrested or charged. And I asked if our officials, our FBI, our security officials, had interviewed this person. I, myself, Mr. Chairman, am a former criminal justice official with the State of New York for ten years, and with all due respect, I cannot accept the bare assertion that this was a hoax without proof. And we have not seen any proof."

And who, indeed, would provide such proof? Congressional hearings—and there were many—are valuable tools for putting an issue on the public agenda, but a slow and tortuous path to the truth. The FAA was investigating the crash, the Scottish authorities had begun a Fatal Accident Inquiry, and of course there was a criminal investigation, which was already being described as the largest criminal investigation in history. But there was no systematic effort to address the questions Cummock, Hudson, and others had been asking for months. "When we ask these questions, we're left with bland assertions that everything that was supposed to have been done was done," Hudson told the *Washington Post*. "When we ask what that was, they tell us they can't tell us for security reasons."

The solution they hit on was an independent commission, a body with full investigative powers and no obligation to anyone else's reputation. This was a time-honored way for government to deal with the occasional Platonic questions that had to be elevated above the give-

and-take of ordinary politics: Who shot John F. Kennedy? Did the Reagan administration trade arms for hostages? What caused the space shuttle explosion? The old-fashioned term for such a body is "blue-ribbon panel"—a council of distinguished men and women whose honesty was beyond question, and with sufficient ties to the establishment so that no matter what embarrassing facts they uncovered, they could be trusted to avoid drawing any inflammatory conclusions. The very fact that *this* commission was being sought by a loosely organized band of citizens, driven by anger and filled with suspicion, was more than enough to frighten the administration. Following the Oval Office meeting on April 3, the family members fanned out to begin their lobbying drive. One of those they met was Bob Carolla, who was a top aide to Sen. George Mitchell of Maine, the majority leader of the Senate. The new administration and Congress had taken office only a few months earlier, and Mitchell was enmeshed in a difficult battle over an increase in the minimum wage, among many other issues, so it wasn't easy to find time for Pan Am 103. The following weekend, Carolla wrote in his diary:

> *Monday—I met with the parents of a young man killed in the bombing of the Pan Am airliner over Scotland this past Christmas. An emotional empathy; feeling their sense of loss; the void filled now by their lobbying; and identifying at a certain level with their lost son, a political science major at [a well-known university]. "Victims of Pan Am Flight 103" want an independent Congressional investigation, which probably is beyond the resources of Congress; also, a disproportionate response—but how do you tell that to parents who have lost a son? The hard language of Washington political/legal/bureaucratese. They do not trust the Executive Branch; but Congressional staff are hoping that the President will appoint a special commission—which, in a figurative sense, will get us "off the hook" and relieve us of the embarrassment of being unable to pursue it ourselves.*

All through the spring and into the summer of 1989, the families worked the Capitol, the talk shows, and the op-ed pages. Hudson's son Stephen, a freshman at Skidmore College, took a leave and moved to

Washington to become what amounted to a full-time unpaid lobbyist. Doors opened for them as soon as they mentioned Pan Am 103, but inside the door there might be only a legislative assistant, who wasn't necessarily happy to see them. Many congressional staffers found dealing with the relatives painful and frustrating. Legislative aides deal mostly with political professionals, who know what they can realistically hope to achieve and how to take no for an answer. But the family members were outsiders, amateurs, pressing their extraordinary demands over strenuous opposition from the White House. And they were angry; the fact that it was righteous anger didn't make it any easier to endure, when it was directed at you. "They were divided into the mad and the sad," recalls Jim Whittinghill, a key aide to Bob Dole, the Republican leader in the Senate. "Some of them yelled, some of them cried, but in either case, as much as you sympathized, it wasn't easy having them in your office. I met with them myself because the senior staffer for national security issues had given up on dealing with them; he didn't want the abuse." Their frustration grew as the disaster, still so fresh in their minds, began receding from the forefront of public awareness. Each day since December 21, thousands of planes had taken off around the world, and none of them had been bombed. The families sensed that the window for action was closing.

In May, finally, a bill was introduced in the Senate by Wendell Ford of Kentucky, who chaired a subcommittee dealing with aviation. It was co-sponsored by Mitchell himself and by Frank Lautenberg of New Jersey, and called for a nine-member commission, including four members of Congress, to investigate both Pan Am 103 and the Soviets' downing in 1983 of Korean Air Lines flight 007 and to issue a report within six months. Paul Hudson considered it a weak bill. It said nothing about other questions he cared about, such as how the families were treated after the bombing and how Pan American and the FAA in its oversight capacity, could have been so lax in dealing with security. Hudson thought it was a mistake to have the same body investigate both Pan Am 103 and the KAL flight, which was shot down by a Russian fighter plane under ambiguous circumstances. And he was upset that the bill did not grant subpoena power to the commission, although it did direct government agencies to cooperate with the investigation "to the extent permitted by law." Bert Ammerman, the other key leader of the family group, supported the bill. Their difference over the legislation reflected a broader difference between them, and within the group as well. Hudson believed that Ammerman was a little too pleased with himself over having a meeting in the Oval Office, a little too eager to shake the hand of power. Those opposed to Hudson thought he was a little too suspicious of the government and too focused on the fine print of the legislation. Around this time, Carolla wrote this about Hudson in his diary:

> *To a degree, I respect his persistence and his unrelenting hardball tactics . . . but after meeting him in person, I find myself thinking that either he is somehow unbalanced (because of his rigidity and lack of perspective) or simply a very nasty person by nature. It is hard to even empathize with someone who comes off so unlikeable. Yet—his purpose is not to be liked, but to get what he wants.*

But Carolla eventually did grow to like Hudson. A month later, after several long days spent working together to draft a substitute bill, Carolla wrote:

> *For the first time, I feel a personal connection with Paul Hudson; perhaps we are finally trusting/listening to each other's intentions; perhaps, too, he is beginning to emerge from what has to have been a hellish grief for his sixteen-year-old daughter.*

The split in Victims of Pan Am 103 would come to a head during the summer, when Hudson and Cummock left to form an organization called Families of Pan Am 103/Lockerbie. But even in May the divisions were apparent to the politicians who had to deal with them. "The bill was in limbo because of the split among the family members," says Carolla. "If you took action one way or the other, one side would get bent out of shape, and they had a lot of moral standing and allies in the press. Everyone wanted to help, but no one wanted to touch it."

The person who came to the rescue was Bob Dole. On the face of it, Dole seemed an unlikely candidate to take up this particular cause.

Exactly one of the victims came from his home state of Kansas, an enlisted man named Lloyd David Ludlow, who had been on his way home to attend his sister's funeral. And although airline safety and international terrorism were important national concerns, they had no particular resonance with the conservative Republicans whom Dole would need to court for the presidential nomination in 1996. In fact, the senator who probably worked the hardest and longest on Pan Am 103 was Ted Kennedy, the nemesis of conservatives. Yet for the next seven years, up through and including his presidential campaign, Dole was one of the leading champions of the families, devoting time and political capital to complex and obscure legislative battles that were, eventually, to put him at odds with practically every government in the world, including that of the United States. All of this, according to Dole's aide Whittinghill, came about as a result of a meeting with Victoria Cummock.

The meeting was arranged by mutual friends in Miami. Actually Cummock had met Bob and Liddy Dole once before through this couple, in a more innocent time when the powerful senator and his prominent wife were "just another couple on the boat" to her. One morning in early June, though, Cummock was in Washington to testify at yet another hearing, when she called her friend, who was helping to look after her children. The friend asked how things were going.

"We're stuck," Cummock told her. "Why isn't anything happening? We can't get in to see Dole, we can't get in to see Mitchell. Didn't you tell me Joe once did something for Dole?"

"Let me call you back," the friend replied. Three hours later, Cummock found herself in the minority leader's office.

Sheer luck and timing had landed her this crucial appointment. But now it was up to her to convince the famously loyal and pragmatic senator to, in effect, side with her over the expressed wishes of a president of his own party. And she would have to do it without Hudson, who understood the legislative process far better than she did. Cummock had spent a frantic few hours tracking Hudson down in Washington, and he arrived at Dole's office just in time only to be told that since the senator was seeing Cummock as a personal favor, the meeting was for her alone. Perhaps that worked in her favor. Another presence in the room could only have diluted the full force of Cummock's grief and outrage. By the time she finished her story she was crying, and there were tears in Dole's eyes also—Bob Dole of Kansas, the embodiment of tough-minded Midwestern reticence. He walked with Vickie through the door to his outer office and introduced her to Whittinghill, and then the Republican leader placed a call to Mitchell. "I'd like you to meet Mrs. Cummock," he said. "I'm going to take her over there now, if that's all right."

Carolla remembers the meeting vividly, because it lasted for forty minutes in the majority leader's office, then continued as he walked to a luncheon speech and resumed afterward. At one point, Carolla says, Cummock apologized for taking up so much of Mitchell's time, and he remonstrated with her: she had a perfect right to ask for his help and it was his job to provide it. Mitchell found Dole on the floor of the Senate that afternoon and after a quick conversation they agreed to introduce a new bill, sponsored jointly by the two Senate leaders. They would seek to pass it by unanimous consent, bypassing much of the legislative process. Cummock and Hudson, Whittinghill and Carolla began meeting to draw up new language.

At that point, says Whittinghill, "all hell broke loose" with the administration. A staff-level meeting with the various agencies involved—Transportation, State, and FBI—turned into a near-hysterical denunciation of the very idea of an independent commission. It would compromise the criminal investigation! It would leak intelligence secrets all over the world! It would be a vote of no confidence by the Congress against our own government agencies! That was followed by a letter to Dole and Mitchell from no less than three powerful cabinet members: Transportation Secretary Skinner, Attorney General Dick Thornburgh, and Secretary of State James Baker III. The three officials opposed a commission "in the strongest possible fashion." The letter stressed, repeatedly and emphatically, the danger that an outside probe might interfere with the ongoing criminal investigation of the bombing. "While we are willing to work with the Congress to address the continuing concerns of the families of Pan Am 103," they wrote, "we are very concerned that any commission or special panel . . . would intrude upon our ability to enhance aviation security and prosecute the culprits of this despicable act." It was far from clear, however, that a congressional investigation would have compromised any secrets essential to a criminal prosecution. The issue for the families was not how the U.S. government obtained, if in fact it did, an early warning of the attack, but why it wasn't shared. It was even less clear how such a probe would have "intruded upon" rather than enhanced the prospects for improved aviation safety. "Intruded" seems to have been the operative word—to the other agencies of government any congressional investigation was viewed as an intrusion.

Dole held his ground. Mitchell did, too, although as a Democrat it was easier for him to stand up to the president; Dole met with Bush regularly on the Republican legislative agenda, and Whittinghill is certain the subject came up in those meetings, because the administration was in a near-panic over the issue. "Dole," Whittinghill says of his former boss, "is a man of honor. Once he makes his mind up on something he doesn't let go." The two leaders prepared to pass the legislation in the face of a threatened veto—although, in fact, Whittinghill and Carolla were sure that Bush wouldn't risk the political fallout from taking on the families directly.

They were right. The administration yielded. In July, John Sununu, Bush's chief of staff, met with Dole and Mitchell to negotiate the terms. The White House would accept a commission to investigate the bombing, but it would be established by the president rather than Congress. He brought a draft of a presidential executive order to that effect, drawn up by Nick Rostow, the NSC general counsel. To Dole, this was a great achievement: the families would get the investigation they sought without an embarrassing confrontation with the president. That was almost a model for how he thought government should operate. Over the next few weeks, the terms of the executive order were worked out between the senators' staffs and the White House. Then Whittinghill called Cummock in to talk to Dole, who broke the news to her in person. But Cummock was in dismay: what Dole considered a legislative triumph, she saw as the negation of four months of hard work. She hadn't bargained for this—to have the administration investigate itself.

"Well, we all know if the president wanted a commission he could have appointed it months ago," she replied bitterly.

"I have to give the White House their way on this," Dole said. "The legislation is not going to the floor. I'm pulling my support."

She turned to Whittinghill. "Okay," she said, "if that's the way it has to be. Only *you* go out there and tell the rest of the family members. They're going to think I negotiated it away. They're not my organization, and they hate me anyway."

On August 4, 1989, Bush issued Executive Order 12686, creating a commission to investigate the crash of Pan Am 103. The KAL flight was dropped from the commission's purview (giving rise, of course, to protests from the families of *those* victims, although there were many fewer of them in the United States). The commission's membership was reduced from nine in the original bill to seven, which meant that the four members of Congress would now constitute a majority. Its mandate included investigating the "practices, policies and laws with respect to the treatment of the families of victims of terrorist acts." That same day, Dole rose in the Senate "to join with the distinguished majority leader to announce that President Bush has signed an executive order to create a commission to investigate the security failure which led to the bombing of Pan Am flight 103 . . . I commend President Bush for this initiative. The majority leader and I have been working with the administration and members of the families of the victims for several months to reach this point." That, of course, overlooked the fact that the families of the victims had in fact been working to reach a different point altogether. In the round of congratulatory remarks on the Senate floor, Lautenberg thanked Mitchell and Dole for their work in bringing about what he called the "*Independent* Commission on Aviation Security and Terrorism." When the report came out nine months later, though, the cover read, appropriately, "*President's* Commission on Aviation Security and Terrorism" (italics added).

Bush appointed Sununu as liaison to the families. This meant they would always have a direct channel to the Oval Office, provided they could get through to Sununu himself—and, as Cummock said, "you know how accessible and congenial Sununu can be." Cummock was not about to drop her role as gadfly. Characteristically, she assumed that if the commission was created by executive order on August 4, it should begin work on August 5. When several weeks went by without anyone even being named to the commission, she began leaving messages for Sununu, which were not returned. In September, by coincidence, she was invited to attend a Republican fund-raiser in Washington, at which Bush and Sununu were going to speak, and she flew up and stationed herself just behind the rope line past which the president would walk into the ballroom. As he strode by, she slipped inside the rope and greeted him.

"Why, Mrs. Cummock," exclaimed Bush, with the manners for which he is famous. "How are the children?"

"They are fine, Mr. President," she replied. "But I'm concerned that no one has been named to the commission you created on Pan Am 103. I've been trying to call Mr. Sununu to discuss this, but I haven't been able to reach him."

From atop the steps, Sununu, who was also famous for his manners, glared down at her.

"John," Bush called up to him. "Mrs. Cummock has been trying to reach you."

"Well," he said through clenched teeth, "you have my phone number."

"Yes," she replied, "but do you have a *better* number? You never answer this one."

Formally, Bush appointed all seven members to the commission, although in practice the four congressional representatives were named by the respective majority and minority leaders of the two houses. For the Senate Democrats, Mitchell chose Lautenberg, and for the Republicans, Dole picked Al D'Amato of New York. To chair the commission, Bush appointed Ann McLaughlin, an eminently respectable Republican ("a member of the Board of Directors for five major corporations," the commission report noted) who had served as secretary of labor in

the Reagan administration. In simple terms, according to Frank Duggan, a former aide to McLaughlin who handled liaison with the families, the commission's task was to "find out everything we could about
the bombing, except who did it." The implicit mandate was to satisfy
the family members. "They told me I had the most important job in the
place," Duggan recalls, "because if the families didn't believe us, nothing else mattered."

And the families were not going to be satisfied easily. One of the
first acts of the commission was to invite the two family groups to submit questions that they wanted the commission to address. Here are
some of the sixty-six items they came up with, as summarized in a
memo from the commission's general counsel, Harry R. Van Cleve:

- Was there a de facto selective warning issued to certain government
  employees? Who knew about the warnings and who did not?

- Was the so-called Helsinki warning really a hoax, and if so, when
  was this determined . . . and what action was taken by the FAA
  and the State Department?

- Are the charges of insensitivity made by Pan Am 103 relatives
  against the State Department's Consular Affairs Office of gross
  incompetence, unresponsiveness, and improper delegation of
  responsibilities valid?

- Was there any connection between this bombing and the cast of
  characters from the Iran-Contra scandal—i.e., Oliver North,
  Ronald Reagan, and George Bush? Was it more of the same
  behind-the-scenes dealing?

And one final question for the commissioners to ponder:

- Were these passengers permitted to be sacrificed to appease the
  Iranians for the Airbus shootdown of July 1988?

Five of the questions were grouped by Van Cleve under the heading
"Traficant/MOSSAD Allegations." That was a reference to Rep. James
Traficant, an Ohio Democrat with a reputation as a conspiracy buff,

who had called a press conference early in November to demand an investigation into possible CIA involvement in the bombing. Traficant got the idea from a private investigator for Pan Am's insurance company, an Israeli American named Juval Aviv, who claimed to have a background in Israel's intelligence service, the Mossad. In a confidential report to the law firm that represented the insurance companies, Aviv had laid out a baroque plot involving "an internal covert operation [within the CIA] à la Oliver North or Edwin Wilson"; a ring that employed baggage handlers at Frankfurt to smuggle suitcases packed with heroin aboard Pan Am flights to New York; and several factions of Mideast terrorists, gangsters, and drug dealers. In Aviv's scenario, the freelance CIA group, together with agents of the Drug Enforcement Agency and West German police, were aware of the drug ring in Frankfurt but let it continue to operate, hoping to gain useful intelligence by keeping it under surveillance. Khaled Jaafar, a twenty-year-old American of Lebanese descent who was killed in the crash, was identified by Aviv as a drug courier. According to the report, Palestinian terrorists, in the pay of one or more Mideastern nations, decided to take advantage of the ring to sabotage an airplane by substituting a suitcase containing a bomb for Jaafar's bag of drugs. The flight they chose, Pan Am 103 on December 21, 1988, also carried a team of CIA agents gathering intelligence on American hostages in Beirut. Their leader, army major Charles McKee, supposedly had uncovered the Frankfurt drug operation and was returning to the States to blow the whistle on the rogue agents. The Frankfurt group had been tipped to the bomb plot and even had obtained a German surveillance videotape of the fatal suitcase switch, but either negligently or deliberately chose not to interfere. This, conveniently enough for their purposes, got rid of Major McKee and his colleagues.

To connoisseurs of conspiracy theories, this story had everything: not just the CIA, but a secret cabal within the CIA; not just terrorists, but drug smugglers in cahoots with terrorists; Swiss bank accounts, illegal weapons shipments, cameos by shadowy German and Israeli agents. On the other hand, if you were the relative of someone killed on the airplane—let alone the mother of Major McKee, a highly decorated officer in Army intelligence, or the parents of Khaled Jaafar—it is hard to imagine a more painful and inflammatory set of accusations. Very few of the relatives ever took it seriously, especially once its origins with the hated Pan Am became public. But it was just what the insurance company and its lawyers wanted to hear. They especially liked the part about how the baggage handler pulled off the luggage switch "only after all the checked suitcases had already passed through security. . . . The only measure for airlines to defeat this method would be for security guards to personally conduct all luggage under their personal view from start to actual loading and then closing of the baggage cargo holds on the plane. Only El Al does this." Clearly, Pan Am could not be guilty of "willful misconduct" if the bomb was put on the plane *after* the luggage had passed security, especially if it happened with the connivance of the CIA. (Aviv implied that the rogue Frankfurt operation reported to a "control" higher up in the agency, who also knew about the bomb, but he was unable to identify him.) Once leaked to Traficant, the Aviv report took on a life of its own. Robert Alpert, who was general counsel for the insurance company, quickly disowned the report and left the company with a warning that it would blow up in their faces. It was investigated many times over, but no credible evidence ever emerged for it; even Pan Am's lawyers now admit it was probably nonsense. Yet as often as it was debunked, it resurfaced in television broadcasts, books, Web sites, and, most notoriously, a *Time* magazine cover story; and even today—after two separate trials that found that the bombing came about in a totally different way—there are people who still believe it.

To be sure, a body which owed its existence to George Bush, Bob Dole, and George Mitchell was not going to traffic in fringe conspiracy theories. But the unsung McLaughlin turned out to be a surprisingly strong and independent inquisitor. Praising its work, *New York Times* columnist A. M. Rosenthal wrote: "It turned out to be a runaway commission. Its members told the President the truth, knowing it would not appeal to him." It held five public hearings (the first four witnesses were all family members: Bert Ammerman, Victoria Cummock, Paul Hudson, and

Joan Dater, whose daughter Gretchen was on Pan Am 103); it conducted hundreds of interviews; and on May 15, 1990, issued a lucid and tough-minded 182-page report. The commission uncovered the embarrassing fact that the high-tech thermal neutron analysis luggage scanners—whose purchase was announced with great fanfare by Skinner in April 1989 and cited again by the White House when it established the commission in August—were unable to reliably detect explosives in the quantity used to blow up Pan Am 103. Deploying the devices "would mislead the flying public by offering a false sense of protection," the commission's report concluded. Nor did the commission attempt to gloss over the ineptitude of the State Department in dealing with the families. It issued what amounted to a reprimand to the assistant secretary of state for consular affairs, asserting that "it is hard to understand" why she "did not even visit Lockerbie to assure the families that their State Department was indeed at their side." " . . . [I]t is difficult to find an area where the State Department took a leading role," the report said. "As a result, the families became increasingly dependent on the Scottish police and Pan Am for information and assistance—while the State Department appeared to be a background crew of paper shufflers."

And the commission was unsparing about the shortcomings in Pan Am's security and in the FAA procedures that were supposed to govern them. "The procedures, both private and public, which allowed the [unaccompanied bags on board the plane] were fundamentally flawed," the report found. In all, the commission made scores of recommendations, both about aviation security measures and the responsiveness of government to disasters, and a number of them were eventually incorporated into law or administrative regulations. But one recommendation, the most strongly worded of all, the one that received the most attention in the press—both for its attention-grabbing content, and because it appeared in the first two paragraphs—would strike no responsive chord in Bush's administration, or for that matter in Clinton's, and go largely ignored. It had to do with national will:

National will and the moral courage to exercise it are the ultimate means for defeating terrorism. The President's Commission on

Aviation Security and Terrorism recommends a more vigorous U.S. policy that not only pursues and punishes terrorists but also makes state sponsors of terrorism pay a price for their actions. . . .

These more vigorous policies should include planning and training for preemptive or retaliatory military strikes against known terrorist enclaves in nations that harbor them. Where such direct strikes are inappropriate, the Commission recommends a lesser option, including covert operations, to prevent, disrupt or respond to terrorist acts.

Rhetoric is no substitute for strong, effective action.

That passage was written largely by J. Brian Hyland, a former FBI agent, whose desk adjoined Frank Duggan's. As Hyland wrote, Duggan kept humming "The Battle Hymn of the Republic" to keep his colleague in a martial frame of mind. Duggan was perfect for the job of family liaison: a lawyer and a reliable Republican pol who had been a railroad-industry lobbyist and assistant secretary of labor; and a native of a rough-and-tumble part of Brooklyn who had put himself through college working as a cop—a big, ruddy, rugged-looking man with an engaging, easygoing manner. Needing someone who could win the trust of mostly middle-class families from the Northeast, many of them Irish or Italian Catholics, McLaughlin couldn't have done better than Frank Duggan.

Duggan followed a few simple rules in his liaison work. He would let the family members talk as much as they wanted, promise to check out anything they told him, and avoid expressing judgments on their theories, no matter how preposterous they might seem. "I would let them talk it all out," he said. "I had just recently been divorced, had nowhere to go, and I was perfectly happy to stay down there at night and talk to people. My role, as I saw it, was to let the people down as easily as I could. They'd hear something on the radio and come back believing that the CIA knew about it, or that the Jews had been warned off the plane, and I would never say, look, you're out of your mind." Duggan, like so many others, found himself caught up in the stories, in the families' sorrows and their rage. He went to meetings of the family groups, a habit that he has kept up to this very day, although the commission went out of business after issuing its report in 1990. Whenever someone new came on to the investigation at Justice or the FBI, Duggan would get them a copy of the families' memorial book, *On Eagles' Wings.* "Keep this on your desk," Duggan would urge them. "I don't want to be morbid, but people are going to call you, and some of them are going to be a pain in the ass. So before you answer, flip open to that page and take a look."

And there came a day in 1992 when Duggan's teenage daughter, Trish, was run over by a driver in a stolen car, and in the hospital she slipped into a coma. Then, some of the care and support that Duggan had lavished on the families flowed back to him. Joan Dater told him, you know, I would take back my daughter in a coma, just to hold her for five minutes. I would give anything for that, just to touch once more her warm living flesh. Duggan could only agree that, yes, his daughter was still alive. After eight terrible months Trish came out of her coma, but she couldn't hear and she couldn't remember very much, and it was clear that she would be handicapped for the rest of her life. Duggan had formed a special bond with George Williams, because they were both former military men who had struggled to give up drinking. And he was borne up by his friend.

"You're not going to drink again over this, Frank, are you?" Williams asked.

"No," Duggan replied. "No, George, you didn't drink over yours, how could I drink over mine?"

When the commission finished its work and issued its report, there was a ceremony at the White House for the family members. Duggan thought it appropriate that each should receive an American flag. He went to John Sununu, but Bush's chief of staff turned down the request. Earlier, Sununu had objected to printing the presidential seal on the cover of the report, but he was too late; the covers had already been printed. So Duggan went to the House of Representatives stationery office and bought the flags himself, and found a Marine to fold them the right way, and was prepared to hand them out to the families, in what he, and many of them, felt was a long-overdue gesture of solidarity by the United States toward its citizens, murdered in a terrorist attack against America.

But about a dozen families turned him down. They didn't want an American flag; not this way, not if it wasn't coming directly from the government with full honors.

Duggan kept the flags that were rejected. And over the years, one by one, the relatives agreed to accept them. It marked their personal reconciliation with the government, and something more: recognition of a growing link between the families' quest for justice and the fight to redeem America's national honor in the face of a tragic and humiliating attack.

5

A Breakthrough

The bombing of Pan Am 103 closely followed another momentous event of December 1988. In its last few weeks in office, the Reagan administration had agreed to open talks with the Palestine Liberation Organization (PLO), reversing a long-standing American policy. In fact, it reversed a policy that just a few weeks earlier had been moving in the opposite direction, when Secretary of State George Shultz had denied PLO chairman Yasir Arafat a visa to address the annual session of the United Nations General Assembly. The State Department had routinely issued such visas to representatives of the PLO since the UN granted the organization observer status in 1974, the year in which Arafat himself had been allowed into New York to speak at the UN. Since then Arafat had been suspected of numerous crimes, including the murder of the American ambassador to Sudan in 1978. Now Shultz had drawn the line, over a three-year-old atrocity not even perpetrated by Arafat himself. The event was the murder of an American, Leon Klinghoffer—shot and tossed overboard in his wheelchair after his cruise ship, the *Achille Lauro,* had been commandeered by a guerrilla faction within the PLO headed by Abu Abbas. Arafat, Shultz wrote in his memoirs, "had, through his continued association with Abu Abbas—whom he did not repudiate—condoned the murder of Leon Klinghoffer." Shultz's indignation grew after reading that Arafat and Abu Abbas had enjoyed a friendly chat at a convocation of the Palestinian National Congress on November 15, during which Abbas had reportedly joked about killing Klinghoffer. On November 26 Shultz wrote to the attorney general recommending denial of the visa. The PLO leader, he wrote, "knows of, condones and lends support to such acts; he therefore is an accessory to such terrorism." Shultz, known to speak cautiously, was choosing a phrase that, in legal usage, meant Arafat could have been prosecuted for Klinghoffer's murder. But Shultz was acting largely on his own; although Reagan supported the move, National Security Adviser Colin Powell relayed President-elect Bush's disapproval. Shultz's stand was opposed even within the State Department, whose Middle East experts had detected a trend toward moderation in the PLO's rhetoric and were rushing to embrace it.

Then on December 14, after several false starts during which he seemed incapable of bringing the words to his lips, Arafat issued his dramatic renunciation of terrorism and his acknowledgment of the existence of Israel, meeting the conditions the United States had laid down in 1975 for recognizing the PLO. Shultz swallowed his outrage, although the PLO for its part offered no apologies, much less compensation, for anything in its bloody past. The PLO's victims discovered, as the Pan Am 103 families would find out for themselves, that justice may be measured out to fit the demands of statecraft.

Arafat's move was applauded as an important first step toward peace, except by those who viewed it as a cynical manipulation of American public opinion. Either way, experts cautioned that in the Middle East there were few words as provocative and inflammatory as "peace." "Every past peace process has coincided with new violence," an experienced American diplomat warned. "Since the stakes are even higher this time around, it is more than likely that someone will try to do something even more sensational." Shultz, in his memoirs, recalled it as a time when "a wave of near-hysteria" swept the region. A few days after Arafat's renunciation of terror, American newspapers carried a story out of Damascus, Syria, about a meeting of radical Palestinian factions determined to miss this historic opportunity for peace. The radicals formed a committee to oust Arafat and replace him with a leader committed to "armed struggle against Israel as the only way to liberate the occupied territories." The stories appeared in the United States on the morning of December 21, about the time the bomb was being transferred to the Pan Am 727 in Frankfurt, en route to London, where it would be loaded aboard the 747 to New York.

Among those either represented in Damascus or attending in person was Ahmed Jibril, the founder and commander of the Popular Front for the Liberation of Palestine–General Command (PFLP–GC). Jibril, who was fifty-one in 1988, was memorably described in 1990 by the journalists Steven Emerson and Brian Duffy in *The Fall of Pan Am 103*. "With his comfortable paunch and colorful sports clothes," they wrote, "Jibril looked more like a hardworking shopkeeper content to keep a few steps ahead of the bill collector than the bloody-minded terrorist officials of a dozen intelligence services said he was." The PFLP–GC, one of about a dozen "rejectionist" groups—not counting recognized states like Iraq, Iran, Libya, and Syria—arrayed against Israel, was an offshoot of the hard-line Marxist Popular Front for the Liberation of Palestine. It had broken with Arafat's Fatah group in the bloody fighting in Lebanon of 1982. Even in that company it was distinguished for audacious, technically proficient, and indiscriminate terror attacks, including the bombings of two airliners on the same day in 1970. One, a Swissair flight bound for Tel Aviv, crashed, killing all forty-seven aboard; the other managed to land safely after an explosion at 10,000 feet. In November 1987 Jibril had been in the news again when he sent two commandos on suicide missions aboard powered hang gliders from Lebanon into Israel; one of them, landing near an army base, managed to kill six soldiers before he was shot to death himself.

And Jibril would be in the news often again in 1989 as the leading suspect in the bombing of Pan Am 103. He had, in the classic formulation, a motive, in seeking to disrupt Arafat's opening to the United States and strengthen his reputation as the most rejectionist Palestinian of all; and he had the means, Semtex bombs hidden in radio-cassette machines. In October, in an operation code-named "Autumn Leaves," West German police had broken up a cell of PFLP–GC operatives on suspicion of planning an attack on a U.S. airline. Among those arrested (and quickly let go) were Jibril's top aide, Hafez Kassem el-Dalkamouni, and the chief bomb maker, Marwan Khreeshat, whom Jibril had recruited for the job. Just a day after the bombing, in fact, terrorism experts at an Israeli think tank nominated Jibril as the likely suspect. No one considered it beyond him to order the murders of 270 men, women, and children to make a political point.

In Scotland, searchers were combing the ground on hands and knees, gathering bits of paper, flecks of metal, and shreds of plastic and fabric. Among them were fragments of a circuit board and an instruction manual that detectives determined came from a Toshiba portable radio-cassette player. Many of these were found embedded in pieces of clothing that showed explosive residue, mingled with fragments of a brown Samsonite suitcase. Detectives concluded that the clothing, the bomb, and the radio had all been together in the suitcase. That seemed to implicate Jibril as well, because the bombs seized from the PFLP–GC cell in West Germany, along with detonators, timers, barometric pressure devices, arms, ammunition, and airline timetables, had also been concealed in Toshiba radios—although, as it turned out, a different model than the one found in the wreckage.

In early February CBS News announced that it had determined that Jibril was the culprit, citing sources "in the international terrorist movement." A spokesman for Jibril promptly denied it. "We didn't do it, and we're not involved," he told CBS—but unconvincingly, since he went on to say "we don't practice terrorism and we condemn such actions," assertions that were demonstrable lies. But clearly CBS had gotten ahead of the investigation. Other Middle Eastern groups were capable, in both the technical and moral senses, of blowing up an airplane, and investigators had not ruled them out. And even if PFLP–GC operatives had made and planted the bomb, it didn't necessarily solve the case. Jibril did not operate in a vacuum. His headquarters were in Damascus, and he himself was a former Syrian Army officer, so he was assumed to take orders from (or at least clear them with) Syria's president, Hafez al-Assad. Assad was considered capable of almost any atrocity, but he was also famous for his caution, and there was no obvious reason for him to want to blow up an American airplane just then. At almost any time during Assad's thirty-year reign there were stories in the American media about his yearning for better relations with the United States. Although he never did the one thing that would have made it possible—end his support for Palestinian terrorist groups—he did manage to forestall any direct American military action against his country. Moreover, Syria was allied with Iran, which had vowed to take revenge on the United States for shooting down an Iranian Airbus in July 1988. The Iranian leaders had refused to accept Reagan's apology or the American explanation that the crew of the *Vincennes*, patrolling the Persian Gulf to protect shipping from Iranian harrassment, had mistaken the airliner for an Iranian fighter jet. Instead, they concluded from the date of the tragedy—July 3—that the plane had been shot down in honor of America's Independence Day.

Jibril had also received financial backing from Libya, whose erratic leader, Muammar Kaddafi, had once made the cover of *Newsweek* as "The Most Dangerous Man in the World?" The question mark showed that the magazine didn't necessarily buy the claim, which was being pushed by the State Department. Libya was on the list that the State Department compiled annually of state sponsors of terrorism, along with Syria and Iran (and Cuba, North Korea, and South Yemen, which were not suspects in the Lockerbie case.) On February 5, a few days after the CBS report fingering the PFLP–GC, the *Washington Post* ran a long, seemingly well informed story about the investigation, whose thesis was summed up in this less-than-clarifying observation:

> Jibril's faction remains a clear suspect—along with the Libyan-backed Abu Nidal Organization and pro-Iranian Shiite extremist groups that U.S. antiterrorist experts say could have been operating alone or together—with or without direction from Syria, Libya or Iran.

Even when they are wrong, the newspaper stories of the period are of interest, because they reflect what American officials were thinking and saying at the time. And they were the source of news for the public, including the relatives. The family members' subsequent struggle was shaped by what they were told by the *New York Times* in the morning and by Dan Rather at night. Over the course of the first half of 1989, various organizations and their respective state sponsors moved up or down in the hierarchy of suspicion. In April, CBS scored another scoop by identifying a passenger alleged to have unwittingly brought the bomb on board the plane in his suitcase—Khaled Jaafar, the young Lebanese American man from Detroit. This was several months before Jaafar was identified by Juval Aviv, the investigator hired by Pan Am's insurance company, as a drug courier whose bag of heroin was swapped for one containing a bomb, but the story might have given Aviv the idea. The CBS report was corroborated the next day by several newspapers, raising expectations of a breakthrough, but then nothing seemed to come of this development. The two suitcases Jaafar had checked on the flight in Frankfurt were recovered, and neither was the brown Samsonite that had held the bomb. Just a month later he was dismissed as a suspect in a long story in the *Los Angeles Times* laying out the latest theory of "U.S. intelligence authorities": that an "Iranian Revolutionary Guard faction probably commissioned the crime, the PFLP–GC carried it out, and a defunct Palestinian splinter group called the Arab Organization of May 15 provided the bomb technology."

As the *L.A. Times* story indicated, Iran was coming under increasing suspicion during the first half of 1989, which is why many of the family members were shocked when, in mid-July, the United States announced that it was prepared to pay compensation for shooting down the Iranian airliner a year before. The offer came a few weeks after Iran initiated a complaint in the International Court of Justice in The Hague, seeking compensation and a finding that the United States had acted illegally. It also followed the filing of a lawsuit in Los Angeles Superior Court by relatives of four of the victims, seeking $31 million in damages. Aware of the obstacles to suing the United States government, the lawyers ingeniously found a theory—that a flawed radar system on the destroyer caused the crew to confuse the airliner with a fighter jet—on which to portray the disaster as a matter of product liability, thereby enabling them to add General Electric, Raytheon, and Honeywell as defendants.

The American offer of compensation was carefully worded so as to be as neutral as possible. The United States would not pay for the destruction of the airplane itself. Payments—ranging from $100,000 to $250,000 for each of the 290 victims, with the higher sums going to wage earners who left behind dependents—would be made only to "an appropriate intermediary," such as an international charity, to assure that the Iranian government didn't receive any of it. And the United States specified that the offer was to be an *ex gratia* payment. This meant that although it was footing the bill for the damage it inadvertently caused, America neither admitted any legal culpability nor recognized any moral responsibility to pay for the consequences of what it deemed a "lawful act of self-defense."

In fact, the offer merely reaffirmed and elaborated a promise made a year earlier by President Reagan to compensate the victims' families. Although it couldn't have been foreseen at the time, diplomatic obstacles would prevent any money from actually changing hands until 1996. Nevertheless the idea of paying money to Iran, or even Iranians, struck the Pan Am 103 families as an excess of *gratia* by their own government. The possibility that the Iranian families might actually receive up to $250,000—compared to the $100,000 Pan Am's insurers were offering—was doubly infuriating. Rep. Marge Roukema, a New Jersey Republican, denounced it on the floor of the House as "a cruel slap in the face" to the American families. Paul Hudson wrote to Bush to protest the offer. On November 22, the president replied:

Dear Mr. Hudson:

I want you to know that Barbara and I think constantly about you and the other Pan Am 103 families. You have suffered a grievous loss, and we and all your fellow Americans share with you in that loss and admire your courage. Not a day goes by that I am not reminded of my responsibility to you as your President to bring those responsible to justice.

Unfortunately, the Pan Am 103 investigation has gone on for some time and is, by no means, completed. However, new and important information continues to be found. As a result, we are not yet ready to bring charges against anyone, and I am certainly not prepared to order government action based on the information we currently have. I wish that it were otherwise, but such investigations take time, and we must take care in this important work.

Regarding Iran, as I have said before, we are working to draw that country back into the community of nations from which it has excluded itself for the last decade. This is a gradual and deliberate policy. However, it can only be completed when Iran changes its behavior by securing the release of U.S. hostages and ending its support for terrorism.

With regard to our compensation offer, we believe it is important—purely as a humanitarian gesture—to offer payment to the families of the victims even though our shooting down of the Iranian airliner was clearly accidental. Regardless of the actions of others, the United States stands behind its responsibilities and the strong moral tradition on which our nation was founded. . . .

Draw Iran "back into the community of nations"? As Bush acknowledged in the same sentence, its isolation was a course Iran itself had decided upon; no one had pushed it in that direction. And what of accountability for past crimes? The investigation was still continuing, and any fair-minded person would be willing to wait for the evidence; but by the same token how could the president talk about reconciling with Iran before assessing its guilt? All well and good, Cummock thought, when Hudson showed her Bush's letter, for Iran to end its support for terrorism, but a little late for John Cummock and 269 others. They had become last year's victims; the hostages held by Iranian-backed militias in Lebanon were today's news.

In a broader sense, Bush's remarks reflected his administration's (and his predecessors') ambivalent policy toward terrorism: often espousing toughness without readiness to run its risks, always ready to "engage" rather than to seek retribution or accountability. Perhaps nowhere was this more evident than in dealing with Iran. A "gradual and deliberate policy" of warming up to it seemed tantamount to a promise to forget its crimes against American citizens. Cummock fired off her own reply to Bush, dated January 20, 1990—exactly a year after the president took office. His actions over the past twelve months, she wrote, "have given me every indication that you are willing to look the other way to Iran's barbaric behavior, and that American citizens are expendable in order to attain a bigger foreign policy objective."

To give Bush his due, both Syria and Iran have posed versions of the same dilemma to American foreign policy for decades. Assad had shrewdly managed to position his nation as the forever-missing piece in the jigsaw of Middle East detente, perennially poised to open talks with Israel, and, therefore, perennially to be courted. Iran, on the other hand, since its Islamic revolution of 1979, had been a country hostile not just to America as a nation, but to the very idea of a secular pluralistic democracy. But Iran was not Libya, an isolated desert country with a population of about 5 million; it was a rich, well-armed nation of 65 million, espousing a religious ideology commanding the allegiance of millions more around the world. Hence, apart from a series of naval skirmishes in 1987 and 1988 over Iran's preposterous claim of sovereignty over the Persian Gulf, the United States has never been bold enough to inflict significant military retribution on Iran.

Ronald Reagan is remembered as having been tougher on terrorism than Bush. But it was on his watch in October 1983 that a suicide bomber blew up the U.S. Marine barracks in Beirut, killing 241 American soldiers in what was then considered the largest single terrorist attack against America in history. (A minority of scholars hold that it's not terrorism if the victims were soldiers.) The Reagan administration did not wait around to weigh the evidence of who was responsible. Within three weeks intelligence sources confirmed what everyone suspected anyway, that a large explosive-laden truck could have passed through the Syrian-controlled Bekáa Valley toward its American target only with the connivance of Syria and the backing of Iran. The French, whose barracks were also attacked at about the same time, didn't even wait for that confirmation; they promptly launched a retaliatory air strike on Syrian positions. But the remaining Marines simply hunkered down until they were evacuated weeks later. No action was taken except some ineffectual shelling of the Lebanese hills by the battleship *New Jersey*—not even when Syrian missiles shot down two American fighter planes in December. Despite Reagan's avowed determination not to be driven out of Lebanon by a terrorist attack, Syria and Iran knew within twenty-four hours of the shoot-down that America had no stomach for a sustained engagement.

The Syrians presumably wanted to teach the Western powers a lesson, and they succeeded, better with some than others. British prime minister Margaret Thatcher saw the experience as a lesson in the futility of "retaliatory action which changes nothing on the ground . . . one must avoid taking on a major regional power, like Syria, unless one is prepared to face up to the full consequences of doing so." But Shultz, even ten years after the event, could hardly bring himself to talk about it—not even in his almost-1,200-page memoir, *Turmoil and Triumph: My Years as Secretary of State,* which spends two full chapters on terrorism but relegates to two sentences and a footnote the terror bombing that killed 241 Marines in Beirut, and the (unnoted) lack of an American response.

On September 19, 1989, a DC-10 operated by the French airline UTA on a flight to Paris from Chad crashed in the North African desert. All 171 people aboard—including the wife of the American ambassador to Chad—were killed. The wide dispersion of the wreckage on the ground suggested that a bomb was responsible, and the French began a criminal investigation. The front-page articles recalled the explosion of Pan Am 103 nine months earlier, but in the absence of a direct connection between the two tragedies the story quickly disappeared from American newspapers.

In December 1989 a new suspect in the Pan Am bombing made his appearance in investigators' files, and shortly thereafter in the media: Mohammed Abu Talb, a member of yet another Palestinian militia, the Popular Struggle Front. Talb was already in jail in Sweden, awaiting sentencing for murder stemming from a series of terror bombings in 1985 and 1986. The Popular Struggle Front had attacked synagogues and American and Israeli offices, not airplanes. But investigators had found "numerous personal and coincidental ties" between Talb and the PFLP–GC cell that was building airplane bombs in West Germany. In his apartment they found a calendar for 1988; a circle was drawn around the date December 21. And they discovered that a few months before the bombing Talb had traveled to a place where two of the threads of the investigation were beginning to converge, the Mediterranean island nation of Malta, 200 miles from Libya. Talb himself was eventually dropped from the list of Pan Am suspects—December 21 turned out to be the date his pregnant sister was due to deliver—but as new clues emerged Malta was to loom larger and larger in an investigation that still had two years to run.

One of these clues came from the sodden ground of Lockerbie itself, part of the immense haul of debris that had been gathered and examined there in the months after the crash. Years later the Scottish tribunal summing up the evidence that led to the murder suspects in the bombing of Pan Am 103 described this crucial find:

> Thirteen very severely damaged fragments, many extremely small, of blue fibrous material. One fragment consisted of two overlaid pieces of material, one being a blue fibrous material and the other being knitted white ribbed material. Between these two pieces there was trapped the remains of a label printed in different colours containing information about age, height, composition and "made in Malta." This composite fragment matched closely in all significant respects the labelled neck section of a Babygro Primark brand. The material of the other fragments also matched the material of the same brand. Adhering to these various fragments were fragments of black plastic, wire, paper fragments from the Toshiba owner's manual, and fragments of the divider of the primary suitcase.

In short, a few scraps of fabric and a scorched label from a baby's jumpsuit. Scottish detectives visited the clothing factory in Malta in

March and determined it was from a lot of 500, which had been sold to retail stores in Ireland and in Malta itself. Inevitably, the mention of Ireland excited the attention of British investigators, although a moment's reflection would have raised the vexing question of why the Irish Republican Army, with so many supporters in the United States, would have wanted to blow up an American airplane. But the Babygro took on new significance after the emergence of a second clue, a printout from the computer system that tracked baggage through the Frankfurt airport. The German federal police had this printout in their possession soon after the bombing but for reasons that have never been explained did not turn it over to the Scottish detectives until August 16. It appeared to show that a piece of luggage had been transferred onto the first leg of Pan Am 103 from Air Malta flight 180, originating in Luqa Airport, Malta. A piece of luggage—but no passenger. None of the interline passengers aboard Pan Am 103 had arrived on Air Malta; none of the passengers on the Air Malta flight had been ticketed through to London or New York on Pan Am. Detectives rushed back to Malta in late August and began fanning out among the shops that sold the Babygro jumpsuits. At a store called Mary's House, they struck pay dirt. The shopkeeper remembered quite well selling the Babygro. He remembered it, in part, because the shopper had bought an odd miscellany of clothing—a child's jumper, a tweed jacket, several pairs of men's trousers in different sizes, and several shirts. Those descriptions matched other fabric scraps that had been recovered from the ground in Scotland. And the shopkeeper remembered the purchaser rather well. He looked, he thought, like a Libyan.

That by itself was not too surprising; Malta was close to Tripoli and there was considerable traffic between the two countries. But for Libya to come up in the investigation of a terror bombing set off bells in Washington and London. For twenty years the country had been run by the eccentric will of Kaddafi. As a young captain he had led the coup against the not-overly-lamented King Idris, to whom the Allies had entrusted Libya (and its oil) after the Second World War. Since then he had promoted himself to colonel, but he held no official position in his own government, ruling by exhortation, proclamation, and, according to the U.S. State Department, the simple expedient of assassinating his opponents, both those inside the country and those who had escaped. His philosophy was a farrago of Islamic mysticism, revolutionary Marxism, and personal megalomania. He saw himself as the savior of oppressed people as diverse as the blacks of South Africa (a favor South African president Nelson Mandela was to return years later) and the American Indians (who, he informed President Reagan in a letter, were mostly "of Libyan origin"). Kaddafi yearned to be a major power on the world stage. At one time or another in the 1970s he had proposed federating or even merging his country with Egypt, with Sudan, with Tunisia, and with Syria, but the affection was not returned. Egyptian president Anwar el-Sadat called his neighbor to the west "a vicious criminal, 100 percent sick and possessed of the demon."

But Libya produced oil—nearly $25 billion worth in 1991—and that translated into big money, for which there were always takers happy to overlook a few eccentricities or assassinations. Spurned by his fellow Arab leaders, Kaddafi envisioned himself at the head of a mighty pan-African union. More ominously, he had amassed a fleet of Russian MIG-25 fighter planes and obtained uranium toward the construction of an "Islamic bomb" in Pakistan. And he had turned his country into a refuge and arsenal for revolutionaries, guerrillas, and terrorists from four continents, ranging from the Japanese Red Army to the Provisional IRA. According to the State Department, in the Middle East Kaddafi was the prime sponsor of the Abu Nidal Organization and also supported the Palestine Liberation Front, the Popular Struggle Front, Palestine Islamic Jihad, and Jibril's notorious group, the PFLP–GC.

Of course, some of the same groups, and others just as bloody-minded, were supported by Syria and Iran. But Libya had the distinction of actually having been attacked on its home soil by the United States. That followed months of escalating tensions between the two countries, beginning in December 1985 with bloody commando attacks on the El Al ticket counters in Rome and Vienna. Twenty people, including five Americans, were killed in the attacks by the Libyan-backed Abu Nidal group. On January 7 President Reagan severed all American trade and economic ties with Libya. Kaddafi threatened to "pursue U.S. citizens in their country and streets." In March Reagan sent an American armada across Kaddafi's "Line of Death" in the Gulf of Sidra, where Libya claimed sovereignty well beyond the internationally recognized twelve-mile limit. Predictably, Libyan forces fired at the American ships, touching off a skirmish in which U.S. forces sank several Libyan missile boats and destroyed a land-based radar site.

Then, early in the morning of April 5, a bomb went off in the LaBelle discotheque in West Berlin, which was crowded with off-duty American soldiers. Two people were killed and more than 150 wounded, including many Americans. American intelligence had intercepted messages between Tripoli and its embassy in East Berlin proving that Kaddafi was behind the attack. On the evening of April 14, Washington time, American planes from carriers in the Mediterranean and bases in Britain raided the Libyan cities of Benghazi and Tripoli. Kaddafi's own house was heavily damaged in the attack, along with the French embassy, which was hit by mistake. More than forty civilians were killed in the neighborhood adjacent to the Azzaziyah Barracks, where Kaddafi himself was staying that night. The official American position was that it had no intention of killing the Libyan leader himself, which would have been a violation of both American and international law, although if the roof had happened to fall on his head, Reagan said later, "I don't think any of us would have shed tears."

The Libyan bombing was the high point of the American military response to terrorism. The Reagan administration heralded it as a huge success. President Reagan's standing in public opinion polls soared, although a poem read on Libyan state television ominously, if cryptically, warned that the president would be "killed in a contemptible manner, instantly, like a pig . . ." The Tokyo summit of the seven Western industrialized nations in May put terrorism high on the agenda. The Group of Seven issued ringing commitments to take action, individually and collectively, against state-sponsored terrorism. Shultz, meeting with a large U.S. press contingent, was full of confidence. Asked what message he had intended to send to Kaddafi, he replied curtly: "You've had it, pal." That phrase was played on television and caught the headlines, and Shultz may well have thought his headaches with Libya were behind him. Veterans of the Reagan administration, even those who presumably know better, still promulgate that as the quasi-official version. As late as 1993, Howard Teicher, senior director for political-military affairs in the National Security Council in the Reagan years, wrote in his memoirs that "a political objective of the mission had been achieved. [Kaddafi] as well as the other state sponsors of terrorism, notably Syria and Iran, could no longer take for granted that the United States would continue to endure terrorist attacks against America with impunity." And on October 13, 2000, former secretary of state Lawrence Eagleburger appeared on CNN's *Crossfire* to defend the concept of military retaliation against terrorists (in that case, Islamic militant Osama bin Laden). As an example of a successful military strike, he mentioned "President Reagan's response against Libya when they—on the bombing of the bar in Germany—we haven't seen much of Mr. Kaddafi since." Even as he spoke, two of Mr. Kaddafi's intelligence agents were on trial for putting a bomb aboard Pan Am 103—two and a half years after Reagan ordered the bombing of Libya.

Kaddafi, it seems, didn't get the message America intended for him. He may have been paying attention to European public opinion, which manifested itself in anti-American demonstrations in several allied countries. France had pointedly refused permission for the land-based bombers to overfly its territory, requiring a 1,200-mile detour, and even Reagan's staunch ally, British prime minister Margaret Thatcher, came under political attack at home. Kaddafi may well have concluded that the United States wasn't going to pay this political price a second time. Libyan-sponsored anti-American terrorism didn't stop after the American bombing; it merely shifted to "front companies and other organizations to hide Libya's hand," according to a 1991 State Department report titled "Libya's Continuing Support for Terrorism." The report charged that "the Libyans sponsored a series of anti-US operations immediately after the US air strikes in April 1986 . . . Tripoli was responsible for the shooting of a US embassy communicator in Sudan . . . Two Libyans were apprehended on 18 April 1986 as they attempted to attack the US

Officers Club in Ankara with grenades . . . The Libyans confessed that they were ordered to cause the maximum number of casualties, particularly women and children."

Thus when Libya surfaced in the Pan Am investigation, few American diplomats or counter-terrorism experts were surprised. It was, in fact, welcome news for the Bush administration, which had no appetite for a confrontation with the other leading suspects, Iran and Syria. On March 10 National Security Adviser Brent Scowcroft finally answered Cummock's letter to Bush. He reminded her that the investigation into the Pan Am bombing was still continuing, and cautioned her that press reports blaming the PFLP–GC and Iran were merely "speculative." On April 30 the State Department's annual report "Patterns of Global Terrorism" was released, listing Iran and Syria as well as Libya among the six nations accused of supporting terrorist activities. According to news stories, White House officials had asked the State Department to postpone the report, but it turned out the April 30 deadline was mandated by law as part of the State Department's reporting requirements to Congress. The White House was embarrassed by the report; it came out on the very day President Bush publicly thanked Iran and Syria for helping to release an American hostage in Lebanon.

It was at about this time that a new development was to shift the investigation decisively in the direction of Libya. The Scottish judges' decision traces the history of yet another charred scrap of fabric picked up on January 13, 1989, near Newcastleton, logged into the records of the investigation four days later, and finally examined on May 12, when it was found to be the badly damaged and charred neckband of a Slalom brand shirt. Embedded in this material was a fragment of a circuit board, half the size of a thumbnail. It appeared that the elastic in the fabric had melted and fused in the heat of the explosion, sealing the fragment inside and protecting it as it fell to earth, and assuring it would be spotted by searchers who might otherwise easily have overlooked a chip of green plastic that fell to earth somewhere on 845 square miles of greenery. In September, at last, investigators turned their attention to this infinitesimal clue and discovered that it did not match any of the wiring from the Toshiba boom box in which the bomb was believed to have been hidden. Only one other electronic device could have been in such proximity to the explosion, investigators reasoned. It must have been a part of the bomb itself.

Detectives fanned out all over the world, searching among the most ubiquitous products of contemporary industry, electronic circuit boards, for one showing the same distinctive pattern of tracks. In early January 1990 Detective Superintendent Stuart Henderson, the deputy head of the Scottish task force, sent a photograph of the board to one of the FBI's top explosives experts, Thomas Thurman, asking for his help in identifying it. Thurman says Henderson asked him to keep his inquiries within the bureau, and he complied. Over most of the next six months he worked on trying to match the photo to records in the FBI's huge database of IEDs ("Improvised Explosive Devices," or bombs). The shape of one edge of the fragment reminded Thurman of the circuit boards in travel alarm clocks that had been used in bombs by Japanese Red Army terrorists. He asked agents in Malta to send him one of every kind of travel clock they could find in the shops there, and when they arrived he took them apart and spread them out over his workbench, but they didn't match, either.

In June, Henderson came to America for a conference of American and British investigators at the FBI compound in Quantico, Virginia. Thurman brought up the circuit board and asked Henderson's permission to consult another agency. He doesn't remember if he specifically mentioned the CIA, but that was the agency he had in mind. Henderson assented. A few days later, Thurman visited CIA headquarters and met a friend there, a brilliant forensic analyst. He was handed a stack of photographs of bomb components the CIA had retrieved from all over the world. None matched. On an impulse, he asked, "Did you save any of the hardware?" A single device, a few inches square, was brought for him to examine. Thurman removed the circuit board and put it under a low-powered stereoscopic comparison microscope, with his photograph alongside it. An instant after, he jumped up from his bench. The photograph precisely matched the specimen he was examining, down to the little manufacturing imperfections that indicated they were not just the same item but from the same batch. The device, he was informed, was from a timer seized in Senegal in 1988, and it matched another that had turned up in Togo two years before that—in both cases in the possession of agents linked to Libyan intelligence. It was an MST-13 timer produced by the Swiss firm of Meister and Bollier (or Mebo)—one of a batch of twenty that, as Mebo's director Edwin Bollier later admitted to FBI agents—had been manufactured expressly for Libya.

Thurman had made a decisive breakthrough. But he was in a delicate situation, because he wanted that timer, and he wasn't sure the CIA was going to give it up. The CIA and the FBI ultimately serve the same government, obviously, but they occupy different realms, geographically, legally, and epistemologically. The FBI is a criminal investigative body, subordinate to the Department of Justice, although in practice often more independent than its political superiors might care for. It deals in provable assertions backed by evidence that meets the burden of proof demanded in a criminal trial. The CIA is an intelligence organization. It deals in probabilities, in estimates of capabilities and assessments of intentions, and it employs methods that were never designed to survive a suppression hearing on search-and-seizure. The Pan Am bombing was remarkable in the degree to which the CIA actually did cooperate with a criminal investigation. In an unprecedented breach of practice, the agency even allowed an informant to testify at the trial of the two suspected bombers. But back in 1990 when Thurman asked to have the timer, he had to promise that he was not planning to use it as evidence that might show up in court but only as a lead to help track down the source of the fragment recovered in Lockerbie. "You can have it," he was told. "But you didn't get it from us."

The CIA, of course, was also carrying on an investigation into the bombing, with its own methods and for its own purposes. The nation sends its military into action based on intelligence, not criminal evidence. The 1986 air strike on Libya had been based on communications intercepts; Reagan didn't wait for the perpetrators of the bombing to be arrested and tried. But the bombing of Pan Am 103 had been treated as a crime, not an act of war, dating back to the very beginnings of the investigation, when, indeed, it might have been one. Later, there would be opportunities to reverse that decision, but those opportunities were not taken. The investigation into what the families regarded as an attack on America was from beginning to end conducted under the auspices of the Dumfries and Galloway constabulary. Whatever the other implications of that course, by forcing the investigation into paths that could be retraced in open court, it helped determine the outcome. Those paths turned out to lead only to Libya.

And yet at the very heart of the mystery of Pan Am 103, for the families, at least, there remains the unresolved and perhaps unresolvable question of the culpability of Jibril and his patrons in Iran and Syria. Very few people outside of Libya itself doubt the guilt of Abdel Basset Ali Al-Megrahi, the Libyan agent who was indicted, tried, and convicted for the bombing. Almost all Western experts on Libya assume that his orders must have been cleared—if they didn't actually originate—with Kaddafi himself. But among the families and in intelligence circles it is widely believed that Megrahi was implementing a plot conceived by Jibril, on authority from Iran and with the acquiescence of his patron, Syria.

In this scenario, after the German police broke up the PFLP–GC cell and seized their bombs, Jibril handed the job off to Libyan intelligence. The argument has the virtue of logical coherence; the alternative requires the assumption that in the fall of 1988 there were two separate cadres of terrorists (the PFLP–GC and the Libyans) independently planning to blow up airplanes flying out of Germany with bombs hidden in Toshiba radios. And there is at least circumstantial evidence for it. American intelligence sources say that Iran transferred $11 million into an account controlled by Jibril at a Hungarian bank a few days after the bombing. If this scenario is true, then by the same standard Shultz had applied to Arafat in calling him an "accessory" to terrorism, Iran and Syria were as much accessories to murder. Moreover, Iran and Syria, or their respective leaders, would be guilty even if they did nothing to advance the plot once it had been turned over to the Libyans; under American criminal law, parties to the original conspiracy are absolved only if they take specific steps to repudiate it.

One of those who thinks that Iran must be implicated is retired CIA officer Robert Baer, whose twenty-one-year career at the agency was mostly devoted to fighting Middle Eastern terrorists. Baer had spent 1986 to 1988 in Beirut, infiltrating Iranian-backed terror groups, before being reassigned to Paris in September. He left behind his friend and roommate, Chuck McKee, who was on his way home on December 21 aboard Pan Am 103. "This was too sophisticated an operation for Libya to have pulled off alone," Baer says. "The bomb had to travel on three different planes through three airports." Baer believes the White House was only too happy to focus on Libya, and that attitude filtered down to agents in the field, who stopped pursuing evidence against Iran and Syria. "The most closely guarded secret in Washington, and the most shameful, is that we look the other way when it comes to Iran's responsibility for these acts," he says. "We only want to pick a fight with those we can beat." In 1996, when Baer met Victoria Cummock, the conversation brought her to the brink of tears. "He voiced what Paul Hudson and I had been saying to each other all through the end of 1990 and into 1991," Cummock says. "We were getting the State Department briefings, and we both noticed there was less and less in them about Syria and the Iranians. Then we stopped hearing anything about them."

Some of these whispers found their way into print. Syndicated columnists Jack Anderson and Dale Van Atta reported in mid-1990 on "a private pact" between Bush and British prime minister Margaret Thatcher to "downplay" the investigation. "Both had learned that Iran may have paid Palestinian terrorists to do the job," they wrote. "Bush and Thatcher agreed that they were powerless to strike back against Iran, so the information would be best kept under wraps." The summer of 1990, of course, corresponds to the period when investigators began finding evidence against Libya. But something else happened then as well: Saddam Hussein invaded Kuwait, and overnight every other geopolitical consideration in the Mideast took a back seat to defeating Iraq. Iran, which had for years been at war with Iraq, now gained in importance as a counterweight to Saddam. And once again the United States found itself courting Iraq's neighbor and enemy, the eternal linchpin of American ambitions for peace in the Middle East, Hafez al-Assad of Syria.

So do you believe Baer, who brings both moral certainty and the credibility of a longtime field operative to his account? Or do you trust the officials in Washington, who for the most part have closed ranks behind the assertion that information never turned up to link Jibril, Iran, and Syria to the bombing? Vincent Cannistraro, the CIA's deputy chief of operations for antiterrorism in 1988, says he does not rule out the possibility of Iranian or Syrian involvement but has yet to be convinced of it. He disputes the significance of Iran's $11 million payment to Jibril; Iran was sending money to Jibril all the time in those years. Nor did he ever experience any political pressure to keep away from Iran or Syria. It would be unheard-of for politicians to dictate the course of a field investigation, he maintains. Even the suggestion is infuriating to the State Department. At a tense meeting with the family groups shortly after the indictments came out, Deputy Secretary of State Lawrence Eagleburger angrily denounced a family member for asking if the reason Iranian and Syrian involvement wasn't found was because investigators were discouraged from looking for it. He regarded that as tantamount to an accusation of lying. "He got very irate and launched into a tirade," recalls Stephanie Bernstein, a young mother of two whose husband, Michael, had died on the plane. "He said, 'How dare you impugn the integrity of the president I work for!' People were very offended."

Eagleburger might have been touchy because the president he worked for had blithely exonerated Syria with an offhand remark the very day the indictments were announced. "The Syrians took a bum rap on this," Bush declared, even while his own Justice Department was promising to keep pursuing the case wherever it led. "We started off with a hard-on to go after Iran, knowing what we did about Autumn Leaves," says Larry Johnson, then an official in the State Department's Office of Counter-Terrorism. "But we were getting nowhere, and then we did a 180-degree turn once we found out about the timer." Some family members are still trying to find out what got left behind in that 180-degree turn. It is unlikely that they will ever know. For others, it is quite enough to know who pulled the trigger.

6

Tracking Libya

The information implicating Libya was, of course, secret. Neither the public nor the families were told at the time that the focus of the investigation had moved to Libya and away from Iran and Syria. As far as they could tell, a year and a half had gone by since the bombing and the investigation appeared stalled. But the family groups also had a new cause to focus on in the summer of 1990. Following the report of the McLaughlin Commission in May, Sen. Frank Lautenberg and his three congressional colleagues on the commission introduced bills based on its recommendations. The report's essential recommendation was to pay more attention to the danger of terrorists putting bombs on airplanes, and the bill was an elaborate exercise in translating that demand into bureaucratic infrastructure. It created a new post, "Director of Intelligence and Security," in the Department of Transportation, with duties including preparation of an annual Aviation Security Report. It authorized the FAA to add an "Assistant Administrator for Civil Aviation Security" and to hire security directors at specified high-risk airports. It required improved background screening and training for airport security workers, and it mandated expedited research on bomb-detection devices to screen luggage. And it tried to assure that relatives of victims never again went through the unique torments suffered by the Pan Am 103 families, by establishing procedures for the State Department to follow in contacting family members.

It's hard to imagine who could have seriously opposed a bill based on the widely praised report of a bipartisan commission, intended to appeal to Americans' common decency and desire not to be killed in an airplane bombing. At least it was hard for Cummock to imagine, but she was learning that by itself the obvious, undisputed desirability of a measure was not sufficient for it to be actually enacted. "When we started out trying to do something to prevent this from happening again, people told me, it'll take an act of Congress, and I said, okay, great, where do we go for one of those?" she recalled, many battle-scarred years later. "Now when someone says that, I go *Eeeek! Why don't you try for something simple, like a proclamation from the Pope?*" As a matter of fact, even Cummock's own group, Families of Pan Am 103/Lockerbie, opposed the bill in its original form, and only endorsed it after strengthening amendments were added. (The original family group, Victims of Pan Am 103, supported the bill from the outset.) Predictably, the airline industry took the position that the security of its passengers must be assured at all costs, as long as those costs didn't come out of its profits. The various bureaucracies whose lives would be affected by the bill wanted their say as well. So even without much overt opposition, the bill took more than three months to pass—exceptionally fast for a significant piece of legislation, although it seemed excruciatingly slow at the time. For much of that time Hudson, Cummock, and the other family members (aided now by a professional lobbyist) fought what Cummock called "the Battle of the Clauses—all the little phrases like 'to the extent practical' and 'consideration will be given' that they put in there when no one's watching, so that in the end it doesn't mean anything anyway." Cummock continues to be a skeptic about American airline security, and she is in a position to know, having served on an aviation-safety commission chaired by Vice President Al Gore. However, whether or not the assistant administrator for civil aviation security was the person responsible, the fact is that from 1988 until September 2001 there were no successful attacks on American airlines.

This bill could not have been passed without the families, who struggled in 1989 to establish the commission, and again in 1990 to pass the legislation, and who provided the moral authority necessary to overcome the immense inertia of the federal government. "No matter what the experts say, no matter how desirable something like this is in the abstract, to actually pass it takes blood on the ground," says Paul Hudson. "Our family members were the blood." They could say, truthfully, that they weren't doing it just for themselves, which immediately set them apart from most people who lobby the government. The passengers on Pan Am 103 weren't going to be brought back by an act of Congress, but the family members threw themselves into it with the same passion that Suse Lowenstein brought to her sculptures of mothers struck down by grief: this was *their* memorial to their loved ones. "It seemed to me a very Jewish thing to do," says Stephanie Bernstein, whose husband, Michael, had been a prosecutor in the Justice Department's Office of Special Investigations, the unit that tracked down Nazi war criminals for deportation—by coincidence, the same office that Allan Gerson had helped establish in 1979, although the two had never met. Michael Bernstein had given up a lucrative practice with the prestigious Washington law firm of Covington and Burling to take this comparatively low-paying government job, and Stephanie saw the time she spent waiting in congressional offices or leaving messages for reporters as honoring him in a way he would have appreciated. "Our biggest selling point," she says, "was that we're not doing it for ourselves, this is for the public good. Who could be against that? Except the industry, of course."

It turned out, though, that the biggest threat to the bill wasn't opposition from industry, or, in fact, opposition of any kind; it was the sheer complexity and perversity of the legislative process. The bill had, in principle, the support of both Dole and Mitchell, and strong backing in the House as well, but sometime in the fall it seemed to lose momentum; days, then weeks, went by without it moving toward the floor for a vote. Hudson was watching the calendar; there were only so many legislative days left before adjournment. The family members who had worked so hard for the bill were growing restless, and as the end of October neared they began to move from lobbying to demonstrating. They began a phone assault on Dole's office, calling again and again, frantically, so that for a few hours every time a staffer hung up the phone it would immediately ring again, and every time he picked up the phone to place a call he'd find a Pan Am 103 family member on the line. Finally a sympathetic Senate aide explained to them what was happening: the bill was the object of a "silent hold," a maneuver, not taught in high-school civics classes, by which a legislator can in virtual secrecy block a bill until he gets a favored amendment attached. In this case, he learned, it was a Republican from a Western state who sought a change in regulations affecting truck weights on interstate highways and chose the Aviation Security Act as the way to achieve it.

When Hudson found out, he called his wife, Eleanor, who was on the couch in her living room in Albany, New York, keeping track of legislative developments by telephone. All through the struggle, armed only with her phone and her memory, she had been a crucial resource for the family members in their lobbying; she seemed to keep in her head the complete list of Pan Am 103 victims and their family trees, so that when someone needed to approach a particular legislator, Eleanor could usually be counted on to come up with a sister or aunt of a victim who lived in the relevant state. Now, hearing from Paul that all their work over the past five months was in danger of coming to naught over an unrelated issue having to do with trucking, she was galvanized. "They were killing my work," she says. "How dare they? I gave up my husband for two years, my son dropped out of school, our business was falling apart—this couldn't be allowed to happen." Without even knowing for sure the capital of the state involved, she called directory assistance and asked for the phone number of the leading television station. When the operator said that she needed more to go on than that, Eleanor poured out her heart to her. Ordinary people seemed never to turn down a Pan Am family member. Eleanor got the number and called the station and asked to speak to the news director.

"Do you know what your senator is doing to these people who lost their sons and daughters on Pan Am 103?" she demanded.

Around the same time, Jane Schultz, whose son, Thomas Britton Schultz, had been killed on the flight, was buttonholing George Bush as he campaigned for Republican candidates in Connecticut. Whether because of Eleanor's call, or because Bush interceded with the leadership, or some other maneuver—events were moving very fast—within hours the hold was dropped and the bill proceeded to a speedy passage. As the vote was tallied, Dole, catching sight of the family members in the gallery, gave them an exuberant thumbs-up. Afterward there was a reception for the senators and family members who had worked on the bill. Bob Monetti, whose son, Rick, died on the plane, remembers exactly his feelings on that day. "I'd been thinking, we're going to get this passed, and then I'm going to feel better," he recalls. "And then it passed, and everyone was all excited, and I thought: So? What now? I still have the rest of my life to get through."

The case against Libya picked up speed in early 1991, around the time Syria was sending its soldiers to march (none actually fought) in the Gulf War alongside American troops. In February, the shopkeeper in Malta who had sold the Babygro jumper picked out a photograph of a man who resembled the purchaser. It was a photograph of Abdel Basset Ali Al-Megrahi, a highly placed agent of the Libyan intelligence service, the JSO. In April, detectives searched the offices of a Maltese travel agency run by Al Amin Khalifa Fhimah, who had been the manager of the Libyan Arab Airlines (LAA) office in Malta at the time Pan Am 103 went down. They found Fhimah's datebook for 1988; in December, a week before the bombing, he had made a note to pick up Air Malta luggage tags. Luggage tags are ordinarily kept under tight security by airlines, out of fear of precisely what did happen to Pan Am 103, but Fhimah had retained access to secured areas of Luqa Airport.

By that time, it was no longer a secret that investigators were focusing on Libya. French authorities had found evidence that the 1989 UTA bombing had been ordered by Kaddafi's government, which had been nursing a grievance against France for supporting the government of Chad against a Libyan-backed insurrection. At the end of October, a French judge issued arrest warrants for four Libyan intelligence officials, including Kaddafi's powerful brother-in-law, Abdullah Senoussi. The French claimed to have information that both the UTA and Pan Am bombings were decided on at a meeting in Tripoli in September 1988. If true, that would tend to exonerate Jibril and Iran in the Pan Am bombing, because it implies Libya was planning the attack even before the PFLP–GC cell in Germany was rounded up; Jibril would have had no reason to hand off the job to the Libyans until after the arrests, in October. But American investigators never confirmed this September meeting.

The murder indictments against Megrahi and Fhimah, announced simultaneously in Washington and Scotland on November 14, 1991— almost three years after the bombing—marked a decisive turning point in the families' search for justice. Henceforth terror would have a face, the saturnine and heavy-lidded visages of Megrahi and Fhimah, and the families' anger would have an object, Muammar Kaddafi. The indictments would also represent an affirmation of American intentions to treat the bombing of Pan Am 103 as a crime rather than an act of war. Although in public American officials did not rule out a military strike to punish Libya, it never came under serious consideration. A well-placed State Department official describes this as "a personal decision made by George Bush." But it happened to coincide with the interests of two of the most important bureaucracies within his administration. One was the Department of Justice, especially its Criminal Division, headed by Assistant Attorney General Robert S. Mueller III. Justice was gung-ho to prosecute one of the greatest crimes of the century. Deputy Assistant Attorney General Mark Richards was put in charge of the case, overseeing a task force headed by veteran prosecutor Brian Murtaugh. "Their attitude was, we tough cops will go in there and put these guys away before the candy-assed diplomats can sell us out," says one top State Department official who met with prosecutors during that period.

The military, by contrast, "was nowhere in these meetings," the official says. "They were there but they just didn't raise their head." The lesson the Pentagon seemed to have taken from its victory over Saddam Hussein ten months earlier was that it was fine to go into combat if you could exactly replicate the conditions of the Gulf War. The underlying philosophy of the "Powell Doctrine," which set up a list of rigorous conditions for deploying military force, was that the pursuit of mere political goals around the globe was an unworthy use of American military power. The military's unique, sacrosanct mission was the defense of America's vital national interests. Certainly some people defined the national interest broadly enough to encompass justice for Americans killed in a bombing and the deterrence of future terrorism. But the Pentagon tended to define it in terms of direct threats to American security, not abstractions such as "justice" or "teaching terrorists a lesson." From the military point of view, Libya, a country with a population roughly twice that of Brooklyn, manifestly wasn't a serious danger to the United States, regardless of what two people named Megrahi and Fhimah might have done in 1988.

Apart from the particular internal political dynamics of the Bush administration, the Lockerbie bombing presented a test case for American policymakers and foreign policy pundits: should America retaliate against state-sponsored terrorism and, if so, should it be done selectively, determined by its needs and interests? Leaving aside moral questions about the risk of killing innocent civilians, the practical argument against a military strike is that it may invite another round of retaliation. The United States did bomb Tripoli in 1986, after all, and 270 people apparently paid the price in 1988. Moreover, evidence of Libyan activities after 1986 show that it was wishful thinking for Shultz to believe that bombing could work as a one-time proposition. Terrorists must be convinced that each provocation will bring a certain, and presumably escalating, response. The argument for retaliation is that the long-term gain in American credibility will have a deterrent effect that will eventually save more lives than it costs. But events in the real world don't always conform to the scenarios played out in think tanks. States that sponsor terrorism don't usually announce their intentions at press conferences. It took three years and the most extensive criminal investigation in history to identify Libya as the perpetrator of the Pan Am bombing, and, even so, it depended on the recovery of fingernail-sized bits of evidence. What if the next plane were to blow up over the ocean, and you never found out who did it? Could the United States bomb Libya again just on suspicion?

In the final analysis, the decision not to bomb Libya in 1991 at the time of the U.S. indictments reflected the political zeitgeist of the period, which found its expression in Bush's vision of a "New World Order." It was a period of rapid and exhilarating change in the world. The Soviet Union, which had helped support the Kaddafis of the world, had disappeared from the political map, and in its place was a humbled and compliant Russia. Historic peace negotiations were underway in the Middle East; the last of seventeen American hostages held in Beirut would soon be home. It was possible to imagine a world in which terrorism would recede as a threat, and for Bush, much more agreeable to look forward to that future than back at a bombing now almost three years old.

All this analysis begins, of course, with the assumption that Megrahi and Fhimah didn't decide on their own to bomb the plane. White House spokesman Marlin Fitzwater told reporters it was "impossible for us to believe that the [Libyan] government was not involved and that this is not a case of state-sponsored terrorism." Acting Attorney General William P. Barr declared that the investigation "is continuing and will be pursued unrelentingly until all responsible are brought to justice." The detectives had done their job, which was to identify the direct perpetrators. The next move, in a typical case, would be to bring them in for questioning and get them to turn in their superiors. Regrettably, American intelligence officials say, the next level up of JSO officers, to whom Megrahi would have reported, was to suffer exceptionally high attrition in the 1990s owing to a rash of unexplained automobile crashes, accidental drownings, and horseback-riding mishaps. But this was hardly a typical case, anyway. Megrahi and Fhimah had left Malta on the first flight back to Tripoli on the morning of December 21, 1988, and when the indictments came out three years later, they were still in Libya. As Scotland's chief prosecutor, Lord

Peter Fraser of Carmyllie, put it, they were "not likely to be arrested in the normal way."

At this very moment, though, there were a handful of officials in Washington, clustered in the National Security Council and the State Department's Office of Counter-Terrorism, who saw in the indictments the seeds of a great opportunity for American diplomacy. One of them, Ambassador Richard A. Clarke, in charge of the White House Counter-Terrorism Office, was still working at the NSC well into the Clinton administration, in an office in the Old Executive Office Building with a big combination lock on the door and a sign behind his desk that said THINK GLOBALLY, ACT GLOBALLY. From the global perspective neither Megrahi nor Fhimah were of any importance by themselves, except as the means to achieve a long-sought goal of American foreign policy, the isolation and neutralization of Kaddafi. Of course, Kaddafi was unlikely to ever turn them over to the West, nor would they surrender on their own, but that was not a problem, certainly not one that cried out for a solution. To the contrary, it was desirable to leave things just as they were. Libya would be their prison, and the United States would do its best to keep Kaddafi in there with them.

Thus American strategy proceeded down two tracks. At the Justice Department the demand for Kaddafi to surrender the two suspects for a trial in the United States or Britain was taken seriously as something to be worked for, and, although it was considered unlikely, preparations were made and careers advanced on the prospect of a criminal trial. To others, this was legalistic thinking, an illustration of how the law sharpens the mind by narrowing it. They had larger purposes than a trial in mind. And Kaddafi obligingly played into their hands by refusing to turn over the men to the West. "The evidence against Libya," he ringingly proclaimed, "is less than a laughable piece of a fingernail."

On November 27 the United States and Britain followed their demand for extradition with a statement circulated as an official document in the UN General Assembly and Security Council. (France issued its own letter related to the suspects in the UTA bombing.) The United States and Britain incorporated some new demands into a side letter. Libya now was required to

- Surrender for trial all those charged with the crime; and accept responsibility for the actions of Libyan officials

- Disclose all it knows of this crime, including the names of all those responsible, and allow full access to all witnesses, documents and other material evidence, including all the remaining timers

- Pay appropriate compensation

It doesn't take a constitutional scholar to notice that this statement begins by calling for a trial and concludes with a demand for "appropriate compensation," which presupposes the outcome of that very trial. This anomaly didn't trouble those who drafted the letter, since they never expected, or even intended, for Libya to agree. Indeed, the terms appeared to have been chosen to make it as difficult as possible for Kaddafi to comply. The next step was to go to the Security Council.

Libya fought back on the grounds where it thought it was strongest, which, ironically for an outlaw nation, turned out to be on the basis of international law. Even American officials admitted privately that Libya had a case, although not necessarily a winning one. Libya had no extradition treaty with the United States or Britain, so the demand to "surrender" the suspects for trial was an extra-judicial one on the face of it. Libyan law, like that of many other countries, did not permit the extradition of its nationals for crimes committed outside its borders. And the 1971 Montreal Convention for the "Suppression of Unlawful Acts Against the Safety of Civil Aviation" specifically provides for trial in the courts of the country of the accused as an alternative to extradition. Libya, France, the United States, and Britain were all signatories. Libya announced that it stood ready to try Megrahi and Fhimah as soon as the other countries did their duty under the convention and turned over the evidence. If that didn't satisfy its accusers, it offered to turn them over for trial by an impartial third party, although Kaddafi's idea of an impartial third party was the Arab League.

Unfortunately for Libya, its fate now rested in the UN Security Council, where the United States and Britain were laying the groundwork for what would be some of the toughest economic and political sanctions ever applied against a sovereign state. In the Security Council, the law began and ended where the superpowers said it did, assuming they could muster the nine votes (out of fifteen) necessary to pass the relevant resolution. Then, according to the terms of the UN charter and as envisioned by its founders, all member states were required to treat the resolution as legally binding. Here Libya labored under two disadvantages. The first was political. The Soviet bloc, formerly a reliable supporter of revolutionary third-world governments such as Kaddafi's, wasn't answering its phones in 1992. And the Arab bloc wasn't taking Kaddafi's calls either. The Gulf states still felt some residual obligation toward the United States for having gone to war on their behalf, and most of the other Arab leaders considered Kaddafi a dangerous lunatic anyway. "Libya would go to the Arab this and the Islamic that, and they made sympathetic noises but never really lined up behind them," recalls an American diplomat posted to the UN in the early 1990s. "If you can't win your own bloc around here, you're basically dead." The second problem was that most countries believed Libya probably did it. Blowing up an airliner, like going after diplomats, is a form of terrorism that can rouse strong feelings at the United Nations, which under other circumstances can be extraordinarily understanding of the "root causes" of even the most appalling violence. It helped that France—not ordinarily known for its acquiescence to American interests or pressure—was pressing a parallel case. And there were the indictments to consider. Even countries at odds with the U.S. government harbored some grudging respect for the independence of the American and British judicial systems.

Still, the votes were close and hard-fought. Never before had the Security Council condemned a member nation as a state sponsor of terrorism; in years past, one side or the other in the Cold War could be relied on to veto such an insult to any of its friends, allies, or proxies. Nor for that matter had any state ever been condemned by the Security Council for aggression, until Iraq in 1991 (the vote against North Korea in 1951 actually came about through a onetime device used by the UN General Assembly). And Iraq and Korea had been engaged in actual aggression on the ground when the UN acted; Libya was being

condemned for events three years in the past. By the terms of the UN
Charter, Security Council resolutions imposing sanctions are reserved
for urgent threats to international peace and security. Here, this
mighty weapon was enlisted to enforce a demand for the surrender of
two individual criminal suspects, who could hardly be said to be
threatening international peace in 1992. So American diplomats laid
the legal groundwork carefully. They bided their time until January,
when Cuba and North Yemen, whose two-year terms as non-
permanent members were expiring, would no longer be on the Security Council. Then, following up the demands of the November letters,
they introduced a resolution (731) deploring "international terrorism
in all its forms" and urging Libya "to provide a full and effective
response" to the American, British, and French statements. Thus the
stringent terms of the letters, including the demand for "appropriate
compensation," were incorporated into the resolution without actually
having to restate them. The tactic was intended to take advantage of
the fact that some delegates might not pay very close attention to the
fine print of what they were voting on. "We were asking for a lot here,"
says Bruce Rashkow, who was the senior legal adviser to the State
Department for UN affairs in 1992, "and this was a way not to have to
answer questions like, 'have you exhausted all other approaches?' or
'why are you bringing this to the Security Council in the first place?'
Instead of having to argue them into accepting each of those points, we
could just say, look, they have to comply with the letters. We're just
asking for cooperation."

   In March, the United States and Britain introduced Resolution 748,
which called on the Libyan government to "commit itself definitively
to cease all forms of terrorist action and all assistance to terrorist
groups," substantially broadening the language of the earlier resolution. The two allies were in a hurry to pass this resolution quickly,
because Libya had brought its own case against them in the International Court of Justice. Libya's argument was that it was prepared to
try Megrahi and Fhimah in its own courts, as provided in the Montreal
Convention, but was being thwarted because the Western countries
refused to turn over their evidence. Moreover, it was invoking the new

but not unreasonable proposition that not even the UN Security Council was above the law—that extradition and the sanctions that flowed from it were questions for the International Court of Justice sitting in The Hague, where Libya was likely to get a far more receptive hearing. A favorable ruling for Libya in The Hague would have greatly complicated the efforts to round up enough Security Council votes to move to the next step of sanctions.

But justice in the International Court of Justice is notoriously slow. To assure that the resolution passed before the Court had a chance to issue its ruling, American and British diplomats began a round of intensive but quiet, one-on-one diplomacy ("bilaterals") with the Security Council member nations and the countries with business interests in Libya. This was an indication of the importance the two Western countries attached to the matter; most UN votes are negotiated within the building, but when Washington cares enough about something it speaks directly to foreign capitals. The pitch ("démarche" in diplomatese) was a combination of subtle pressure and overt appeals to self-interest. "My pitch to [the Italians and Egyptians] was, we're going to put Kaddafi in a box, and give him just enough air to stay alive, and you're going to be the straw that he sucks that air in," said a senior American diplomat who took part in the campaign. The "box" was built of sanctions that cut off all air traffic to and from Libya and prohibited arms sales to the country. Adopted under Chapter VII of the UN Charter, the most stringent provisions of which deal with aggression and threats to the peace, these sanctions were mandatory on all UN member nations. Henceforth, foreign visitors would have to arrive overland from the nearest Egyptian airport, requiring a five-hour drive through the desert, or aboard a ferry from Malta. A third Security Council resolution, 883, was passed a year and a half later, closing loopholes in the earlier versions, freezing some Libyan assets abroad, and banning sales of equipment for Libya's oil industry.

One thing was not done, however: an embargo of Libyan oil sales abroad, which would have brought the country to its knees quickly, if it could have been enforced. That was the rub, though; Libya sold 1.4 million barrels of oil a day, mostly to Europe, and American allies such as Italy would have been brought to their knees as well. (The United States, which enforced its own, much stricter sanctions, essentially did not trade with Libya at all, and American oil companies were not supposed to operate there, at least openly.) Over the next five years, proposals for an oil embargo would periodically surface in Washington, make news for a day or a week, and then quietly disappear, to the great dismay of the families. Through their organizations and their allies in Congress, they would monitor the sanctions religiously and continuously press for stricter enforcement and tougher regulations. But despite all the political pressure they could muster, the price of trying to make the Europeans go along with an oil boycott was just too great for any administration to pay.

The other danger of an oil embargo, as some saw it, was that it might work. That was not what some of the originators of this policy had in mind. A trial for Megrahi and Fhimah was the last thing they wanted; it would be Kaddafi's way of escaping his box. Worse yet, Libya might be "destabilized." For Kaddafi to lose his grip on power would be a disaster. "There are only two other groups of people who'd like to run Libya," says one official who was deeply involved in devising the sanctions strategy. "The Rome café set of émigrés and dissidents, who'll never run anything, and a bunch of some of the scariest and most extreme fundamentalists you'll find anywhere in the world. So there's no call for getting rid of Kaddafi, as such. We just wanted to neutralize him."

On those terms, as a diplomatic stratagem, sanctions were a great success. Starting with indictments of two obscure intelligence agents, the Bush administration managed to get the UN Security Council not only to condemn Kaddafi's whole terror apparatus, but also to contain it. During the seven years the sanctions were in effect, Libya put their cost at $33.6 billion, roughly equivalent on a per capita basis to $1.5 trillion for the United States. American analysts give estimates that range down to about $18 billion, but even at that level the damage was substantial. Although the country continued to produce and sell oil during that time, very little new exploration and development took place, and its petroleum infrastructure, starved of spare parts, deteriorated significantly. Over the same period, Kaddafi kicked out most of the terror groups he had been sheltering and ended his support of organizations such as the Provisional IRA. Almost a decade after he helped devise and implement the strategy at the NSC, Ambassador Ted McNamara, now head of the Americas Society, reflected on what he had accomplished:

> Ten years later, I still believe we did as good a job as we could have done. The sanctions were an extraordinarily effective mechanism, especially when you look at the alternative of a military strike. They took Kaddafi out of the terrorism business for a decade while he worked out this problem. He got into the terrorism business in the first place so the world would pay attention to him, and instead the whole world boycotted him. He imagined himself becoming a big player in Africa, but Africans couldn't even take an airplane to see him. It ruined it for him.

Naturally, this strategy only worked as long as it went unacknowledged. In public, the sanctions—which were regularly renewed by the Security Council every three months for the next seven years—were always described as a means to force Kaddafi to turn over the suspects, and that's how many of the family members saw it, although McNamara sought to make them understand the bigger picture:

> Sure, we wanted justice for the victims, but we also wanted no more victims, and that's what we got. There's been no repeat of Pan Am 103 and there almost surely would have been one if we'd done another military strike. I told the families so many times: there were a lot of other families that won't have dead children as a result of this. But I never really got the feeling they understood.

It's hard to generalize about the family members on this point; they were divided among themselves about how best to deal with Libya. Stephanie Bernstein, who had her own sources of information among her late husband's colleagues at the Justice Department, knew that a trial was unlikely but regarded the sanctions as an acceptable means of bleeding Kaddafi. At the other extreme there were those like George Williams, who would have been happy to see the Kaddafi problem turned over to the 101st Airborne. At least one relative asked Frank Duggan's advice about hiring a private assassin. Duggan, out of government at the time, and in line with his policy of always taking the family members seriously, responded that it could be done, although the plan never went any further.

In the middle was a majority who endorsed sanctions for their announced purpose of having a trial—ideally, one that wouldn't stop with Megrahi and Fhimah but would hold Libya accountable at the highest levels. Or, if the facts led to Syria or Iran as the culprits instead, then they would follow them there. What mattered, when nearly everything else in life that mattered was lost, was the redemptive power of truth. But to those charged with devising American policy toward terrorism the truth required no further proof; they were long familiar with the limitations political considerations imposed on what could be said in the full in the light of day and what was better left for the long twilight struggle. They were not after the "truth" of the courtroom, where the criminal justice system gave the defendant every benefit of the doubt. That presupposed a court system and rule of law that bore no resemblance to the world they lived in. For seven years they tracked every boat that called on Libyan ports and every African foreign minister who made the trek to Tripoli for Kaddafi's lucrative embrace. What mattered to them could be seen in reconnaissance photos and read in intelligence reports, and in that realm, things were going well.

7

Assessing Damages

The FBI and the Scottish police, the British Air Accidents Investigation Branch and the Federal Aviation Administration, the McLaughlin Commission and various committees and subcommittees of the House and Senate were not the only organizations investigating the bombing of Pan Am 103. Within a day of the crash, Pan Am itself, and its insurance company, had dispatched investigators to London and Frankfurt. Close on their heels were the plaintiffs' lawyers, who saw in the disaster the makings of a historic lawsuit against Pan Am. The lawyers, of course, had a specific interest in finding evidence about "willful misconduct" by Pan Am, and they spent a lot of time interviewing baggage handlers, gate agents, and security personnel—in part following leads that were developed by the German newsmagazine *Stern*. This was still largely unexplored, although potentially lucrative, legal territory. "Suits arising from terrorist activities against airlines is an infant industry," the prominent New York trial lawyer Aaron J. Broder remarked in 1985, after the TWA jet hijacking, "but it should take off now." In the Lockerbie case, the plaintiffs' lawyers would reconstruct on their own a good part of the case that was eventually brought against Fhimah and Megrahi, and they outlined at trial a scenario that was consistent in every important detail with the one that would be laid out years later by the Scottish prosecutors.

As the families discovered to their dismay, a plane crash brings lawyers on the run. One day after Alexander Lowenstein's remains were identified in Scotland, a New Jersey lawyer wrote to his father offering his "deepest sympathy" and a special one-time-only discount on "the customary one-third fee most other attorneys routinely charge." Lowenstein sent the letter to the New Jersey State Office of Attorney Ethics, and after appeals all the way to the U. S. Supreme Court, the lawyer was duly reprimanded for conduct "patently offensive to the common sensibilities of the community."

The long-lost cousins and college friends who showed up on the families' doorsteps in the first few days did not, for the most part, have any delusions about trying the cases themselves; their plan was to get a retainer signed and refer the client to someone who knew what he was doing, in exchange for a small share of the fee. In the end almost all the families found their way to one of a half dozen or so specialists in aviation tort law, and of these, roughly half belonged to one firm in particular, Kreindler & Kreindler of New York City. When the various cases—210 in all—were consolidated for trial in the Eastern District of New York, the firm's senior partner, Lee Kreindler, was named by Chief Judge Thomas C. Platt to head the committee that would actually run the case. The trial would be conducted by Kreindler and his son, Jim Kreindler, by Michel Baumeister of Baumeister & Samuels, and by another father-son team, Frank Granito Jr. and Frank Granito III, of Speiser, Krause, Madole, Nolan & Granito. All of these were New York firms in the relatively tiny world of aviation tort law, and the lawyers knew each other well as collaborators and occasional rivals—as, indeed, they knew most of the lawyers on the other side, representing the insurance companies. The suit was filed under the name of one of Kreindler's first clents, Denice H. Rein, whose husband, Mark Alan Rein, had been a forty-four-year-old investment banker and the father of their two children—someone, not coincidentally, whose case was likely to amount to a very large sum of money.

Kreindler had joined his father's small general practice shortly after graduating from Harvard Law School in 1949, and essentially invented the field of aviation tort law just three years later. That was in a case involving a National Airlines DC-6 that crashed on takeoff from Newark Airport and hit an apartment building, killing 31 people aboard the plane and on the ground. Kreindler proved that the propeller on the plane's number 3 engine had gone into reverse pitch after the cockpit crew had mistakenly feathered it. Until then, lawyers had generally sued airlines on the well-known doctrine in tort law of *res ipsa loquitur*, "the thing (injury) speaks for itself." This was a way of saying that since the airline exercised total and exclusive control of the airplane, it was necessarily responsible for flying it into the ground. The airlines' defense would consist of trying to show that their impeccable standards of training and maintenance made just such an accident impossible—therefore, assuming (for the sake of argument only) that if it actually did occur, it could only have been an act of God. This struck Kreindler as evading the issue on both sides. Air accidents have causes, he reasoned, just as the ones that occur at stoplights do, only more complicated. Mounting his own investigation into the National crash, he concluded that the absence of a tiny screw had allowed the propeller to overtravel into reverse pitch after the crew attempted to unfeather it. On the glass-topped conference table in his office, which raises and lowers on a mechanical pedestal by remote control, to this day sits a metal cylinder about eight inches across, a slip-ring assembly for the same propeller model that malfunctioned on that airplane. After winning that case Kreindler went on to become a leading authority and practitioner in aviation tort law. This is a field that does not reward false modesty. Just nine months before Lockerbie, Kreindler had won a jury award of nearly $8 million for the estate of Philip Estridge, a near-legendary IBM executive who led development of the personal computer, who had died with his wife in a 1985 Delta Air Lines crash near Dallas. It was the largest jury verdict ever for a death resulting from a plane crash. Kreindler's reaction was that he was "pleased, but not elated"; he told the newspapers he thought he could have gotten much more, as much as $25 million.

Plaintiffs' lawyers work on contingency fees, meaning they are paid a percentage of whatever their clients collect, if anything. Since a small case takes almost as much work as a big one, they have an obvious incentive to sign clients with the most lucrative claims, which in this case were, basically, the widows and children of the men sitting in first class. After a year or so went by, Victoria Cummock was one of the few who hadn't chosen a lawyer, and Kreindler made it his mission to sign her. He invited her to visit the firm in New York, and when she said she couldn't leave her children he offered to fly them up too, and when she still demurred, he made an appointment to meet with her over lunch in Miami. "He pulled out a retainer for me to sign, already filled in with his percentage," she recalls, "and when I didn't jump at it he reached in his briefcase for another one, with a lower percentage, and then another one, and I just kept saying I was going to think about it. He was very persistent." Cummock resisted Kreindler's charm, but the episode opened her eyes to the fact that contingency fees—usually around a third of the recovery—are actually negotiable. Or they are, that is, if you have a case potentially worth in the eight figures.

Kreindler is, naturally, a great believer in the tort system, which he thinks deserves much more credit than it has received for saving passengers' lives by making airlines pay for their mistakes. He has been a tireless campaigner against various no-fault schemes that would offer fixed compensation to families after a crash, a reform that would have the effect of rendering trials, and consequently trial lawyers, redundant. And he is an eloquent defender of the principle that every tortious loss and injury, physical or emotional, tangible or intangible, deserves compensation. In 1989, he engaged in an exchange of views in the *New York Times* with an insurance-industry lawyer who dared to suggest that "court judgments and money awards are not the answer to everything." Money, the industry representative wrote, is "useless for making up for a decedent's family's genuine grief, loss of companionship, and so on." That belief strikes at the very essence of what Kreindler does. "Since money is the accepted medium of exchange," he replied, "it is also the only way to evaluate losses. . . . Despite what the critics say, money can make family members who have suffered a grievous loss feel better"—and all the more so when the family members' gain is at the expense of the rich corporation that caused the accident.

Long before the lawyers had figured out how to prove their case against Pan Am, they had to be thinking about the end of the process, when they would try to get as much money as possible out of the insurance company. The nominal amount sought in the suit was $7 billion, a figure chosen primarily for its attention-getting value, and because it was high enough that the jury verdict couldn't exceed it even if every one of the 270 people who died was an IBM executive. By the time the case was actually tried in 1992, Pan Am was bankrupt, and for practical purposes the ceiling was the airline's $750 million liability policy. Within that limit, though, there would be great variability among the cases, and much scope for legal maneuvering. Damages come in many different varieties—harder or easier to win, more or less lucrative, depending on the exact circumstances of the plaintiff and the jurisdiction in which the suit was brought. The family members were entitled to file suit in any court that they could plausibly, or even implausibly, assert exercised some kind of jurisdiction. The choices included their own home states, or the home states of the victims, or New York, where Pan Am had its headquarters, or even Florida, the headquarters of Pan Am's security subsidiary, Alert. After the liability trial was concluded in Brooklyn, Judge Platt could send the cases back to those state courts to decide, according to the law and standards of the community, how much money to award.

What this meant to the family members was that just having a relative killed in the crash did not automatically entitle them to any amount of money in particular, at least beyond the insurance company's original take-it-or-leave-it offer of $100,000. Did the death of Denice Rein's husband or the Cohens' daughter constitute a real, compensable loss? If so, they would have to prove it. It was not sufficient to show that the people who died were loved and missed. Such losses were barely recognized in tort law; instead, its tendency was to atomize the relationship into a discrete bundle of transactions, and assign a monetary value to each. And the one the law gave the greatest weight to was the one factor with the least significance in emotional terms: the relationship between a wage earner and the people he supported.

Assuming that the plaintiffs established Pan Am's liability for the crash, the one thing the law unambiguously provided was that the family of a breadwinner should receive the money he would have earned if he'd lived. In most jurisdictions courts also recognized the loss of tangible "services" by the victim, such as cooking and household repairs, to which a dollar value can be assigned. But what about the "services" that can't be replaced on the labor market—a category for which the law had created its own specialized vocabulary: a parent's "nurture," a spouse's "consortium," a child's "companionship"? "The expansion of wrongful death damages to include sentimental as well as economic losses did not take hold until after the Industrial Revolution, at approximately the same time the concept of children as chattel whose labor was owned by their parents waned," a federal court wrote a few years later. "The result of this gradual and relatively recent shift is that the scope of [such damages] varies tremendously from state to state." In 1989 just nine states, New York not among them, allowed parents to recover damages for the loss of a child's future companionship and affection. Moreover, the Supreme Court in a 1974 case had drawn a tendentious distinction between "loss of companionship," which was compensable, and "grief," which was not. By squinting hard at this proposition, one could discern the high court's reasoning. The former constituted the loss of a positive benefit, while the latter was just a state of mind. But, as Aaron J. Broder observed, it was a pointless exercise: "The jury is going to weigh the plaintiff's grief anyway; you can't separate them and for the court to try and draw this distinction makes the law an ass."

All of those were claims brought by family members for their own losses. But there was another category of claims brought on behalf of the victims themselves, or their estates. They had suffered losses, too— the pain of their injuries (assuming they didn't die instantaneously), the emotional distress of impending death (if it could be shown they were aware of it), and the loss of enjoyment of the remainder of their years (as calculated according to mortality tables). People who survive air crashes get compensated for these things, so why discriminate against the ones who had the misfortune to die? And, finally, there was a kind of claim brought, in effect, on behalf of society itself: punitive damages, which were meant to punish the defendants and deter future misconduct. (Although the process benefits society at large, the actual damages are paid to the family members.) Punitive damages are the Holy Grail of tort claims because they are limited only by the degree of misconduct and the wealth of the defendant who would have to pay them.

Yet this system, the proud product of centuries of common law, struck the family members as just another way of prolonging their torment. The insurance company's refusal to budge from its $100,000 offer and its insistence on appealing the verdict against Pan Am all the way to the Supreme Court meant that most people didn't get any money until 1995 or 1996—too late for some, like Hudson, whose real-estate business collapsed and whose law practice went neglected for years after Lockerbie. The process of fixing damages turned into an undignified squabble over the value of the lives that were lost. Since so much depends on the victims' projected future earnings, the plaintiffs' lawyers invariably impute to him a future of Carnegian achievement, while the other side is obliged to argue that he would have stayed in the same job until retirement. Or until death, and it's fair game for the insurance company to try to show that the victim might not have lived all that long anyway. In court, the widow of a highly paid executive (not Cummock) who was killed on the plane estimated his weight at 220. The insurance-company lawyer informed her during cross-examination that it was actually 247.

But the greatest source of bitterness arose over the handling of the "non-dependency" cases—those in which the victim wasn't supporting anyone else, which included almost all of the college students who were killed. Obviously, college students are a cost to their parents, not a source of support. Pan Am's lawyers stopped just short of suggesting that the families were therefore ahead of the game. "If they could show $275,000 in lawn-mowing services, that's something Your Honor could take into consideration," a lawyer for the insurance company remarked, a comment that drew gasps of outrage from the family members in the courtroom. Even the invidious distinction the law tried to draw between "loss of companionship" and "grief" worked against the parents of the students; spouses provide companionship till death do them part, but grown children move away. The parents had the lion's share of the one thing the law didn't acknowledge as worthy of compensation, and that was heartache.

Long before any of those factors came into play, though, there was a preliminary struggle over punitive damages. Were they permitted under the Warsaw Convention? This arcane point of law had never been settled definitively. Punitive damages were almost never awarded in plane crashes, most of which have an element of pilot error in them, and the assumption (at least until the 1999 EgyptAir crash) was that no one in the cockpit crew would be on a suicide mission. But Pan Am 103 was an exceptional case in many ways, and it seemed to the plaintiffs' committee that punitive damages would flow naturally from a finding of "willful misconduct." In June, 1989, Pan Am filed a motion opposing claims for punitive damages. The committee responded with their own briefs. By coincidence, the same issue was being raised at the same time in a lawsuit against Pan Am arising from a 1986 hijacking at Karachi International Airport in Pakistan. The two federal judges—Platt, in the Lockerbie case, and John Sprizzo, in the Karachi suit—ruled on the matter in the same month, January 1990, and reached opposite conclusions. Judge Platt ruled for Pan Am, holding that punitive damages were not allowed; Judge Sprizzo, for the plaintiffs in the hijacking case. Not surprisingly, therefore, the losers in both cases appealed. The decision by the Second Circuit Court of Appeals, titled *In re Air Disaster at Lockerbie, Scotland on December 21, 1988,* hinged on three words in the original French-language text of the Warsaw Convention. The relevant phrase provided that in case of an accident "le transporteur est responsable du dommage survenu." When the treaty was sent to the U.S. Senate for ratification in 1934, "dommage survenu" was translated as "damages sustained." Was this the correct rendering? Did it matter? Yes, it mattered, the court ruled:

> Plaintiffs argue that "du dommage survenu" means "damages occurred" or "arrived" or "happened," not "sustained," and thus

[the Warsaw Convention] contemplates punitive damages. Pan Am contends that the proper translation is "sustained," but that the exact translation does not matter because punitive damages do not "happen" or "occur" any more than they are sustained; rather, punitive damages are imposed by a jury or a court.

After reviewing in detail the history of the sixty-year-old treaty, the Second Circuit agreed with the defense lawyers on the narrow linguistic question. But federal judges also enjoy the privilege of deciding cases on broader public-policy grounds. Here, too, the court sided with Pan Am, ruling that punitive damages would undercut the whole purpose of the Warsaw Convention: to establish a uniform system of liability that wouldn't bankrupt the airlines. No other nation allowed punitive damages under the convention. Moreover, Judge Richard J. Cardamone wrote, "allowing punitive damages recoveries might well defeat the goal of making airlines insurable." The airlines would be in a Catch-22 situation, because many jurisdictions don't allow corporations to insure against punitive damages—on the theory that if you don't have to pay the judgment yourself, it isn't much of a punishment or deterrent. But, Cardamone concluded, "if an airline could not find an insurer able or willing to sell insurance for punitive damages, it might well choose to go out of business, or at least out of the international market, rather than risk bankruptcy with every flight."

So punitive damages, which could have run into billions of dollars, were not allowed. To reach this point took until March 22, 1991—two years and three months after Pan Am 103 crashed on Lockerbie.

All through that time, U.S. Aviation Underwriters, the insurance syndicate that was in charge of Pan Am's defense, kept its $100,000 offer on the table. In a 1994 speech to an aviation-law convention, Kreindler recalled that in the early months, when the facts were still murky and the case might have gone either way, most of the suits could probably have been settled for "relatively low multiples" of that amount. But USAU never budged. Shortly after he was appointed to head the plaintiffs' committee, in early 1989, Kreindler called John Brennan, chairman of USAU. Brennan told him USAU was proceeding on the principle that "there is no way any airline, in this day and age, can effectively protect itself against a terrorist attack." Moreover, the terrorism was directed not at Pan Am but at the United States government, and the government should pay. The discussion ended there, as all conversations on this topic were to end for the next six years. A few months later, when Kreindler heard that the insurers were talking about settling the cases filed in Scotland by residents of Lockerbie (who, not being airline passengers, were not covered by the Warsaw Convention) he asked if that meant USAU was softening its stand. "It doesn't affect the passenger cases, Lee," USAU's claims chief, Robert Alpert, told him. "The passenger cases won't be settled until the Supreme Court of the World denies our last application."

That was the official position, which Alpert was obligated to maintain, even as he privately came to believe that it was both morally indefensible and self-defeating. "It was my belief in early 1989 that there was virtually no chance Pan Am would walk out of a courtroom in New York without a finding of willful misconduct," he said, years later. "We could have advised the families of the victims that the insurers were prepared to pay full compensatory damages, settled as many as could have been settled and tried the remaining few. It would have saved the insurance industry a couple of hundred million dollars and gotten money into the hands of people who needed it." Alpert made that case to Brennan, and ultimately to the top executives of General Re, the insurance giant that owned USAU, and when he was overruled, he left the company in disgust.

Even the insurance company couldn't deny that Pan Am's security in Frankfurt was asleep at the switch. But in explaining his refusal to negotiate, Brennan insisted that right up until the time the indictments were handed down Kreindler had failed to show how the mess in Germany specifically led to a bomb getting aboard a different airplane in London. And when the theory did emerge—involving Megrahi and Fhimah checking a suitcase tagged to go from Malta to Frankfurt to London to New York—Pan Am's lawyers scoffed at the notion that the terrorists had entrusted their plot to a suitcase traveling through three airports over ten hours. "Too many things to go wrong," a lawyer said, summing up the defense thinking. "Everything we know about terrorists tells us they don't work that way."

But the Malta theory was a masterpiece of lucidity compared to the one propagated by the defense—that Gothic tale of double-dealing drug smugglers and rogue spies, spelled out in lurid detail in the report by the dubiously credentialed Juval Aviv. The journalist Christopher Byron, who exposed USAU's machinations in a series of articles in *New York* magazine, doubts the defense team ever seriously planned to present this scenario in court during the trial. Instead, they used Aviv's report as the basis to subpoena memos, minutes, tapes, and surveillance reports from the CIA, the FBI, the State Department, and the National Security Agency, seeking information about the Drug Enforcement Administration's mythical "Operation Corea." Of course, the chances were nil of getting these agencies to release these mountains of secretly obtained evidence, let alone evidence about something that didn't exist. But that was part of the strategy. Aviv's report predicted, accurately, that government lawyers would try to quash the subpoenas on national-security grounds. That, in turn, would allow Pan Am to portray itself as the victim of a government cover-up, unable to mount a defense because the key evidence was locked up in Washington.

And they didn't stop there. In December 1990, based in part on the Drug Enforcement Administration (DEA) drug-sting scenario, Pan Am sued the United States government for third-party indemnity—in effect, asking the taxpayers to pick up the cost of any judgment the family members might win. The claim was based on two assertions: first, the drug-sting bag-switch scenario; second, that the government had received warnings about the bombing but negligently failed to pass them on to Pan Am. Both the plaintiffs' committee and the government itself opposed the claim. For more than a year that issue haunted the upcoming trial, until, just before the jury took its seats in the courtroom in Brooklyn, Platt asked USAU's lawyer, James Shaughnessy, if he could produce any evidence for his claim, and Shaughnessy admitted that, in the absence of government cooperation, he couldn't. Whereupon Platt dismissed Pan Am's complaint.

The Aviv tale also had a life well beyond the courtroom. Although USAU's lawyers have always denied leaking the report, it quickly found its way to James Traficant, the Ohio congressman, whose interest helped bring it to the attention of the press. Both NBC and ABC News broadcast versions of it in 1990. (The ABC story was reported by Pierre Salinger, who was the only American journalist allowed to interview Fhimah and Megrahi, as well as Kaddafi, and seemed to have been convinced of their innocence.) In the fall of 1990 the victims group, which had adopted as its motto "The Truth Must Be Known," called for another round of congressional hearings into the allegations. A subcomittee of the Committee on Government Operations obliged, summoning DEA officials to tell what they knew about "Operation Corea." Their answer was nothing. "There was no DEA operation code-named 'Corea,' 'Courier,' or anything similar to that name," Assistant Administrator Stephen H. Greene testified on December 18, 1990. "DEA had no operation, under any name, which facilitated the free movement of drug couriers from the Middle East or Cyprus through Frankfurt and onward to London and the United States. And DEA had no operation which circumvented airport security at Frankfurt, or any other city." That helped quell speculation about Aviv's scenario until it surfaced again in the spring of 1992, just days before jury selection in the Pan Am liability trial was to start, this time on the cover of *Time* magazine. The story inside bore the provocative headline (with the traditional hallmark of a newsmagazine exclusive, a question mark) WHY DID THEY DIE?

The *Time* story was a dubious piece of journalism on the face of it, and in retrospect it looks even worse. A photograph of an innocent Georgia businessman somehow turned up with a caption identifying him as "David Lovejoy, a reported double agent for the U.S. and Iran." *Time* acknowledged that Aviv's report "was written off as fiction by many intelligence agents." But the magazine used it anyway as the basis for "a four-month investigation" that found "new questions about the case." There was not much sign, though, that the investigation had found any new *answers*; each time the article approached anything like a revelation, it took refuge in the newsmagazine writer's best friend, the conditional tense:

- The fatal suitcase *"may not have been* transferred to Pan Am Flight 103 in Frankfurt, as charged in the indictment of the two Libyans. Instead, the bomb laden bag *may have been* substituted in Frankfurt for an innocent piece of luggage."

- "The rogue bag *may have been* placed on board the plane by Jibril's group with the help of . . . a Syrian drug dealer who was cooperating with the U.S. Drug Enforcement Administration in a drug sting operation."

- "Jibril and his group *may have* targeted that flight because on board was an intelligence team led by Charles McKee, whose job was to find and rescue the hostages [held in Lebanon]." (All emphases added.)

Since McKee had spent the preceding months in Beirut, one might think that a Palestinian terror group would have found easier ways to kill him than to smuggle a bomb aboard a 747.

Time introduced a new source—Lester Coleman, a former journalist, press agent, and paid informant for the DEA. Coleman was also a fugitive; he'd been indicted on charges of attempting to obtain a passport under a false name and had fled to Europe, a fact that *Time* dutifully reported but evidently did not consider a serious impeachment of his credibility. In 1990 he'd contacted Pan Am, claiming to have information that supported Aviv's theory about the bombing. James Shaughnessy, the chief outside counsel for USAU, had interviewed Coleman in London and taken down his account in an affidavit, which Pan Am filed with the court in support of its effort to shift the blame for the bombing to the U.S. government. The coincidence of the *Time* article appearing just at the start of the trial led to howls of outrage from Kreindler and his colleagues, who saw it as a cynical attempt to mislead and confuse potential jurors. The U.S. Attorney's office evidently agreed. It began an investigation of Shaughnessy, Brennan, and Coleman. Shaughnessy, the lawyer, was never charged. Brennan was never charged in the Lockerbie case, although the investigation that began there led to his indictment and conviction on fraud charges in an unrelated aviation case. (The conviction was overturned on appeal.) But Coleman's affidavit was so patently phony that in September 1993 he was indicted for perjury, something almost unheard of in a civil case. Those with a sufficiently conspiratorial turn of mind viewed Coleman's prosecution as continuing evidence of the government's wide-ranging cover-up. Coleman himself seemed to endorse that view, shortly before returning to America to face the charges in 1996, when he bravely proclaimed to a British newspaper: "They can arrest me, but they cannot silence me." His martyrdom ended on an ignominious note the following year, when he pled guilty to five counts of perjury.

Dragged kicking and screaming to trial, conceding nothing, fighting to the end to uphold its preposterous claim that the U. S. government was actually responsible for the bombing, Pan Am made a conspicuously unsympathetic defendant. Of course, it was also bankrupt and out of business by that time. Its defense was in the hands of USAU and its lawyers, primarily Shaughnessy and one Clinton H. Coddington, one of the top insurance lawyers in the country, who was brought in from California to run the defense at trial. Without much of a defense to offer, Coddington's role was limited to minimizing and ridiculing the plaintiffs' case, and—in case Pan Am lost—attempting to goad or manipulate Platt into making a mistake that would require the verdict to be reversed on appeal. Holding the money, USAU was happy to see the process prolonged. Coddington brought to the task a pompous and condescending manner, an ostentatious silver drinking cup from which he alone sipped while everyone else made do with paper, and a finely honed indifference to his own popularity. One day, deep into June, the following exchange took place:

MR. CODDINGTON: Your Honor, I do take exception to Mr. Baumeister's uttering expletives in the courtroom. You maybe

didn't hear it, but I did, in response to the witness's testimony. It
is serious misconduct.

THE COURT: I didn't hear him say anything.

MR. GRANITO III: It was in response to my handing him a note,
not to the witness's tesimony.

MR. CODDINGTON: I don't think he ought to take the Lord's name
in vain in this courtoom, no matter who gives him anything.

MR. GRANITO III: What he said, Your Honor, is "gee."

THE COURT: Stop quibbling . . .

To the family members attending the trial, Coddington was the
personification of the indifferent corporation callously turning its back
on their loved ones. "My skin is not as thick as it should be, considering
how long I have done this, but it's somewhat thick," Coddington told
the judge at one point. "I've had plaintiffs mutter to me and approach
me. I had a gentleman . . . he came up to me in the men's room and put
his arm round me and said, 'How much money are you getting paid to
do this?' "

To the family members, the trial was less a disinterested search for
the truth than a contest, run by arcane and occasionally irrational rules.
They had waited three and a half years for this vindication, for Pan
Am to stand exposed in all its shameless greed and incompetence, and
found themselves sitting through a wrangle over what pseudonym to
use for a German airport employee who was afraid of testifying under
her own name. Kreindler had referred to her as "Mrs. X" in his opening statement but the defense lawyers weren't going to fall for that
trick:

MR. SHAUGHNESSY: We think instead of using Mrs. X maybe they
could use Mrs. Schultz.

MR. BAUMEISTER: Mrs. Y.

MR. SHAUGHNESSY: No, a name.

MR. CODDINGTON: So as not to highlight it with intrigue. We
would stipulate to the German name for Doe.

THE COURT: Schmidt.

Coddington insisted, and the judge agreed, that no witness should be allowed to utter the words "willful misconduct" in front of the jury, since that was what the jury was supposed to be deciding. Kreindler brought this up at a sidebar: "Do you object, Mr. Coddington, if I now tell [the witness] under no circumstances in any answer to any question should he use the term willful misconduct? Because that's what I would like to do in light of this colloquy."

And Coddington replied: "It is your solemn duty so to do, because if you don't and if he speaks of it, I will move for a mistrial and ask that all costs and sanctions be awarded against you personally."

Michel Baumeister was tremendously confident going into the trial; he'd mastered all the depositions, exhibits, and expert testimony and found Pan Am's negligence equal to that of the asbestos and tobacco industries in foisting poisonous products off on an unsuspecting public. There was a great deal of evidence that Pan Am simply couldn't rebut, and Platt wouldn't let them bring up the drug-sting defense at all. So over the course of thirteen weeks, and through the testimony of fifty-eight witnesses, the jury heard in necessary if excruciating detail the path the suitcase took through Frankfurt's computerized baggage-transfer system; they learned how Pan Am's security chief in Frankfurt hired and promoted young women because he liked their looks, and how, after the bombing, he found a weeks-old memo about the Helsinki warning and backdated it to hide the fact that it had never been distributed. In his summation, Coddington was reduced to making the preposterous argument—barely an argument, more just a desperate attempt to sow confusion—that the fact that the bomb suitcase happened to be packed with clothing bought in Malta didn't tend to establish Malta as its origin:

They obviously imported the Czechoslovakian Semtex, the Swiss timing device, the Chinese umbrella, the Japanese player and the U.S. suitcase. They imported all those from those countries, to assemble them to make their bomb bag . . . Why is it when you have these materials found in a suitcase from six different countries somehow it all originated in Malta?

Still, for a while it seemed closer than the lawyers had predicted; the jury was out for three days and for much of that time seemed nowhere near a decision. When the verdict came in—guilty of willful misconduct leading to the deaths of the passengers on Pan Am 103—Platt commiserated with Shaughnessy:

> . . . you all did a professional job. I know it's not easy to lose. Mr. Shaughnessy, I will say this to you, you had a tough case.
>
> MR. SHAUGHNESSY: Thank you, Your Honor.
>
> THE COURT: I told you that from the start of the case, you had a tough case. You tell that to Mr. Coddington, I know he felt quite differently . . . I know Mr. Brennan felt differently, but this was a heavy case on the side of the plaintiffs.

That was July 10, 1992—a little more than three and a half years since the bombing. But the case had a long way to go yet. Pan Am was certain to appeal the verdict. Moreover the whole process of assessing damages hadn't even begun; unless USAU relented and began making serious offers, there would have to be at least a few trials to establish a range for future settlement talks, and those verdicts could be appealed as well. Platt decided to make a start on these trials now, while he still had a jury sitting, so the Appeals Court could rule on the damages and liability issues at the same time. That might shave a year or two off the process.

Kreindler, as head of the plaintiffs' committee, got to choose the first damage cases to try. This was his payoff for more than three years of work, and naturally he wanted cases that would demonstrate the full magnitude of the family members' loss and illustrate his philosophy that money really can make a difference to them. Certainly Mark Rein, who was treasurer of Salomon Brothers when he died, had the potential to be a very rich man, but just how rich would largely depend on the stock market. Calculating his lost earnings was a job for a Nobel Prize–winning economist (who, as history shows, would almost certainly have underestimated how much money would be made on Wall Street in the 1990s anyway). Platt was in a hurry; the jurors had been sitting since April and were growing restless. Two of them had already been excused and he was proceeding with the ten still on the case. But Kreindler also represented two attorneys for PepsiCo, Harry Bainbridge and Robert Pagnucco, who had been on Pan Am 103, returning together from a business trip to Europe. Executives of large corporations, which promote people along predetermined paths with regular salary increments, make for exemplary disaster victims. So Kreindler, together with his son and partner, Jim, tried those two cases. (USAU replaced Coddington and Shaughnessy with another team of lawyers for this phase of the proceedings.) Then, as a representative of the back of the airplane, they chose Walter Porter, age thirty-five, a native of the small Caribbean nation of St. Vincent and the Grenadines living in Brooklyn. For Bainbridge and Pagnucco the verdicts were for around $9 million, roughly two-thirds for loss of earnings and the rest for the three other categories Platt instructed the jury to consider: loss of services, parental care, and companionship. Porter's verdict was a fraction of that, a total of $1.85 million. Porter was a union electrician and a calypso singer of some local renown—he was returning from a performance in England when he was killed—but his future earnings potential didn't measure up to that of the two executives. In calculating future earnings, the jury is told, it can only project forward based on the evidence from the past; even though Porter was voted "best new artist" by the *Caribbean Entertainment Journal* in 1985, they were not allowed to speculate that he might actually be a future Harry Belafonte.

What was a little surprising, and disappointing to Jim Kreindler, was that the awards in Porter's case for loss of services and companionship were proportionately smaller as well. He had a wife and one child, as did Bainbridge (whose son was born a few months after the bombing); and he was an electrician, so he arguably was more useful around the house than all of PepsiCo's lawyers put together. It appeared, Kreindler said, that in all three cases the jury came up with a figure for lost income and then calculated the non-pecuniary damages so they came out at about half of that. "It was starting to look as if the jury was just getting burned out on the case," he says, "and so we ended it there; originally Judge Platt had talked about having ten damage trials."

The jury in its wisdom had spoken, and the system moved on,

spitting out a million here, ten million there in its fitful attempts at justice. At a later stage in the case, in a case brought by Aaron J. Broder, a different jury in the same jurisdiction would award *$5 million* in lost companionship to the widow of an oil-company executive who had died on Pan Am 103, and that couple didn't even have a child. That compares to $1,250,000 awarded for the same thing to Bainbridge's widow, who was about the same age—is it really conceivable that her husband's companionship was four times as valuable to her as Bainbridge's was to his wife? Who could believe that? To be sure, the trend in jury awards is ever upward. The three years that elapsed between the two trials might have accounted for some of the difference (although, since USAU kept appealing all the verdicts, the earlier judgments weren't necessarily paid any sooner than the later ones). But the fact is the jury just happened to see it that way, on that particular day, with that particular set of facts and those particular lawyers. That life isn't always fair is something the Pan Am families had learned long ago. Still, it struck them as gratuitous that the jury system managed to perpetuate, and even exaggerate, the inequalities among the victims who, no matter how much they'd paid for their tickets, all died together.

There was one other brief trial to get through, to decide whether to compensate the victims for conscious pain and suffering. This was a relatively new concept in aviation law, which Broder had helped pioneer in a case arising from the crash of a DC-10 on takeoff in Chicago. The accident occurred when one of the plane's engines fell off just seconds into the flight, and Broder argued that his client, in a window seat just behind the wing, would have had a perfect view of the unfolding disaster. The jury put a value of $10,000 on the emotional trauma, which lasted only a few seconds until he was killed, along with everyone else on board. More recently there had been awards in the vicinity of $1 million for passengers aboard the Korean Air Lines flight 007 shot down over Russia in 1983, but that plane had flown on for a considerable time after it was hit. (The exact length of time was, of course, subject to legal wrangling. "We claimed twelve minutes, they allowed us eight," recalls Hans Ephraimson, who was the head of the American family group for that disaster.) The passengers aboard Pan Am 103, depending on where they had been sitting, mostly fell in two minutes or less, except for the ones who were sucked out of the fuselage and, depending on whether their clothing slowed them at all, may have taken as long as three minutes before they hit the ground. Judge Platt was not pleased to discover that people from different parts of the plane might need to be treated differently, and he told the lawyers as much:

> I am not going to have separate trials for three or four different sections of the aircraft. This is the wrong venue for this operation. I am the wrong judge. I will import a judge from someplace, from North Dakota, who has nothing to do. He could do this for a year, little trials for different sections of the plane.

Platt suggested that a reasonable offer from USAU would be $10,000 per passenger for pain and suffering, "but Mr. Brennan [the chairman of USAU] is not reasonable." If they went to trial, he added, and the jury awarded $500,000 a head, Brennan would have no one to blame but himself. Kreindler, of course, quickly bridled at the suggestion that $500,000 was an outlandish sum:

> I think a verdict in one of these cases, for example, Pagnucco, even if it is seconds—reviewing his life, his children, his career and everything else—$500,000, in my opinion, is not enough.

But in the trial, USAU's lawyers were able to make much of the fact that the experience of the passengers was different, depending on where they were in the plane. Since people leave their seats and move around during a flight, it wasn't possible to say for sure where Bainbridge and Pagnucco had been at the moment the bomb went off. The jury chose to believe that this was an unresolvable problem, and Platt, eager to put this part of the trial behind him, decided that for this purpose a single standard would apply to everyone on board the plane. As far as the law was concerned, there was no pain and suffering on board Pan Am 103.

And there matters stood, again. In mid-August, Kreindler had taken time out to write a seven-page letter to Sen. George Mitchell, opposing a plan to replace the tort system with automatic, fixed compensation for airplane crashes, paid for by a surcharge on tickets. He called the proposal "a fraud on the traveling public . . . tantamount to requiring medical patients to take out damage insurance to protect themselves from medical malpractice, before visiting their doctor." Of the just-completed Pan Am liability trial, he wrote it was "probably the best example in history of why the fault system is necessary in international aviation . . . It was the litigation itself, or, to put it more generally, the fault system, that uncovered the record of horrendous willful misconduct that the jury verdict acknowledged." It was also, though, the fault system that had taken more than three years to reach this point, with no money having yet changed hands and little prospect of it doing so in the near future. USAU promptly appealed the verdicts to the Second Circuit Court of Appeals, where arguments and rehearings took two more years. A three-judge panel handed down a decision on September 12, 1994, nearly six years after the bombing.

The judges upheld the liability finding, and most but not all of the verdicts on damages. Judge Platt, they ruled, had neglected to instruct the jurors that in calculating damages for lost parental care and guidance, they should consider only the period until the child reaches adulthood—a legal standard not entirely supported by common sense, which teaches us that children stop listening to their parents long before they reach legal majority. (For analogous reasons a portion of the Pagnucco damages for "loss of society" was set aside, since some of the Pagnucco children were adults.) But the two-to-one decision was quite a bit closer than the plaintiffs' lawyers would have liked. The majority opinion called the trial "fair," on balance, but far from perfect. The dissent, from Judge Ellsworth Van Graafeiland, was a particularly blistering one, based largely on a reading of the evidence that persuaded him that Pan Am did, indeed, receive and rely upon an oral intepretation of the FAA regulations permitting them to substitute X-ray inspections for physical search of unaccompanied baggage. But it also contained this arresting sentence, all in capitals: "NO ONE

KNOWS WHEN, WHERE OR HOW THE BOMB GOT ON THE PAN AM PLANE EXCEPT THE PERSON WHO PUT IT THERE." Van Graafeiland went on to say that "having reviewed this proposed testimony of Pan Am's experts that the district court kept from the jury, I am convinced that had the jury been permitted to hear this evidence, there is a strong likelihood it would have rejected plaintiffs' contention that the bomb which exploded began its deadly journey in Malta."

Of course, as matters appear to us now, they would have been wrong; the Scottish court, with precisely that question before it, having heard even more evidence than was available in 1992, found that the bomb did indeed begin its deadly journey in Malta. But at the time, that opinion served to bolster USAU's determination to keep up the fight, demanding a rehearing *en banc* (before the entire Second Circuit), and when they lost there, appealing to the Supreme Court. Their tactics prompted an outburst from Platt about their "shocking" foot-dragging. "Don't you understand there are widows and people suffering while you people have been doing this?" he scolded them. Only when the Supreme Court denied the insurance company a hearing—which took until January 1995—did USAU begin serious settlement talks, which dragged on until the following year.

Platt appointed two "special masters" to oversee the negotiations. And that was one more painful hurdle for the family members, especially the ones who had lost children. They came, in some cases with scrapbooks and photo albums, the lonely repositories of their children's hopes and dreams, and confronted a bored-looking lawyer from the hated insurance company, who knew, whether or not the parents realized it yet, that it was all pointless. USAU was going to make one global offer for all the cases brought by parents, and the parents would either accept it or take their chances on a trial. The only exceptions were a handful of cases filed in Florida (where a judge ruled that the damages would be assessed under Scottish law, which was somewhat more favorable to the plaintiffs) and an even smaller few where the parents were able to make a convincing case that they were financially dependent on their children. As for the rest, nothing the parents could say about their children mattered one tiny bit. The door had been slammed on their children's futures, and what lay behind it would never be explored. Sitting in an office with a dramatic view of the Pan Am building, Bob Monetti described the day of his half-hour meeting with the special master as "the worst day of my life, other than the day Rick was killed. When they asked me at the end if I had anything else to say, I said yes, I wish I'd known this was taking place in an office and not in a courtroom, because then I could have brought in a gun and shot you dead right in your chair."

The special master who heard the non-dependency cases, a retired federal magistrate named Sol Schreiber, made a well-meaning attempt to establish a sympathetic bond with the parents, but it was a hopeless task; they were unreachable in their grief, certainly by anyone who approached them under the aegis of the judicial system. Schreiber was nursing a grief of his own, the recent death of his wife of thirty years from cancer. "I understand how you must feel," he told them, but of course he didn't, and they were insulted and outraged that he should compare his own commonplace loss to their own exquisite pain. Eventually one mother set him straight. "When you lose a husband or wife, you bury them in the ground," she told him. "When you lose a child, you bury them in your heart."

But with prodding by Schreiber and under the baleful eye of Platt, USAU had accepted the inevitable and begun to put some money on the table. The offers kept inching up, from $100,000 to $200,000 to $275,000—a figure one mother described to the newspapers as "insulting and inhumane"—to $400,000 and ultimately $575,000. At that point Kreindler advised his clients that the risks of going to trial outweighed the possibility of getting a larger verdict. It was, Schreiber asserts, at least twice the going rate for non-dependency wrongful-death judgments in New York State up to that time. In principle, any of the plaintiffs could have turned it down and demanded a trial, but they would have been going into battle with a reluctant lawyer, facing a judge who wanted to put Lockerbie behind him forever—and against the wishes of the other families, since USAU was threatening to withdraw the offer if it didn't get near-unanimous acceptance. Daniel and

Susan Cohen were the last holdouts; they bridled at the very word "set-tle," with its overtones of compromise and giving in. But there was no longer a principle at stake; they would, as they wrote in their book, be fighting over money, and in the end they probably wouldn't have got-ten any more of that, either. So, like the others, they signed their names to a form forever releasing and discharging Pan Am from any and all claims, demands, damages, suits, debts, dues, reckonings, bills, prom-ises, covenants, extents, and executions of every kind, which they had, had ever had, or in the future could have, "for any matter, cause or thing whatsoever from the beginning of the world to the date of this Release," arising out of or in any way connected with an aircraft bomb-ing which occurred on December 21, 1988, over Lockerbie, Scotland, thereinafter referred to as "the Occurrence."

But the legal system had a few final indignities to inflict on the fam-ilies. One of Pan Am's insurance underwriters had declared insol-vency, and as a result there was a shortfall in the settlements. The law, in its infinite concern for insurance-company stockholders, did not in this situation require the other underwriters to pick up the slack; instead the loss was borne by the plaintiffs, amounting to $1.3204 per $100, so that a $575,000 settlement was actually $567,407.70. That was further reduced by about $12,000 for the plaintiffs' committee's com-mon expenses for things like investigators, transcripts, and expert wit-nesses. That amounted to a total of around $2.5 million, duly audited by a second special master appointed by Platt, who had to rule on what was a fair cost per page for making photocopies (20 cents) and what class of travel to allow lawyers flying back and forth to Europe (busi-ness). Finally the relatives had to pay their lawyers' fees, which varied from lawyer to lawyer and from case to case but were typically around 30 percent, so that the $575,000 ended up closer to $400,000. To what shall we compare this sum? To the $5 million to $10 million, after fees, received by the families of most of the businessmen on the plane? Or to the $100,000 the insurance company first offered, a sum which would have been worth, at a conservative compound interest rate of 6 percent, nearly $160,000 by the time the families actually received their settle-ments? To the amount of direct financial support the parents actually expected to receive from their children, which was, in most cases, nothing at all? Or to what the parents would have paid, if only they could, to see their children walk through the gate at JFK, full of stories about their adventures and plans for Christmas, to hug them and hustle them into their cars and drive off into the ordinary night of December 21, 1988?

As for Victoria Cummock, anyone who could stare down John Sununu was not going to be intimidated by an insurance-company lawyer. She hired a lawyer from Speiser, Krause, Madole, and got her case remanded to a Florida court. She followed the New York cases closely and wrote down a figure she wanted to achieve. The amount is secret, but based on the range of other settlements it was very likely between $10 million and $20 million. "I said to them, I think this is a fair amount, and if you don't agree, then I'll see you in court. With my children. I had all my documentation ready to go. Luckily John Cummock was a fanatic on keeping receipts.

"We had a court date set on a Monday. My lawyer called on Friday and said, they're up to half of your number, and I said nothing doing. He called me Sunday night and said, I've got them up to 80 percent, all you have to do is agree not to say anything in public. I said, forget it.

"He shows up in my driveway Monday morning and says, they'll meet your number to the nickel, all you have to do is sign this agreement. And I said, I'm not signing anything like that. I'm not going to gag myself. Get in the car and let's go to court.

"And he's frantic now, he's literally blocking the driveway to keep me there. You've got to sign, he says, you have to get on with your life. I said, here's a phone. You call Pan Am and tell them I'll take the offer, in cash, in thirty days. I accept the condition that I can't talk about the amount. But that's the extent of the agreement. I'm going to say what I want for the rest of my life.

"He says, I can't do that. And I said, you can't not do it, because if you don't, we're going to trial and I'll get myself a new lawyer. So he makes the call, he talks to them for a minute and then hands me back the phone.

" 'They accept,' he says."

8

Smith's Complaint

Bruce Smith, alone among the close relatives of the victims, had no stake in the outcome of the trial. If anything, he regarded it as a distraction from the goal of holding Libya accountable. By 1992 Smith was flying Airbuses for Delta Airlines, which had purchased Pan Am's transatlantic routes, but he would never feel at home in a Delta uniform or in the thoroughly automated and computerized cockpit of an Airbus, which he regarded as a distinct comedown for a 747 pilot. The willful-misconduct verdict against Pan Am meant nothing to him personally because he had long since accepted the insurance company's settlement offer of $100,000. And he had dropped out of the family groups. He didn't need them for emotional support, he didn't care much about their ideas about aviation safety, and they didn't want him there anyway. Once, early on, he had come straight from the airport in his captain's uniform to a hotel where the families were meeting. That fixed his reputation, in the minds of many of the family members, as an apologist for Pan Am at best, and at worst a spy. It didn't help that he dismissed the trial as an irrelevancy. Whatever their failures, Pan Am's ground crews and baggage handlers didn't put the bomb on the airplane, Libyan terrorists did—a point he made over and over to newspapers, to public officials, and to any of the other family members who would listen. Yet even Victoria Cummock, who saw the truth in this argument, wasn't prepared to focus on Libya until after she settled her suit against Pan Am. That left Smith feeling like a voice in the wilderness—until, one morning as the trial was nearing its end, he chanced to pick up a copy of the *International Herald Tribune* dated July 2 and read an op-ed column under the headline "Libya: Pay the Lockerbie Families Now." Exactly what he believed! But other than through the UN sanctions, he had no idea how to force Libya to live up to its obligations. The author of this piece, however, did:

> Justice demands that Libya be made to pay—now. Whether Pan Am may be ordered to shoulder responsibility hardly detracts from Libya's primary responsibility. . . .
>
> The White House, despite its UN efforts against Libya, has been reluctant to take the extra step needed to give bite to the Council resolutions. It should urge the Council to establish immediately a UN claims commission to compensate Libya's victims.
>
> There is a precedent. After the Gulf War the Council condemned Iraq and established a claims commission through which Iraq is required to compensate victims of its Scud-missile attacks and other aggression.
>
> The Council could authorize a terrorist victims' claims commission to make awards to Libya's victims. These could be enforced against Libyan assets by a court of law.

The author was Allan Gerson, who was identified as chief counsel to the United States delegation to the United Nations from 1981 to 1985. Smith had never heard of him, but he had numerous contacts in the State Department from his work establishing the counter-terrorism rewards program. From his hotel room in Paris Smith started dialing Washington.

"Who's this Gerson?" he asked.

"He's in private practice now," he was told. "He's hooked up with Abe Sofaer at Hughes Hubbard & Reed."

Those names meant nothing to him either.

"Sofaer," he was informed, "is the former legal adviser to the State Department."

I really have to talk to these guys, Smith decided. He found a number for Hughes Hubbard & Reed (HHR) in Washington and asked to speak to Allan Gerson.

The idea behind the article had come to Gerson unexpectedly, at a conference on the Lockerbie case at Albany Law School at Union University of New York at Albany. In 1991 Gerson found himself for the first time since shortly after law school in private practice, with a venerable Wall Street firm better known for representing blue-chip banking and corporate clients than anything Gerson did. HHR's discreet brochures featured the stern visage of founding partner Charles Evans Hughes, distinguished statesman and jurist: governor of New York State (1907–1910), secretary of state (1921–1925) and chief justice of the United States (1930–1941). Gerson went there to practice public international law, which deals with transactions among states, and between private citizens and states—a field so specialized that he had it practically to himself, along with a handful of international law professors and senior legal advisers who had made the transition to private practice. Before he was hired, two partners took him to lunch and asked what, exactly, he thought he would do at the firm. He had to think a moment before answering, "I look for solutions that lie outside the ordinary way of doing things."

He was brought to HHR by his good friend Abraham D. Sofaer, who had joined the firm himself only a year earlier, after five years as the legal adviser to the Department of State. Among Washington lawyers, Sofaer is never spoken of without glowing tributes to his brilliance, generally balanced by rueful acknowledgments of his arrogance. He was born into a prosperous, cosmopolitan Jewish family in Bombay, India, in 1938; his parents were Iraqis and spoke Arabic at home. His career in the American bar had been a series of triumphs: editor in chief of the law review at New York University Law School, clerk to Supreme Court justice William Brennan, professor of law at

Columbia University, and U.S. District Court judge in the Southern District of New York. An admiring profile of him in the *Washington Post,* nine months into his tenure at the State Department, called him "one of those rare people in Washington who has become more important than the official post he fills." He understood, better than some of his predecessors, that the implicit role of the legal adviser is to find a legal justification for what the political leadership had already decided to do. But Sofaer went beyond the mere drafting of opinions to become an influential policy adviser to Schultz. Although his tenure at State was an unusual detour in what had been a model judicial career, he was still widely regarded among lawyers and judges as someone who might someday sit on the United States Supreme Court.

Gerson had met Sofaer in 1979 at a poker game on Martha's Vineyard, and the two men had become good friends. Gerson was seven years younger than Sofaer, a foot taller, and tended toward the contemplative, whereas Sofaer was fierce; but they had the same internationalist, strongly anti-Communist views, and as immigrants from exotic parts of the globe they had a shared sense of being outsiders playing an insider's game. Sofaer had just been appointed to the federal bench, and on his frequent trips to Washington he would stay with Gerson and his wife, Joan Nathan, who were living in Chevy Chase. When Gerson came to New York he'd visit Sofaer in his apartment on upper Fifth Avenue. With their families they would get together for Shabbat dinners and for holidays. But there was a secretive side to Sofaer; up until the day he decided to leave the bench to go to the State Department, Gerson never even knew his friend was thinking about the job.

Gerson joined HHR with great expectations, one of which was to start making serious money. He was forty-six then, and he'd spent almost his entire career in government, academia, and, most recently, the conservative think tank the American Enterprise Institute. Conservative think tanks pay no better than liberal ones, and in any case not enough for someone whose three children attended one of Washington's expensive private schools. Making serious money was, of course, part of Sofaer's agenda, too. He was the lead partner in the Washington office, with a mandate to bolster what until recently had been a somewhat overlooked appendage of the big New York–based firm. Gerson, who was taking a leave from his teaching post at George Mason University, was "Of Counsel," the title usually given to lawyers who join a firm in mid-career, apart from the handful of stars who come in as partners, like Sofaer. He was expected to generate his own clients and bill them for his time at $300 an hour or more, which he would share according to a formula with the firm.

But his clients weren't the usual run of corporations doing SEC filings, suing, and getting sued that keep most lawyers busy in firms like HHR. One of his first clients was an American citizen who had been arrested in Saudi Arabia on suspicion of murdering his wife. The man, Earnest Sands, was a retired Army sergeant working in Saudi Arabia as a civilian Defense Department employee. He returned to his house one day to find his Filipino American wife dead in bed, and shortly afterward was brought in by Saudi police for questioning. To his son, he described his interrogation as consisting of being locked for fourteen hours in a stifling cell and harangued by interrogators seeking a confession. The case had some very peculiar elements. The woman's pinky had been amputated (a way of disgracing a devout Moslem), and her larynx cut out. Sands maintained, at the time and ever since, his absolute innocence.

The case came to Gerson by way of one of his mentors in international law at Yale, Michael Reisman, who had been approached by Sands's family in the States. There was no dispute that the Saudis had the right to investigate and prosecute a crime committed on their soil. Every American official Gerson approached at first told him the same thing, that their hands were tied because the Saudis insisted on handling the case themselves. But to Gerson it was obvious that the United States had an obligation to protect its citizens from a third-world judicial system which had not yet discovered the concept of due process. And he thought he knew why the government wasn't living up to its obligation. "It appears," he told a reporter for the influential Washington weekly *Legal Times,* in a front-page story, "that the importance of maintaining smooth diplomatic relations with the host country has outweighed the need to press vigorously for the release of an American ex-serviceman who is caught up in the machinations of a medieval system of justice."

But Gerson was wrong; the American government wasn't bowing to Saudi pressure. The truth was even more shocking to him: the State Department was keeping Sands there on its own. His colleague David Dorsen flew to Riyadh and met the mayor. "We know all about the case," Dorsen was told, "and we have no problem with letting your client go. It's your government that wants to keep him here." Dorsen was dumbfounded, and so was Gerson when he got the news. He called a friend at the State Department who he knew had worked on this matter and invited him to deny it.

"If we bring him home," the friend told him, "you'll get him off. You know that. You will plead that an American court has no jurisdiction over him because the crime was committed abroad. And as a result you will free a murderer, and we don't want to free a murderer."

Gerson couldn't believe what he was hearing. "You want to keep him there until he confesses?" he erupted. "How do you know he's guilty?"

"We know he did it," the official replied smugly. "He lied in interrogation about a sweetheart he had on the side."

"I learned in high school that it's better to let ten guilty men go free than convict one innocent one," Gerson shot back.

"Well, that's not how I learned it. It's always more complicated than that."

So Gerson began to look for solutions "outside the ordinary way of doing things." He decided public attention might help Sands's cause, so he brought it to the attention of his former boss at the U.S. Mission to the United Nations, Ambassador Jeane Kirkpatrick, now a syndicated newspaper columnist. She devoted one to Sands, which ran in some newspapers under the headline "American Citizen, Islamic Justice." He looked for a way to bring political pressure to bear. Sands had no strings to pull, but Gerson's father-in-law had been a major backer of Rhode Island senator Claiborne Pell, then the chairman of the Senate Foreign Relations Committee. Pell wrote a letter on Sands's behalf. Finally Gerson and Dorsen pulled a rarely used legal maneuver, threatening to obtain a writ of mandamus against the secretaries of State and Defense. This is a judicial order meant to force a public official to discharge his duty—in this case to do everything in their power to get Sands out of Saudi Arabia to face a fair trial here. The next day Sands was recalled from reserve status to active duty, and flown back under military guard to the United States, where he was arrested and held for a court-martial.

Gerson was sure that the government's behavior was unconstitutional, and he recommended to Sands that he challenge the court-martial. But the American Bar Association had recently loosened its rules on client solicitation (the practice once more colorfully known as "ambulance chasing"), and two young lawyers with backgrounds in military justice contacted Sands and persuaded him that the quickest way to freedom was to have the trial. "You're gambling with your life," Gerson told him solemnly. But Sands, who didn't want to wait around for a year or more while the constitutional issues were argued, took the risk and was acquitted.

There's a footnote to the Sands story, which in a small way sheds some light on the obstacles a private citizen must overcome in pursuing justice against a government, even his own. Long after Sands was home, a package showed up on Gerson's desk from the State Department. It contained excerpts from the cables between the State Department and the American embassy in Riyadh, requested by Gerson at an earlier stage in the case and long since forgotten. When Gerson saw them, he realized he had a gold mine of evidence for a civil suit against the government. The entire scenario was spelled out in a series of exchanges, in which the embassy reported that the Saudis were willing to let Sands go, and the State Department responded: keep him there. But the federal government is ordinarily immune to suits by individuals charging misconduct by its officials. Their only recourse is to persuade Congress to pass what is known as a private bill, authorizing them to sue. The House Judiciary Committee would be the place to start, and as it happened, Gerson's colleague Dorsen knew the ranking minority member, Rep. Henry Hyde of Illinois. Hyde held a hearing on Sands's ordeal. But then came the 1994 congressional elections, when the Republicans unexpectedly took control of the House. Hyde became chairman of the Judiciary Committee. This ordinarily would have been good news for anyone relying on his help in getting something through Congress. But it turned out to be a fatal setback, because Hyde was now too busy and too prominent to sponsor a private bill, especially one so potentially controversial and embarrassing to the government. So ended the Sands case, in a fizzle of missed opportunities instead of a thunderclap of justice. The indifference the government displayed toward his client's rights, and the arbitrary way that shifting political fortunes destroyed his chance to sue, helped shape Gerson's growing militancy about holding governments accountable for human rights, including the government of the United States.

Gerson's other clients were equally unconventional. He represented the family of American missionaries in Belize, the former British Honduras, the parents of which were accidentally killed when a British tank on maneuvers ran over their car. The British government offered the couple's children a set compensation of $10,000, which is what the local law would have provided had they been run down by a Belize postal truck. In a series of polite but increasingly pointed exchanges, Gerson pressed the argument that London's deference to the legal system of its own former colony appeared to have no other purpose than saving money. Ultimately he negotiated an increase in compensation to $330,000.

He represented the owner of the *Lucky Star,* a foreign vessel that was seized by federal agents in international waters with the largest shipment of hashish ever intercepted in international waters. Under American law, the search, even though carried out without advance consent, could be retroactively legalized if the government of the vessel's flag country agreed to waive its objections. The vessel was registered in a small Caribbean nation. Gerson met with the prime minister, who said, somewhat testily, that the American ambassador had handed him the paper and showed where to sign.

Excellent, Gerson thought; he's unhappy about being pushed around. "Then you can withdraw the waiver," Gerson told him.

"You expect me to go against the United States on drugs?" the prime minister exclaimed in horror, with the example of Noriega still fresh in his mind.

So he didn't win that one, but still, it was a heady time for Gerson. In the aftermath of the Gulf War, he cast about for a way to leverage some of his high-level contacts in Arab capitals, dating back to his years at the UN. Billions would be spent on post–Gulf War reconstruction, and he thought he could help Egyptian construction firms win a share of it. He flew to Cairo for meetings, and returned home by way of Tel Aviv, where Sofaer was meeting with Israeli government officials. The two lawyers took a long late-night stroll down the boardwalk in Tel Aviv, congratulating themselves on how much they'd achieved in the rarefied field they'd chosen. Who else did this kind of thing? They were on top of the world, but that was before either of them had given more than a passing thought to Lockerbie.

Pan Am flight 103 had entered Gerson's life in the spring of 1992 by way of a law student named Mark Zaid, who had recruited him for a conference on Lockerbie, terrorism, and aviation security. Zaid, who had attended the University of Rochester along with two of the students who had been killed in the bombing, was in his third year at the law school of Union University at Albany, New York. He is a lifelong connoisseur of conspiracy theories, a compulsive investigator and skeptic, and a leading lay expert on the Kennedy assassination, although frequently at odds with other assassination buffs over his preference for facts over baroque speculation. Terrorism was a natural outgrowth of his interests, and he volunteered to line up an international law expert for the conference, which was organized by a friend, Joel Schwarz. An acquaintance who knew of Gerson's work in the Justice Department recommended him. Gerson, who was busy in Washington, tried to beg off, but Zaid told him he wouldn't have to prepare anything: he could just come and listen and speak up if he had something he wanted to say.

The experience was an eye-opener for Gerson. A number of family members attended, including Paul Hudson. As he began to speak, someone handed Hudson a note, which he read aloud, announcing that a 747 had just crashed over the Atlantic. It was a hoax meant to heighten the immediacy of his talk, although a number of people in the audience thought it was in poor taste under the circumstances. It was during a session devoted to the upcoming Pan Am trial that Gerson had his fateful brainstorm. Hughes Hubbard & Reed had been representing Israel in its claims against Iraq for damage caused by missile attacks during the Gulf War. The UN Security Council had established a commission to pay these claims from Iraqi oil revenues. A fund was established to collect one-third of the proceeds of such sales, although Iraq refused to sell any oil under its auspices and instead was smuggling petroleum out of the country. Nevertheless the UN commission labored on, processing claims in the hope that one day Iraq would comply. It seemed to Gerson that the principle was sound, and a great innovation in international law, which had previously been concerned with punishing aggression, not compensating its victims. It occurred to him that families of passengers killed by state-sponsored terrorism were as deserving as the victims of international aggression. Libya, unlike Iraq, was freely and legally exporting oil and had plenty of revenues that could be attached, as well as assets around the world, including bank deposits frozen by the U.S. government since 1986. Out of this idea came his op-ed article, which ran in the *New York Times* on July 1, and a day later in the *International Herald Tribune*.

To Gerson, the article was essentially a think piece, and a way to keep his name in front of the public, part of his job as a professor and a Washington lawyer. It was, however, read far more widely and with more interest than he imagined, in a number of places, including the State Department, the National Security Council—and Libya. It struck a particular chord with Lee Kreindler, whose case against Pan Am was about to go to the jury. Kreindler was infuriated by the article. He had spent three years building a case against the airline, not the terrorists. The last thing he wanted was to remind the jurors that "those who planted the bomb . . . are not in the courtroom." The suggestion that someone else could or should be made to pay—let alone a country with more oil than Texas—struck him as akin to sabotage of his efforts to wring millions of dollars out of Pan Am's insurance companies. Of course, it's entirely possible none of the jurors—who were continually cautioned by the judge not to read anything about the case—ever saw the article. Certainly, Gerson had no intention of influencing their verdict. But so much was at stake for Kreindler, so delicate was the balance on which millions of dollars hung, that for years afterward, long after fate had thrown them together as allies, he could barely bring himself to write or utter a civil word to, or about, Gerson.

Bruce Smith, though, had a very different reaction to the article. Smith had persisted in his belief that Pan Am was a victim of terrorism, just as the families were. In late 1991, right after the indictments came out, he had attempted to file his own claim against Libya for lost companionship and earnings. He had valued Ingrid's companionship at $100,000 a year, and multiplied that by his own additional life expectancy of thirty-one years; he added a little more than $900,000 for Ingrid's lost earnings and tripled the sum to make it punitive, arriving at a grand total of just over $12 million. A lawyer advised him that claims against a foreign government must be filed with the State Department—where, for lack of a better venue, it was referred to the office of International Claims and Investment Disputes. In January the State Department advised him that the United States and Britain had demanded "appropriate compensation" from Libya, but "since Libya has not yet agreed to pay compensation, it would be fruitless to present it with detailed claims now." That struck Smith as an unusually circular and self-defeating argument even for a government bureaucrat. "What you wrote there," he told Gerson on the phone from Paris, "is exactly what I've been looking for. I want to retain you to make it happen." A few days later Smith was in New York; he hopped a flight to Washington and found himself in a conference room at HHR with Gerson and Sofaer.

Gerson made sure Smith understood what he was signing up for. Unlike tort lawyers, HHR didn't work on contingency. Smith would pay $300 an hour for as much time as Gerson put in on the case, and to the extent Sofaer got involved, it would be even more. If the two of them met at the State Department with an assistant secretary of state for an hour, it could run close to $1,000.

Smith said that would be all right. He had taken his Pan Am pension of $350,000 in cash when the airline folded, and he was prepared to spend all of it to fight Libya. After getting approval from the New Business Committee of Hughes Hubbard & Reed, Gerson wrote Smith on July 20, offering his services "to bring to fruition the idea proposed in my *New York Times* piece . . . to achieve passage of a UN resolution establishing a claims commission calling for Libyan compensation to the families of victims of Pan Am 103. I believe the expertise of myself and Judge Abe Sofaer offers a reasonable chance of securing passage of such a resolution." Smith countersigned the letter and sent it back to Hughes Hubbard & Reed, of which he became a client, although not one whose name would appear in any roster of clients in future HHR brochures.

The more Gerson thought about the possibilities, the more the case intrigued him. For one thing, the universe of possible clients wasn't limited to Smith; any of the relatives, whether they were suing Pan Am or had already settled, would be eligible to bring a claim before a UN commission. Smith put Gerson in touch with Paul Hudson, who in turn agreed to bring it up with some of the other family members. The more clients who joined Smith, the less costly it would be for him. There was another potential client as well, one which was well accustomed to paying corporate lawyers. This was the insurance syndicate headed by USAU, which would be spending at least $24 million if everyone took its minimal offer—and many times that amount if multi-million-dollar judgments stood up on appeal. And that didn't even include the amount paid by Lloyd's of London, which had insured the aircraft itself for $40 million. The insurance companies would be entitled to make a claim against Libya to get that money back, too.

On the other hand, the obstacles were considerable. As individuals, the family members of the victims had no standing with the United Nations. The proposal for a claims commission would have to come from a member state—in this case, obviously, the United States. At the very end of August, Gerson met with Assistant Secretary of State for International Organizations John Bolton. Bolton liked the idea in principle, but said it wasn't likely to get very far unless it was pushed from the very top. He suggested that Gerson write a summary of the proposal along with draft language that he, Bolton, could suggest for inclusion in President Bush's opening speech to the General Assembly when it convened in September. That was gratifying, in one sense, but Gerson, who knew how many ideas compete for mention in a major presidential address, warned Smith not to get his hopes up.

Gerson drafted a passage for inclusion in Bush's speech, and Bolton ran it by Lawrence Eagleburger, the acting secretary of state, and sent it on to the White House. Claiborne Pell, who was chairman of the Senate Foreign Relations Committee, wrote to Bush supporting the idea, and so did several influential senators: D'Amato and Moynihan of New York, Chuck Grassley of Iowa, and Dennis DeConcini of New Mexico. But there was no way to tell whether the idea was going anywhere. Somewhere in the White House, Gerson knew, his idea was in the hands of a special assistant to the president, who might or might not even bring the matter up for Bush's consideration. Gerson himself could do nothing more.

The day of the speech came; the next day he looked in the *Washington Post,* but there was no mention in it of a claims commission, and when Bolton sent him the text of the address, it wasn't in there. Gerson never found out exactly what had happened to the idea. "Probably someone in the White House just looked at it and said, it's those jerks in the State Department, and threw it away," Bolton says. "Yet if Bush had said it, they could have found a dozen families to go on the news and chant hosannahs to him, a month before the election."

But there is another possibility: the idea may have been deliberately killed by someone in Bush's National Security Council. Forming a UN claims commission would constitute movement in the standoff between the United States and Libya, and there were powerful forces in the White House opposed to precisely that. Interestingly, just a day after Gerson's article appeared in July, the *New York Times* published a letter responding to it from an official of the Organization of African Unity, which was presumed to be speaking for Libya. Far from rejecting Gerson's idea, the OAU official seemed to endorse it. But he

Victoria Cummock and Bruce Smith on the porch of her home in Florida. Victoria co-founded and served as president of Families of Pan Am 103/Lockerbie and served on the President's Airline Safety Commission. Bruce, a former Pan Am captain, was first to initiate the lawsuit against Libya.

On 21 December 1988, a terrorist bomb destroyed Pan American Airlines Flight 103 over Lockerbie, Scotland, killing all on board and 11 on the ground. The 270 Scottish stones which compose this memorial cairn commemorate those who lost their lives in this attack against America.

Pan Am 103 cairn at Arlington National Cemetery commemorating the "attack against America" and listing all 270 victims.
Top: Base of cairn with inscription.
Bottom: Francis Klein, master builder and father of flight 103 passenger Patricia Klein, putting finishing touches on the cairn's last stone.

Co-author Allan Gerson beside cairn memorial plaque
at Arlington National Cemetery.

Memorial to Oklahoma City Federal Office Building bombing
(under construction).

WE COME HERE TO REMEMBER
SE WHO WERE KILLED, THOSE WHO SURVIVED AND THOSE CHANGED FOREVER.
MAY ALL WHO LEAVE HERE KNOW THE IMPACT OF VIOLENCE.

Suse Lowenstein's *Dark Elegy* series sculptures.
The life-size sculptures feature mothers and wives of victims posing nude
in expression of collective grief at the bombing of Pan Am flight 103.

$4,000,000

REWARD

Diplomatic Security Service

On 12/21/88, Pan Am Flight 103 from London to New York exploded over Lockerbie, Scotland killing all 259 on board and 11 more people on the ground. A massive investigation over the next three years culminated in the indictments of two suspects, who are both Libyan nationals and intelligence officers.

Abdel Basset Ali Al-Megrahi, one of the two suspects, is believed to be in Libya. The Libyan Government, against which the United Nations has invoked resolutions and sanctions, has been unwilling to turn Al-Megrahi over to the United Kingdom or United States for trial.

The United States Department of State and the U.S. airline industry are offering a reward of up to $4,000,000 for information leading to the apprehension and prosecution of Al-Megrahi. The U.S. Government also can provide for the protection of identity and the possibility of relocation for persons and their families furnishing such information. If you have information about Al-Megrahi or the Pan Am 103 bombing, contact authorities or the nearest U.S. Embassy or consulate. In the United States, call your local office of the Federal Bureau of Investigation or 1-800-HEROES-1, or write to:

HEROES
Post Office Box 96781
Washington, D.C. 20090-6781
U.S.A.

ABDEL BASSET ALI AL-MEGRAHI

DESCRIPTION

Date of birth:	April 1, 1952
Place of birth:	Tripoli, Libya
Height:	Approximately 5'8"
Weight:	Approximately 190 lbs
Hair:	Black curly, clean shaven
Eyes:	Dark brown
Complexion:	Light brown
Sex:	Male
Nationality:	Libyan
Occupation:	Formerly Chief of Airline Security, Libyan Arab Airlines, in Malta
Aliases:	Abd Al Basset Al Megrahi, Abdelbaset Ali Mohmed Al Megrahi, Mr. Baset, Ahmed Khalifa Abdusamad

Program developed and funded by Air Line Pilots Association and Air Transport Association in coordination with U.S. Department of State

Wanted poster with photograph of bombing suspect Abdel Basset Ali Al-Megrahi. Bruce Smith helped spearhead the "Heroes" Rewards Program.

Douglas Rosenthal, lead lawyer at Sonnenschein, Nath & Rosenthal, the firm that served as co-counsel with Gerson in initiating the civil suit against Libya.

Mark Zaid, co-counsel for families of bombing victims, in his Washington, D.C., law office.

Frank Duggan, McLaughlin Commission liaison for the victims' families, in his later office as chairman of the National Mediation Board.

In The

Supreme Court of the United States

October Term, 1996

————————◆————————

BRUCE SMITH, as personal representative
of Ingrid Smith, Deceased,

Petitioner,

vs.

THE SOCIALIST PEOPLE'S LIBYAN ARAB
JAMAHIRIYA; LIBYAN EXTERNAL SECURITY
ORGANIZATION, also known as Jamahiriya Security
Organization; and LIBYAN ARAB AIRLINES,

Respondents,

ABDEL BASSET ALI AL-MEGRAHI, and
LAMEN KHALIFA FHIMAH,

Defendants.

————————◆————————

**Petition For A Writ Of Certiorari
To The United States Court Of Appeals
For The Second Circuit**

————————◆————————

PETITIONER'S REPLY BRIEF

————————◆————————

Douglas E. Rosenthal
  Counsel of Record
Carol Elder Bruce
Lisa A. MacVittie
Jill I. Prater
Sonnenschein Nath & Rosenthal
  1301 K Street, N.W.
  Suite 600, East Tower
  Washington, D.C. 20005
  (202) 408-6400

Allan Gerson
  Special Counsel

Mark S. Zaid
Douglas B. Rutzen
Timothy C. Russell
  Of Counsel

Attorneys for Petitioner

Brief filed before the U.S. Supreme Court on behalf of Bruce Smith.

proposed a commission that would not just adjudicate claims, but also investigate "the circumstantial evidence against Libya"—in other words, an international tribunal with the power to decide that Libya wasn't guilty after all. To America's foreign-policy makers that would have been a clarion call to kill the commission plan before it went an inch further. Sanctions were their strategy, and as far as they were concerned, they were working.

"Well," Gerson said to Smith after Bush's speech, "the commission idea is not going to happen, at least not this year."

"What else do you have in mind?" Smith asked.

There was one other thing. They could sue Libya for damages in an American court, just as the other relatives had sued Pan Am. The idea had been in his mind almost from the beginning, although the Smith retainer letter spoke only of work to promote the UN commission idea. There was a strong case for a lawsuit on symbolic grounds. The evidence would be spread on the record for the world to see. And the judge would weigh it according to the standards of civil lawsuits, where cases are decided by a preponderance of the evidence. That was a much lower threshold than prosecutors would face in proving guilt "beyond a reasonable doubt"—as Americans were to discover when O. J. Simpson was successfully sued for wrongful death by the Goldman and Brown families after he'd already been acquitted of their murders. The judgment cost Simpson millions, and he was shunned by people everywhere. In lieu of a hanging, Smith would accept that for Kaddafi.

The practical problems, though, were daunting. To prove their case, they would almost certainly need at least some of the evidence developed by the FBI and the Scottish police, and there was no assurance they would get it. To the contrary, as long as a criminal trial of Fhimah and Megrahi was still a possibility, prosecutors would likely fight to keep the evidence secret. And if they won a judgment, how would they collect it? Gerson's original proposal had envisioned a commission, with the authority of the UN Security Council behind it, which could monitor Libya's oil exports and distribute the proceeds to the claimants. But would a judgment from a U.S. District Court be so easy to enforce in a foreign country? Would a court in Rotterdam order the seizing of tankerloads of Libyan crude oil? Would it order a Libyan ship mothballed and prepared for delivery to Smith?

And there was a more immediate obstacle: How would he even get an American court to take jurisdiction? Twenty years earlier, this would have been an entirely hopeless task. But in 1979, while Gerson was with the Justice Department's Office of Special Investigations prosecuting Nazi collaborators who had escaped to America, a decision by a U.S. appellate court opened the way for American justice to pursue human-rights abuses in violation of the law of nations anywhere in the world. The case concerned one Joelito Filartiga, who was a teenager in Paraguay in 1976, when he was abducted, tortured, and killed by the police on a remote suspicion that he was connected with an insurgent group. His death was no different than those of hundreds of others at the hands of the Paraguayan police. But somehow the officer who interrogated him, Americo Norberto Pena-Irala, became known to the Filartiga family, and they decided to pursue him in the courts. They followed him all the way to New York City, where he had fled and was living in 1979.

When Filartiga's father, Joel, began contacting American lawyers, they all told him the same thing: he could never get a hearing in a U.S. court because criminal acts committed abroad were considered outside U.S. jurisdiction. Finally he contacted the Center for Constitutional Rights in Manhattan. Intent on expanding the reach of international law, they dredged up a nearly 200-year-old statute, the Alien Tort Claims Act of 1789. Its purpose was to grant jurisdiction to the U.S. courts for torts committed abroad "in violation of the law of nations," if the perpetrator could be located in the United States. The statute had not been used for at least one hundred years, and in early 1979, when the CCR's lawyers filed their suit against Pena-Irala, the amazed judge in U.S. District Court promptly dismissed it. Whatever may have been Congress's intentions in 1789, he ruled, American courts long since had held that the "law of nations" is not a basis for judicial review of the treatment of U.S. citizens, and certainly not their treatment at the hands of a foreign state.

But on appeal, the Second Circuit U.S. Court of Appeals did something revolutionary. The times had changed, it ruled. International law now required courts to give greater consideration to the dignity of the individual and less to the prerogatives of government officials who use torture as an adjunct to law enforcement. Reversing the district-court ruling, the court held that "deliberate torture perpetrated under the color of official authority violates universally accepted norms of the international law of human rights, regardless of the nationality of the parties."

Financially, it was a hollow victory. Pena-Irala was found to be in the United States illegally and was deported back to Paraguay. As a result, he never contested the suit, but neither was there any way to make him pay up, so the $10 million default judgment awarded to the Filartiga family remains uncollected to this day. But the case has been heralded by international human-rights lawyers as a kind of magna carta for victims of official torture and killing. Even uncollected judgments serve important functions, as Yale Law School professor and former assistant secretary of state for human rights Harold Koh has written: deterrence, denial of safe haven in the United States to the defendant, and the affirmation of a code of conduct that civilized nations share. That was what the Court of Appeals had in mind in writing: "Our holding today, giving effect to a jurisdictional provision enacted by our first Congress, is a small but important step in the fulfillment of the ageless dream to free all peoples from brutal violence." In 1989 the Filartiga decision became the basis for a lawsuit against the estate of Philippine dictator Ferdinand Marcos involving more than 10,000 claims of torture, summary execution, and disappearance.

But there was no obvious way to bring Libya under the umbrella of the 1789 law. Pena-Irala and Marcos were sued in the United States because they were in the United States; Kaddafi (and Fhimah and Megrahi) obviously weren't going to turn up conveniently in New York. In fact, Libya had been sued once before in the United States over a terrorist attack—the bombing of a bus in Israel allegedly masterminded by the Palestine Liberation Organization with support from Libya. The parents of one of the victims had sued both Libya and the

PLO in U.S. District Court for the District of Columbia. The suit was dismissed by a judge who held that American courts had no jurisdiction over foreign governments or quasi-national organizations such as the PLO—and this time, the appellate court agreed. In fact, Court of Appeals judge Robert Bork, soon to become nationally known in his ill-fated nomination to the U.S. Supreme Court, hinted in a concurring opinion that he would overturn the Filartiga decision itself if he had a chance. So, as Gerson saw it, the crack in the wall around government-sponsored human rights abuses wasn't likely to open wide enough to admit Smith any time soon.

What stood in the way was the doctrine of sovereign immunity, the principle, descended more or less directly from the divine right of monarchs, which holds national governments above the law, unless they specifically consent to subject themselves to it. It is sovereign immunity that leaves American citizens with a grievance against their own government with no option for redress unless a specific exception to immunity is drawn in the law. When raised by foreign governments, sovereign immunity provides an even stronger defense, one that would almost certainly protect Libya from a lawsuit in an American court— or so went the conventional thinking at the time. Lee Kreindler wrote that he looked into suing Libya around the same time, and concluded it was impossible. But Kreindler was an aviation lawyer. Gerson's expertise was in international law and in human rights. Over the last half century, he knew, there had been a gradual trend toward restricting the formerly absolute nature of sovereign immunity. Gerson thought it might be possible to nudge that process along a bit.

Naturally, the movement in the U.S. Congress to restrict sovereign immunity had been primarily for the benefit of American business, not victims of terrorism. The relevant law, the 1976 Foreign Sovereign Immunities Act (FSIA), incorporated two specific exceptions to sovereign immunity, neither one especially well suited to Gerson's purpose. One covered purely commercial dealings having a "direct effect" inside the United States. This was intended to allow the courts to settle disputes between American corporations and foreign governments over contracts and loans—a situation that only began to arise in meaningful ways with the advent of state-owned businesses. There was no obvious way to bring the bombing of an airplane under that heading, although Gerson was willing to examine non-obvious ways as well. He considered the argument that Libya's financial support of terrorist groups was tantamount to a commercial transaction within the meaning of FSIA. With a sympathetic judge, who knows how far he might have gotten?

But the case law was discouraging; courts were interpreting the commercial exception very narrowly. Gerson happened to know this because he'd been working on just such a case at Hughes Hubbard & Reed. It involved another American caught up in the Saudi judicial system—Scott Nelson, a medical-systems engineer employed in the construction of the King Faisal Hospital in Riyadh. When Nelson made the mistake of pointing out a potentially dangerous flaw in the system of pipes that delivered medical gases to the rooms—pipes that had already been installed behind beautiful and costly marble walls—he was corrected by his superiors on the proper role of consultants in Saudi society. To make sure he understood, he was forced to do deep knee bends at gunpoint with a pipe strapped behind his knees. Back in the United States, and crippled for life, he had hired the well-known Washington lawyer Leonard Garment to sue the Saudi government. Garment had brought in his friend Sofaer for advice on the international-law aspects, and Sofaer had handed over some of the work to a younger associate named Dan Wolf, who had turned for advice to Gerson. In trying to persuade a judge to hear the case, they had argued that Nelson's hiring, by way of an ad placed by the Saudi government in a Texas newspaper, constituted a commercial transaction within the scope of FSIA. This was probably a stronger argument than anything Smith had going for him, but even so it was turned down by the district court. Nelson's lawyers appealed and won a reversal, and Saudi Arabia had appealed that decision to the Supreme Court. There was no way of knowing how the Supreme Court would rule, of course—and in the end, they decided against Nelson—but even so, what troubled Gerson was that the U.S. State Department had entered the case with a friend-of-the-court brief *backing Saudi Arabia's position*.

Gerson understood, of course, that the American government had its own reasons for favoring the principle of sovereign immunity. It was a form of self-protection against foreign courts. Even countries, such as the United States, that don't have a policy of torturing foreign consultants benefit from not having foreign judges looking over their shoulders. And there was also "the Building"—the phrase insiders used to refer to the permanent bureaucracy of the State Department, whose institutional interests stayed the same, irrespective of the politics or ideology of any particular administration. None of these institutional prerogatives was more precious to the Building than sovereign immunity. It was an article of faith, a point of solidarity among all nations, whether benevolent or despotic, democratic or totalitarian—a legal shield against the masses who sought to know too much or to hold their governments accountable for their misdeeds. Gerson was prepared to fight Libya in court, but he didn't want to have to fight his own government as well.

There was a second exception to sovereign immunity in the FSIA, which denied immunity for torts committed within the United States of America. As far as the State Department's interpretation of the law went, this was intended to allow citizens to sue foreign diplomats who ran over them in traffic accidents. Nevertheless, Gerson saw an opening here, in the argument that an airplane owned and operated by an American company and carrying mostly Americans on its way to America was, functionally, part of America. He asked for a study of the question by Malvina Halberstam, an authority on international law at Cardozo School of Law, part of Yeshiva University. She wrote back suggesting at least two possible approaches. One was based on the language of the act, which could be construed as covering torts within the "jurisdiction" of the United States, not just its "territory." It was a settled matter that American-flag civil aircraft are within American "jurisdiction." If that approach failed, Halberstam went on, one could argue that an American airplane was legally part of the "territory" of the United States, by analogy to maritime law, which with blithe disregard of etymology regards a ship at sea as part of the "territory" of its flag nation. "I think it is a difficult argument to make," she warned, "but I don't think the question is completely foreclosed. . . ."

Well, thought Gerson, now we're getting somewhere.

There was a third approach he could try, one which elevated the matter beyond the narrow and picayune parsing of legal passages and definitions and into the eloquent realm of justice, where Gerson by nature was more at home. He envisioned an argument that said, in effect, no American Congress could have ever intended that the FSIA serve as a shield for a state guilty of murdering innocent American civilians. Such a state was guilty of a violation of *jus cogens,* universally recognized principles of civilized conduct, and, as an outlaw nation, had implicitly waived its immunity—just as Nazi Germany did in committing "crimes against humanity." Gerson had been trained in this expansive view of international law, the so-called "Yale School," centered around Professors Myres McDougal and Harold Lasswell. The Yale School advocated a contextual approach to the law, viewing it as a means to enlightened decision-making rather than an end in itself. For precedent Gerson reached all the way back to 1917, and a New York State Court of Appeals decision in *Wood v. Lucy, Lady Duff-Gordon.* In this seemingly mundane contract dispute over the licensing rights to "fabrics, parasols and what not," the great Benjamin Cardozo, a future Supreme Court justice, discerned the principle that "the law has outgrown its primitive stage of formalism when the precise word was the sovereign talisman, and every slip was fatal. It takes a broader view today." To put it another way, in the life of the law many things are by their nature implicit, and judges should look for them beyond the "black letter" of the statute books. To hang that argument around Kaddafi's neck would have been one of the capstones of Gerson's career.

When he reached that stage in his thinking, he began to look into other possibilities, including bringing suit in the courts of Great Britain. The plane, after all, had blown up over Scotland; Smith's wife was English and he had a house there, so there appeared to be ample grounds for jurisdiction. The amount he could recover was most likely small, compared to what an American jury might award, and few if any of the other American families would be in a position to join him. But at least it promised a venue for getting some of the evidence into

the record and establishing Libya's culpability. Gerson had a trip scheduled to Jerusalem to discuss Israeli claims against Iraq, and it would be
relatively inexpensive for him to stop off in England on his way back.
He checked with Smith, who would foot the bill, and then made an
appointment to see Professor Eli Lauterpacht of Cambridge, perhaps
the most prominent international law scholar in England. That was in
January 1993, and he had no idea, when he left on the trip, that on his
return everything would be different.

9

Defection

As 1992 ended, four years after the bombing and a year after the indictments, Kaddafi had begun to pay the price for refusing to turn over Fhimah and Megrahi. UN Security Council sanctions shut down Libya's air traffic with the rest of the world, froze its deposits in foreign banks, and choked off its imports of weapons and airplane parts. By prohibiting the sale of oilfield equipment and technology, the sanctions whittled away at Libya's oil-production capacity, which accounted for nearly 90 percent of the government's revenue. Occasionally an African President for Life would show up in Tripoli for a well-publicized handshake with Kaddafi, but most Western countries observed the sanctions, even those with close economic ties to Libya such as Germany and Italy. The U.S. Treasury Department, which enforced America's own, even tougher sanctions—including an almost total ban on travel to Libya by Americans—announced periodic crackdowns on violators, who faced (in theory, at least) penalties ranging up to twelve years in prison. Western tourism and investment in the country came to a virtual standstill. Under American pressure, Ukraine embargoed a shipment of sixty tons of ammonium perchlorate—an ingredient in rocket fuel—destined for Libya from Russia. A variety of sources, including World Bank figures, document a precipitous decline in economic activity in the years following 1992. Unemployment was running at about 30 percent and inflation at 50 percent. Government employees were going unpaid, a condition that would eventually lead to a short-lived rebellion by army officrs. Kaddafi called for austerity programs—"dangerous," as Libya scholar Ray Takeyh has pointed out, "for a regime that depended for its survival on buying the population's acquiescence."

And there was the distinct possibility that things would get much worse for Kaddafi. In the fall of 1992, the implacable Daniel and Susan Cohen had contacted Democratic presidential candidate Bill Clinton, asking where he stood on Libyan sanctions. Clinton, naturally, was happy to seize an opportunity to promise to do better than his opponent. "If elected," he wrote back, "I will do what is right and necessary to send a message that individuals who engage in and countries which lend support for terrorist activities will pay a high price . . . the United States should make it clear that if [the suspects] are not turned over, it will press the United Nations to broaden the sanctions to include an oil embargo." Within weeks of his election, the family groups staged a rally across the street from the White House to remind the president-elect of this pledge. A thorough boycott of Libyan oil production would have been a mortal blow to Kaddafi. That, however, may have been one reason—besides the objections of America's European allies—why it was never seriously attempted. Fearing Kaddafi's possible successors more than Kaddafi himself, the policymakers in the National Security Council wanted the Libyan leader in a box, not a coffin. But it might not have looked that way from Tripoli, so as the Clinton administration prepared to take power in Washington, Kaddafi convened his top aides into a group called the Committee for the Case of Lockerbie. Its mission was to find a way around the American sanctions without giving in to the humiliating demand for Fhimah and Megrahi's extradition. The instrumentalities would be the Pan Am 103 families, if they could be persuaded to accept an offer of compensation, and a top-notch lawyer who knew his way around Washington, if one could be found who would take on Libya as a client.

Kaddafi may not have been especially wise about American politics, but he could see that cutting a deal with Washington was impossible as long as the families were threatening to chain themselves to the White House fence at the first hint of any reconciliation. But he was disastrously wrong in his calculation of what it would take to buy them off. What the family members sought was Kaddafi's humiliation and punishment. Therefore, almost anything he offered was likely to be turned down; if he was willing to pay it, then by definition it didn't hurt him enough. Most of the family members hadn't even considered suing Libya at this stage, and so hadn't considered what, if anything, they would accept by way of settlement. Some, like the Cohens, would have refused any payment at all. The two who did think about it were Smith and Hudson. Smith had asked for $12 million in the claim against Libya which he had tried, and failed, to file with the State Department. Hudson had drawn up a comprehensive list of damages that by coincidence also worked out to around $12 million per victim, or $3 billion for all 240 fatalities combined. Hudson's reckoning also included figures for lost business by American airlines, "injury to the national dignity" of the United States, the costs of the investigation, punitive damages, and interest from December 21, 1988, amounting in all to $23.2 billion, or two-thirds of Libya's gross domestic product. Hudson's intention was to extract a payment large enough so that by itself it could be construed as an admission of guilt, no matter what Libya called it.

By the same token, though, Libya had a political as well as an economic incentive to hold down the payments. In diplomatic terms, Tripoli would have wanted any payments to be considered *ex gratia*—a humanitarian gesture that does not convey any admission of guilt. As legal adviser to the State Department, Abe Sofaer had negotiated an *ex gratia* payment by Iraq to the families of thirty-seven American sailors killed in 1987 when an Iraqi pilot mistakenly fired two Exocet missiles at the American warship USS *Stark*. The payment was $730,000 for each death, which was considered a very large amount at the time. Libya never made a concrete offer to the Pan Am families, but there were indications that they were prepared to pay as much—or, one might as well say, as little—as $1 million for each of the victims. Libya had no diplomatic relations with the United States, so the main job of the Committee for the Case of Lockerbie was to find an intermediary who could deal with the families and the American government. Kaddafi had refined his tactics since the Carter administration, when his choice of a Washington power broker was the president's brother Billy, a Georgia filling-station owner. "They try to buy what they believe to be influential people," Cannistraro, the former CIA official, said at the time. "They are used to spreading money around and getting their way." Virtually the only form of commerce still taking place between the United States and Libya was a one-way trade in influence peddling. Lawyers were still allowed to sell their services to Libya, provided they applied for a license from the Treasury's Office of Foreign Assets Control. And preliminary conversations, where no money changes hands, didn't require even that formality. By the dozens, along with miscellaneous former government officials and prominent private citizens, they showed up at the State Department to propose solutions to the impasse. In various guises and combinations, they generally involved monetary compensation to the family members and a trial of some kind for Fhimah and Megrahi, although not in an American courtroom. "They drive our Near Eastern Affairs Bureau nuts," the department's spokesman, Michael McCurry, complained to reporters.

Most of them were in it for money, of course; to get the sanctions lifted was worth almost any price to Libya. A few might have had other motivations. Albert Reichmann, a principal in the wealthy Canadian real-estate family, met with Sen. Ted Kennedy, one of the Pan Am families' most outspoken defenders, to ask about ways out of the impasse. It appears that Reichmann, an Orthodox Jew, might have been seeking, on his own, to do a favor for Israel. Israel had no use for Kaddafi, but their worst nightmare was giving Islamic fundamentalists a foothold in North Africa right next door to Egypt. It was an absurd mission for Reichmann to undertake, and Kennedy stalked out of the meeting as soon as he heard what it was about. Washington lawyers frequently must take on unpopular causes, but Libya was in a class by itself. "Life is too short to represent people who get you in trouble," said Thomas Hale Boggs Jr., a partner in Patton, Boggs & Blow and one of Washington's premier movers and shakers. Jonathan Schiller of Donovan, Leisure, Rogovin & Schiller was approached in Geneva by a senior Libyan official, who told him he had something urgent to discuss. They arranged to meet at a nearby hotel, where Schiller believes they were observed by American intelligence agents. "He was seeking my advice on what might satisfy the U.S.," Schiller said. "I told him that I assumed a prompt delivery [of the two accused bombers] on U.S. soil to answer the indictment was a start. That was my free advice to him."

Somewhere in this process, the name of Abraham D. Sofaer emerged. On the face of it, he was the least likely of candidates to represent Libya. He was also the biggest potential prize.

Sofaer was well known to Libya's ruling circle as the author of the legal opinion that justified the bombing of their country six years earlier. Most Americans probably took for granted America's right to punish Kaddafi for his support of terrorism. But international law is vague on the question of when retaliatory force is allowed, and it was not immediately apparent in 1986 that Libya's behavior met the test—even after American intelligence found that Kaddafi had bankrolled the attacks at the El Al counters in Rome and Vienna airports in which five Americans and more than a dozen others were killed. The job of construing the legal fine points fell to the Office of Legal Adviser. "We had to make clear," Shultz wrote in his memoirs, "that Libya could not avoid responsibility for attacking American civilians and others by using Palestinian terrorists to do the job. Abe Sofaer noted, however, that sound as the principle seemed, international lawyers would argue these murders were not 'attacks' on the territory of the United States that enabled us to engage in self-defense under the UN Charter." And it wasn't just nit-picking "international lawyers" who would argue that; America's staunch ally, Prime Minister Margaret Thatcher, warned Washington that retaliatory or preemptive strikes against terrorism were "against international law" and could lead to "a much greater chaos."

Shultz accordingly urged Sofaer to come up with a bolder interpretation, and on January 15, 1986, the secretary of state unveiled it in an address before the National Defense University. Actions such as Libya's, Shultz said, "can amount to an ongoing armed aggression against the other state under international law." He added: "A nation attacked by terrorists is permitted to use force to prevent or preempt future attacks, to seize terrorists, or to rescue its citizens, when no other means is available." Three months later, in the wake of the LaBelle disco bombing in West Germany, America put the "Shultz Doctrine" into effect. The airstrikes ordered by Reagan involved sixteen F-111 fighter-bombers sent to attack targets including Libyan air and naval bases, terrorist training camps, and Kaddafi's personal bunker, residence, and guard barracks. The pilots had been given strict rules of engagement meant to limit the danger of accidental casualties. As a result, only two of the planes actually dropped their ordnance. Even so, as many as forty people were killed on the ground, including Kaddafi's adopted daughter.

It would have been stretching a point greatly to say that Sofaer was personally responsible for the attack on Libya. He had been a functionary in the State Department, and his function was to support what the president and secretary of state had decided to do. But at the very least, he was well known as an influential adviser to Shultz, a hardliner on terrorism, and a friend of Israel. And, of course, at the very time Libya was contacting him, he was the senior Hughes Hubbard partner in charge of Bruce Smith's case, which was progressing toward a lawsuit against Libya for millions of dollars, something about which Libya might, or might not, have known. For those very reasons, though, hiring him would be a tremendous coup, if they could pull it off. If anyone could be expected to sway the family members, the administration and media, it would be someone like Sofaer—a brilliant and well-connected lawyer with an unimpeachable ethical reputation. Libya had been untouchable in Washington for years. With Abe Sofaer as its lawyer, no one could ever say that again.

Did Kaddafi also relish the irony that the man who was instrumental in the attack that nearly killed him would now be doing his bidding? No one knows. But it might have occurred to him that if the whole affair blew up in Sofaer's face, Libya would be no worse off, but Sofaer would be ruined.

The approach would have to be carefully thought out. It was understood that Sofaer would not be motivated by money alone—although money would certainly be part of it. Other lawyers approached by Libya said they had been offered retainers of as much as $1.5 million, and Sofaer would presumably be worth even more. But the Libyans must have known, or could easily have found out, that Sofaer's ego was commensurate with his status as a Washington superlawyer. The way to get to Sofaer was to give him the opportunity to make history.

The Libyans, characteristically, contacted Sofaer through an intermediary—a Washington lawyer named Graham Wisner, the brother of Frank Wisner, the American ambassador to Egypt. And Wisner picked a social occasion to approach Sofaer, a party to raise funds for the victims of an earthquake in Cairo. Years later, Sofaer recalled that "my initial reaction was to say that I would not represent Libya unless it was willing to admit its guilt and satisfy the UN resolutions." Perhaps he didn't put it quite so bluntly at the time. In any case, Wisner got back to him in short order and said that Sofaer's conditions were acceptable to the Libyans.

Gerson was in London in the first week of 1993, returning to Washington on January 7. Early the next morning he called Sofaer at home to tell him of his progress. Lauterpacht, the Cambridge professor, and Lawrence Collins, a prominent London solicitor, had both endorsed the feasibility of a suit in the British courts. The prospect of bringing Kaddafi before the bar of justice had suddenly become real.

"Don't tell me any more," Sofaer interrupted. "I may be on the other side."

"Very funny, Abe," Gerson said. "Now come on, this is serious."

"I *am* serious," Sofaer replied. He explained, briefly and cryptically, that he was weighing a "consensual" arrangement, in which he would try to bring the parties together into agreement. He said nothing about being paid by Libya.

"There will have to be a wall between us," Sofaer said, bringing the conversation to an abrupt end, "and if this thing materializes we will have to reassess our relationship."

So the matter was closed, as far as Sofaer was concerned. If he'd been open to a discussion, Gerson could perhaps have saved them both a lot of trouble. But Sofaer asked almost no one for advice, apart from a very few top HHR partners, bypassing the firm's usual procedures for vetting new business. For days afterward, Gerson puzzled over the conversation, trying to imagine a benign explanation for Sofaer's strange remarks. What did he mean by "the other side"? Opposed to Smith? But Smith was HHR's client—Sofaer was named in the retainer letter as well as Gerson. The "other side," he concluded, could only refer to Libya. But in what capacity? If Sofaer was trying to negotiate a settlement, what was preventing him from going ahead with it on Smith's behalf? But uneasy as he was, Gerson kept reminding himself that this was Sofaer, his friend and mentor, a man he respected and a former federal judge. Surely he knew what he was doing. If he was working on something that had to be kept secret, even from Gerson, he surely had his reasons. Probably it was something sensitive involving the U.S. government.

What Gerson didn't know was that the day before, Sofaer had given Wisner a letter to take back to Libya, outlining an agreement that would form the basis of a subsequent retainer. The letter—which was cautiously addressed "To Whom It May Concern"—would later come to light as Exhibit 9 *In the Matter of Abraham D. Sofaer, Esquire, Bar Docket No. 280–93.*" Under its terms, HHR wouldn't be charging Libya an hourly rate at all; instead, it would bill a flat $3 million a year, deposited in monthly installments with Credit Suisse in Geneva. (Out of that sum, Graham Wisner was to receive $50,000 monthly as a consultant.) Even billing at premium rates, HHR would have had to log a lot of lawyers' time before it could have racked up $250,000 a month in hourly charges. And for what? The operational paragraph in the retainer agreement stated that HHR stands "prepared to assist the relevant parties in resolving by consensual negotiations all pending and potential civil and criminal litigations and other legal proceedings pertaining to the incident involved." But there was no pending civil litigation when the letter was drafted, and the only person even considering it was Smith. There was nothing preventing the Libyans from entering into "consensual negotiations" (what other kind are there?) with Smith, if they chose to. But Libya surely wasn't paying millions of dollars just for assistance in "consensual negotiations" to settle a potential civil action that was still just a cloud on the horizon. Sofaer's letter boasted of the "excellent litigators" HHR had at its disposal, but, he added, "[o]ur efforts will not include any substantial activities as litigators." Nor did he propose to defend Fhimah and Megrahi in a criminal trial. The only criminal trial Libya was interested in was one outside the United States, where HHR's American-trained lawyers wouldn't be of much help. What Libya wanted, manifestly, was Sofaer himself, and what he had to offer them was help in the one area of conflict that couldn't be willed away or papered over by "consensual negotiations." If anyone was worth $3 million to Kaddafi, it was someone who could get the U.S. government to change its bedrock position about the venue of a criminal trial. Certainly Kaddafi wasn't paying Sofaer to change Kaddafi's mind.

There was a wall now between Gerson and Sofaer. They still spoke, although less often and with less ease than before, but Gerson couldn't discuss what he was doing on the Smith case, and Sofaer couldn't bring up his secret meetings in Geneva with Yousef Debri, Libya's chief of external security. If they had, Gerson would have suggested that Sofaer sound out the families before committing to "consensual negotiations" with them. From his limited contact with them, he knew they were unlikely to consent to anything Libya was likely to offer. But HHR's senior management saw things differently: they planned to get their Treasury license and then rid the firm of any obligation to represent Bruce Smith, since they would be negotiating on the other side of the table. Abe Sofaer would work his magic, and they would all be the richer for it. They had no plan, just faith in Sofaer.

A layman without a grounding in lawyers' ethics, regarding it as a

specialized branch of universal ethics such as Plato or Kant would recognize, might have viewed HHR's plan to dump Smith as dubious. But
HHR attorneys, attentive to the fine points of "professional responsibility"—a term which a few years earlier had begun to eclipse references to
"lawyers' ethics" in bar association meetings—believed they had figured
out a way to avoid transgressing the disciplinary code. They realized
from the start—who wouldn't?—that they faced a conflict of interest
problem with Smith, but they considered it manageable. The January 7
letter to Libya concludes with this assurance: "Upon execution of this
agreement, we will seek and obtain the necessary licenses for such activities. We will also immediately take any steps necessary to avoid any
conflict-of-interest issue." So they would deal with it as soon as Libya's
check had cleared, but not before then. The successors to Charles Evans
Hughes were to show just how well they understood their obligations to
their client when a bigger one came along. They were about to affirm
Charles Dickens's view of the law in *Bleak House*: "The one great principle of the English Law is to make business for itself."

Canon 9 of the American Bar Association (ABA) Code of Professional Responsibility, promulgated in 1970 and thereafter adopted, in
some form, by all fifty states, and taught by Gerson at the New England School of Law, enjoined lawyers to "avoid even the appearance of
professional impropriety." Impropriety arises, he told his classes, any
time a lawyer talks to an adversary of the existing client without his
client's knowledge and consent. "Adversary" is broadly construed to
mean anyone whom the client may for any reason consider to be on the
other side, and the obligation begins not just when a suit commences,
but from the day a lawyer is first retained. It is not a defense, he had
emphasized, that the attorney believed he was doing it for the client's
own good. And even if the client later waived his right to object, the
lawyer could still be in trouble, because the "appearance of impropriety" would have already been created. The client is supreme, for better
or worse—a restriction under which many good lawyers have chafed,
including the great Louis Brandeis, whose nomination to the U.S.
Supreme Court was almost derailed when it was discovered that while

representing management in a labor dispute he was secretly negotiating with the workers.

But in 1983 the ABA House of Delegates adopted the Model Rules of Professional Conduct, dropping the ethical considerations of the earlier code and substantially narrowing the "appearance of impropriety" standard by limiting it to the most egregious conduct. The result, in the District of Columbia and other jurisdictions which adopted the model rules, was to make it much more difficult to discipline a lawyer who switches sides. HHR's lawyers took note of this. A waiver from Smith, they were confident, would cure any possible conflicts.

The other thing they needed was a license from the Treasury Department's Office of Foreign Assets Control (OFAC), which administered the American trade sanctions with Libya. The sanctions provided an exception for legal services. This created the minor complication that while Sofaer sought to confine his role to something "analogous to the role of a mediator," as far as OFAC was concerned, HHR was Libya's lawyer, period. Otherwise there would be no license. After consideration, HHR concluded this problem, too, could be overcome.

Not everyone at HHR was pleased with the idea of working for Kaddafi. A highly regarded young associate named Dan Wolf turned down the chance to work with Sofaer on the case, regarding the assignment as "plenty problematic." "Given my background and commitment to human rights," he said later, "I didn't feel it would be appropriate for me to work on the Libya case." David Jacobsohn, a senior partner in the firm's Washington office, thought Libya would be a public-relations disaster for HHR. Twice he took his concerns to HHR's managing partner in New York, Charles Scherer. "I went to him and pleaded with the firm to talk with other knowledgeable people in Washington about the advisability of taking on Libya as a client," he recalled, but Scherer refused to budge. Sofaer was going to take care of it, he assured Jacobsohn. Not long afterward, Jacobsohn left Hughes Hubbard for another prominent Washington firm.

Sofaer himself remained characteristically confident. In an interview years afterward he asserted that "Libya definitely was prepared to compensate the victims' families, and told me so. They would have paid *ex gratia* . . . not technically an admission of responsibility, but morally it represents acceptance of the burden of the damage caused." As he saw it, Smith would come out ahead as well; he would share in this bounty, instead of paying legal bills for a lawsuit which "based on the law as it then existed . . . had very little chance of success on the merits." Sofaer had in mind a settlement on the order of $1 billion, or $4 million for each victim (if non–U.S. citizens were to be covered as well)—"and I had no doubt of the success of my effort, had I been able to act."

It remained only to deal with Smith, who would have to waive his objections to being dismissed by HHR, and with Gerson, who would have to choose between his client and his job. On February 22, Scherer, the managing partner, had written Gerson to renew his "Of Counsel" affiliation with the firm. There were a few changes in his status. Gerson's leave from George Mason University would be up in the fall, and he was planning to scale back his hours at the firm to resume teaching. He would no longer have his own office and full-time secretary at HHR. And HHR gave itself the option of terminating Gerson "if, in our opinion, there may be a conflict between the continued representation of one of your clients and another of the Firm's clients." Gerson, still in the dark about precisely what Sofaer was up to, but holding out hope nothing would come of it, signed the letter.

He was soon to be enlightened, though. In early March, Rick Newcomb, the director of OFAC, told HHR they would receive a license to represent Libya. A few weeks later, Scherer and HHR chairman and senior litigating partner, Bob Sisk, came to Washington to pay Gerson a visit. They walked into his office, looking slightly uncomfortable. Years earlier, Gerson had edited a book on legal ethics, and they noticed a copy on his credenza, which gave them the opening they sought.

"It's good you know something about ethics," one of them said, "because we have an ethical issue to discuss with you."

The ethical issue, as they circuitously divulged, was that the firm wished to represent Libya and divest itself of Smith. Since they were not actively engaged in litigation on Smith's behalf, they saw no ethical impediments.

Gerson did, though. Smith had sunk thousands of dollars into his case. He had come to HHR in part for the same reason as Libya, because of Sofaer's reputation. If he left, who would take him?

When he balked at dismissing his client, Sisk leaned forward over Gerson's desk and said, "You know what your problem is, Gerson? You think you're God."

And Gerson replied, "No, I don't think I am God. But I will tell you a secret. My client thinks I'm God."

It was at that meeting that Gerson ventured his own opinion of what Sofaer was up to. Even without knowing the details, Gerson assumed that "he was trying to do something on a grand scale." Whatever it was, it was likely to be "Kissingerian."

In principle, Smith's waiver was voluntary; he could have demanded that Hughes Hubbard forgo Libya's $3 million and continue to represent him for whatever he had left in the bank. "If Smith had said, I don't want you to do this, we wouldn't have," Sofaer said later. "There was never any suggestion that he was being forced into it." Sofaer speaks from the perspective that it was in Smith's best interests, as well as the firm's, for HHR to try to settle the case from the Libyan side. Under the circumstances, was Smith really in a position to stand in his way? The only question was whether Gerson would follow Smith out the door, and to Gerson the choice was apparent. He called Smith to give him the news, and told him that he would continue to represent him, if Smith wanted him to.

"Are you sure about this?" Smith asked. "Why don't you take a few days to think about it?"

Gerson said he didn't need to think about it. HHR drew up a waiver letter for Smith to sign. "I understand that Allan Gerson is withdrawing from your firm," it began. "I have always considered Allan to be my lawyer, and want him to represent me in the future, rather than Hughes Hubbard & Reed. . . . One of my principal goals in retaining Allan was to find a way to bring Libya into the process of resolving [the Pan Am 103 claims]. Therefore, I consent to your undertaking that representation, and I accordingly waive any objection to your representation of Libya in that connection."

On June 1, Gerson announced his resignation, in a letter to his colleagues citing "divergencies between our respective practices" that "make it advisable for me to separate from the firm." He would continue to use his office until August, as a courtesy.

Meanwhile Sofaer concluded arrangements with his new clients, and on June 24 Credit Suisse reported that the Libyan letter of credit, guaranteeing the $3 million retainer, had arrived. On the last day of June HHR sent out an invoice for $250,000 to the Committee for The Case of Lockerbie, and a day later it was paid. The firm began drafting a press release announcing its new client.

Shortly before the press release was supposed to go out, Gerson got a call from Jim Hoagland, a Pulitzer Prize–winning columnist for the *Washington Post.*

"Congratulations!" Hoagland said.

"For what?" Gerson asked, wondering if Hoagland perhaps had read something he'd written in some scholarly journal.

"For having the courage to do the right thing. I understand you are leaving Hughes Hubbard rather than represent Libya. Tell me about it."

Gerson, taken aback, said it was an "internal matter within the firm" and declined to comment. It seemed to him that someone at HHR must have leaked the story, but he had no idea who. Perhaps someone in the firm's top management in New York or Washington had decided to pull the plug on the idea and chosen Hoagland as his instrument.

On July 14 Hoagland's column appeared under the headline "Gadhafi's Lawyer." (Almost every American publication had its own preferred spelling for the Libyan ruler's name.) Hoagland greatly understated the amount of HHR's fee, but otherwise had the essential story correct. His column has since been reprinted in law-school textbooks on professional responsibility. It began,

Consider it the Washington lawyer's version of the "Indecent Proposal" Robert Redford made on screen to Demi Moore: If Moammar Gadhafi offered you a half million dollars to represent the Libyan government in the bombing of Pan Am 103, would you do it?

Make it more interesting: Would you represent Gadhafi even if you had once worked as the State Department's top lawyer, developing the legal justification in 1986 for economic sanctions against Libya and for the US air raid on Libya that experts believe the Libyans sought to avenge with the Pan Am massacre?

Would you do it even if ungenerous souls would inevitably suspect that the Libyans wanted to hire you precisely because of your high profile on and intimate knowledge of their troubles with the Reagan and Bush administrations, at a moment when the Clinton administration wants to turn the screws more tightly on Libya?

You would if you were Abraham Sofaer, ex-legal adviser to secretaries of state George Shultz and James Baker. Beginning July 1, Sofaer has taken on a job that astonishes and pains many who have long admired him as a staunch conservative in US politics and a strong supporter of Israel.

Sofaer has agreed to represent Libya in the Pan Am 103 case for a fee he declines to disclose. . . .

Sofaer refused to confirm my information that he had met with [Yousef] Dibri in Geneva recently to discuss the contract. He acknowledged knowing Dibri's identity as Gadhafi's national security chief and head of the Libyan government's Committee to Resolve the Pan Am 103 Dispute. . . .

He should have foreseen what would happen. Anyone familiar with the politics of it could have warned him not to take on the family groups, who within a day of Hoagland's column were arranging for buses to Washington to picket outside Hughes Hubbard's offices. Susan Cohen, arch-enemy of compromise, was quoted denouncing Sofaer's behavior as "treason" and "disgusting." Even Sofaer himself now believes that "I should have talked to the families before doing anything. If I could not have convinced them to support my effort, I probably would have dropped the matter, since what is the point in trying to pay people who do not want to be paid?" And it wasn't just the family members who were mad at Sofaer. G. Henry Schuler, a respected Libya expert at the Center for Strategic and International Studies, called Sofaer's decision "outrageous. It creates a terrible, terrible impression and sets back efforts to isolate [Kaddafi] just when the President has pledged to take a strong stand." Sofaer also was somewhat surprised to get a phone call from Lee Kreindler, who called him the day Hoagland's column appeared "to make sure I wasn't planning to come into [the civil case against Pan Am] and make trouble for him and his clients," as Sofaer recounted it later. And then something even worse happened, something that convinced the partners at Hughes Hubbard they had made a terrible mistake that had to be rectified immediately. The State Department and other administration officials stopped returning their phone calls. Denial of access is a mortal blow to a Washington law firm. In fact, as Scherer later testified, "I believe we had learned that they were under instructions not to speak to us."

"And this was a surprise?" he was asked.

"Very much so, because we had previously had very close ties to the State Department, Judge Sofaer having been the legal adviser . . . and they had always been very responsive and forthcoming. And suddenly that avenue closed, and very abruptly, and very dramatically. That's really what led us to conclude that the die had been cast. We just were not going to succeed with them."

Interestingly, Scherer said the families' hostility had been only "a modest factor" in deciding to withdraw from representing Libya. HHR obviously was expecting to do more negotiating with the U.S. government than with the families.

So having cast aside Smith, HHR now had to turn its back on Libya as well, and return the $250,000 that had been deposited only just two weeks earlier. An editorial in the *New York Times* ("A Smelly Retainer Refunded") said Sofaer had been "wise to heed the reasonable reaction against such a tasteless transaction." A few months later, Smith settled up his account with a final check for $2,500. "I feel that you did not fully appreciate my dilemma," he wrote the firm:

Although it was made clear to me that choosing to leave HHR and grant you a conflict of interest waiver . . . was voluntary, it did not seem to me that my relationship with your firm would ever be the same if I refused. HHR no longer wanted me as a client so I had to go. . . . I decided to grant the waiver expecting that we would at least be able to start substantive negotiations with Libya through HHR. Your subsequent precipitous withdrawal from the case nullified even that hope.

Sofaer felt abused and misunderstood. "The press were writing as if I had bombed the plane myself!" he said incredulously, looking back on the affair years later. "It was the most incredible experience! Hoagland, calling me a prostitute because I'm a lawyer doing my job. Lawyers make much more money representing cigarette companies . . . and they should, that's their job. What I did was in the public interest, damn it!"

Sofaer's career as a high-powered Washington lawyer was over; in 1994 he resigned as a Hughes Hubbard partner to follow Shultz to Stanford, where he became, and remains, George P. Shultz Distinguished Scholar and Senior Fellow of the prestigious Hoover Institution on War, Revolution and Peace. But his troubles weren't over. HHR's lawyers had been so sure that getting a waiver from Smith would eliminate any conflict of interest that they had failed to give much thought to another of Sofaer's former clients: the United States of America. On July 21 Sen. Carl Levin, chairman of the Senate Subcommittee on Oversight of Government Management, asked the U.S. Office of Government Ethics to look into whether Sofaer's activities "would violate the lifetime ban on 'switching sides' . . . or any other restrictions on post-employment activities of former government employees." The ethics office found Sofaer had violated no laws. But lawyers practicing in the District of Columbia are subject to the D.C. Board of Professional Responsibility, and the bar counsel there, Len Becker, decided to look into Sofaer's actions on his own.

Becker was a tenacious litigator on leave from his job at the premier Washington firm of Arnold & Porter to do the thankless job of disciplining his fellow bar members, and this was the biggest case to come his way in that time. He accepted that the waiver HHR obtained from Smith probably cured any violation of Bar Rule 1.7, which forbids representation of clients with adverse interests. But there was also Rule 1.11, which states, in part, that "a lawyer shall not accept other employment in connection with a matter which is the same as, or substantially related to, a matter in which the lawyer participated personally and substantially as a public officer or employee." HHR lawyers had dismissed Rule 1.11 as inconsequential, on the grounds that Sofaer had not participated "substantially" in the State Department's handling of the Lockerbie case. Moreover, in the decade since it was adopted, the rule had never once been invoked. In response to a preliminary query from Becker, Sofaer replied that, although he had regularly received top-secret briefings on the Pan Am bombing until he left the State Department in 1990, Libya—which only became the focus of the investigation in 1991—was never mentioned in them.

Eventually Becker's investigation came to center on two events from Sofaer's tenure at State: the decision to bomb Tripoli in 1986, and the handling of a subpoena by Pan Am's lawyers in 1990, seeking State Department documents as part of their effort to blame the bombing on a government plot. Becker investigated for nearly two years before concluding that these events qualified as "participat[ing] personally and substantially" in a "matter" which is "the same as, or substantially related to" Sofaer's work for Libya in 1993. In the summer of 1995 he ruled that Sofaer receive an informal admonition, the lightest penalty the board can apply.

But Sofaer, his pride at stake, refused to accept the reprimand. "What my firm and I planned to do was professionally and morally proper," he wrote in his defense. By challenging Becker's findings, he was forced to defend himself at a two-day public hearing with many of the trappings of a full-blown trial—including a team of defense lawyers from the top-tier firm of Covington and Burling led by David Isbell, the former Chair of the ABA Standing Committee on Ethics and Professional Responsibility. The hearing took place in December 1995. Gerson was among those subpoenaed to testify; the board also issued subpoenas for HHR's records, including contracts and minutes of conversations, putting on the public record a great deal of what otherwise would have been confidential information about how the Hughes Hubbard brass viewed the case. It appears that they believed that their law firm could succeed where the UN Security Council, the U.S. State Department, and the British Foreign Ministry had fallen short.

"I thought it [HHR's representation] was seeking extraordinarily worthwhile ends," Scherer, the New York managing partner, testified:

> It's rare, in my experience, that a law firm can, through lawyers, have what I perceived to be a very beneficial outcome on a very serious problem.
>
> You know, the tensions around Libya were well documented and if there was anything that we could do as lawyers to ease those tensions and bring Libya back into the community of nations, I thought that would be a very desirable goal, and we were also going to be paid handsomely for it, which was of interest.

John Townsend, the managing partner in HHR's Washington office, was even more effusive:

> The ultimate goal would have been to allow Libya to reenter civilized society, to in effect make its peace for the problems that were keeping it a pariah nation and to . . . resolve the problems that were keeping Libya outside the civilized community. In my personal view, that was a very worthy aim.

Sofaer told the hearing what he hoped to accomplish—a compromise agreement to try the Libyan suspects in a third country, and compensation to the families on the order of $1 billion. Nevertheless, he testified,

> Despite my having instructed the Libyans and having gotten their agreement that they would not engage in such activity [negotiating individually with the families to buy off their opposition], I heard that they had contacted a Greek lawyer who represented one of the

families of the victims and proposed that they pay this family a couple of million dollars in exchange for the family's support in quash-
ing the extradition effort.

So I heard about that, I was very upset about it . . . but then I
was informed that's exactly their modus operandi, that's the way
they had gone about treating the families before.

At the close of the evidentiary hearings, Becker summarized his
case against Sofaer: he had worked as legal adviser to Shultz during the
1986 attack on Libya; he had received top-secret briefings about the
investigation into the bombing of Pan Am 103; and he had approved
memos in connection with the Pan Am subpoenas in 1990. These
involvements, Becker charged, gave Sofaer access to privileged government information that could be of use to Libya as a client.

On June 30, 1997—eighteen months after the hearing—the D.C.
Board on Professional Responsibility ruled against Sofaer, who then
promptly appealed the ruling to the District of Columbia Court of
Appeals. He retained new lawyers and enlisted a host of luminaries in
the world of ex–government attorneys on his behalf. Never before had
such legal talent been brought to bear in the defense of one man on so
slight a charge. Of course, not all of this outpouring of support was
motivated by admiration of Sofaer, personally; the outcome of the case
could impact the financial future of many high government officials.
The *amicus curiae,* or friend of the court brief, filed on behalf of Sofaer
in the Court of Appeals listed, among others, a former attorney general
and an acting attorney general, four former counsels to the president of
the United States, a future solicitor general, and assorted general counsels to various cabinet secretaries and deputy assistant attorney generals. But despite the legal firepower behind it, the *amicus* brief's
argument—that competent, well-meaning attorneys would be dissuaded from government service if Sofaer were to be reprimanded—
received an unsympathetic hearing in the Court of Appeals. It ruled
that if attorneys are dissuaded from government service because of such
considerations, all to the good. No one wants attorneys to enter government service with an eye to picking up former adversaries as clients.

The main arguments presented by Sofaer's chief counsel, Sam Dash, the former Watergate chief prosecutor, fared no better. It was simply wrong, the court held unanimously, that Sofaer never really intended to represent Libya fully, but only, as he pleaded, to help it "assum[e] . . . culpability for the 103 bombing." The judges cited HHR's agreement with Libya, providing that "[m]easures will be taken only with your prior consent, and *without admission of liability*" (court's emphasis). They concluded that

> The proposed activities included "investigating the facts and legal proceedings, preparing legal analyses, providing legal advice and proposing legal steps to deal with" the "ongoing civil and criminal disputes and litigation" stemming from the destruction of Pan Am 103—all clearly features of a comprehensive attorney-client relationship. . . .

After his loss in the Court of Appeals on April 22, 1999, Sofaer and yet another new lawyer, H. Bartow Farr III, sought review by the U.S. Supreme Court on denial of due process grounds. Sofaer argued that the test must be not whether a lawyer "may have received" useful confidential information, but whether he actually received it. The petition for review was denied, and by early 2000 the long saga that had began in 1992 was finally over.

It had changed the lives of all those it touched. Sofaer, of course, was long gone from Washington and the practice of law, but his name lived on, not only, as he had presumably hoped, for his brilliance as a judge and a statesman, but also as a cautionary figure for law students, who study the case of *In re Abraham Sofaer* in their classes in ethics. Conferences have been organized around it. As for Gerson, his personal and professional ties to Sofaer were ruptured, seemingly irretrievably. Both men felt betrayed by the actions of the other—Gerson, of course, by Sofaer's jettisoning of him and Smith to take on Libya; Sofaer by what he felt was Gerson's failure to speak up publicly in his defense. If things had worked out, Sofaer still believed, nearly a decade later, Gerson would have collected millions for his client, and a nice fee for himself.

And Smith was left, after expending a small fortune on the case, with not much to show for it, and the prospect of going ahead with Gerson on his own, rather than the large and wealthy and well-connected firm of Hughes Hubbard & Reed.

What had gone wrong? Sofaer, obviously, had bad luck. He could not have foreseen Becker enforcing a provision of the Code of Professional Conduct that had never before been invoked against a government attorney. And since his was the first case to come up under it, he had no reason to expect that his involvement with the Pan Am case, which he regarded as insignificant, would be interpreted by the disciplinary board and the courts as "substantial." In retrospect, he clearly miscalculated the feelings of the families; even he now agrees that it was probably a lost cause to get them to accept an *ex gratia* payment from Libya at that time. But even Dan Wolf, the young associate who wanted no part of the case, is "convinced that Abe was acting out of noble motives." He adds: "I am not speaking about HHR."

Bad luck? A fatal miscalculation, born of arrogance over his own abilities? Or was there something intentional about the downfall of Abe Sofaer? Think back to Hoagland's column in the *Washington Post*. HHR's press release was actually going out as Hoagland was writing his column, but he had called Gerson about it several days earlier, and he had details that weren't in the announcement. How did Hoagland know that Sofaer had been meeting secretly with Yousef Debri, the Libyan chief of external security? Who, among the very few who knew about that, would have had a motive to torpedo the deal? In HHR, Wolf and Jacobsohn, who opposed representing Libya, wouldn't have known about it. In the government, officials in OFAC, which had to approve the contract, certainly knew that Sofaer was talking to Libyans. But Debri's name was written in the contract only in Arabic, and they wouldn't have known what to make of it; and OFAC, a nonpolitical, low-profile government agency, had no obvious axe to grind in the matter.

But the Treasury officials could have passed the information to others in the government, who had a great interest in seeing to it that Sofaer's efforts did *not* succeed. There was a powerful group within the

American national-security establishment that was perfectly content to leave the sanctions in place, and could only have viewed HHR's grandiose dreams of reconciliation with Kaddafi as undercutting years of work aimed at excluding Libya from "the community of nations." When Sofaer met with Debri in Geneva, given the time difference, the information could have been in National Security Council briefings that same morning. Leaking it to a columnist known to be sympathetic toward the Pan Am families would have been an obvious step.

Libya, too, might have seen the benefits of getting rid of Sofaer. As he had discovered, they were undercutting him already by dealing directly, against his instructions, with a lawyer for one of the families. It may have occurred to them that Sofaer couldn't really deliver, and that $3 million a year was a high price for failure. And, lest anyone forget, Sofaer—friend of Israel, hard-liner on terrorism, instrumental in the 1986 bombing of Tripoli—was the enemy. They did have, as Sofaer discovered, quite late in the game, a peculiar modus operandi of dealing with those they hired.

So who blew the whistle on Sofaer? If you were laying odds, you'd make it even money on someone in the White House or State Department, five to one on a source within HHR . . . and four to one, or thereabouts, on Libya itself. Hoagland knows, but he's not talking.

10

Revolving Courts

When Gerson left Hughes Hubbard & Reed, he struck out on his own, for the first time in his career, with only Smith (and, for a while, Sands) as his clients—two unknown Americans going into battle against sovereign nations, with Gerson as their champion, the proprietor of a law firm with not much more to its name than its name. A former client put him in touch with a sympathetic real-estate developer who had an empty suite of offices at 1201 Connecticut Avenue, and he offered it to Gerson, as a lawyer would say, *pro bono*. Gerson wasn't alone for very long, though. Around the time he was moving in, he got a call from Mark Zaid, who had lured him into the world of the Pan Am 103 families originally. Like Frank Duggan, the McLaughlin Commission's "family liaison," Zaid had found it difficult to extricate himself from Lockerbie. After graduating from law school he had begun a small practice in Albany that specialized in filing Freedom of Information suits on behalf of the family groups, seeking files on the bombing from nearly every agency in the federal government except the Forestry Service. This was a fairly unrewarding form of practice, since he was paid nothing for it, and his supplementary work as an occasional public defender and in family court didn't amount to a great deal of income either. But in any case, Zaid was sure his real destiny lay in Washington. Without a job lined up, and unaware of the controversy about to break over HHR's head, he drove down over the July 4th weekend and took up residence on a friend's sofa. One of the first things he did was to look up Gerson.

"You want to help me sue Libya?" Gerson asked.

"Sure, how's the pay?"

"Excellent. We just have to win."

But Zaid, smart and energetic though he was, wasn't going to supply all the help Gerson needed, either. Gerson himself would be returning to full-time teaching in the fall with an extra course load to make up for missed time. He needed to affiliate with a big firm that could throw some bodies at the case—associates to research the law, a counsel of record to file papers, experienced litigators to appear in court. Certainly Libya, if it showed up to defend the case at all, could be expected to mount a formidable defense, and it could afford to hire any lawyer or team of lawyers that would work for it. And while Gerson anticipated a drawn-out fight over the threshold question of whether an American court even had jurisdiction, he had to be prepared for the remote possibility that Libya might waive sovereign immunity and offer to proceed right to trial. In that case a judge might order an expedited hearing, and he would have to come up with evidence supporting the complaint. It occurred to him that one of the chief arguments for bringing the suit—that it would put Libya's culpability on the record— cut both ways: if he failed to mount a convincing case, Libya could claim it had been exonerated. That responsibility led to another reason to bring in a second firm. He would need the help of the Department of Justice, which held the evidence behind the criminal indictments. A decision to release it would be made at the highest levels, and here Gerson was at a disadvantage, as a Republican asking for help from a Democratic administration. He needed not just a big law firm, but a big *Democratic* law firm—or, at least, one with a major Democratic figure aboard, since Washington law firms pride themselves on being able to work both sides of the political aisle.

A natural choice was Lloyd Cutler, former White House counsel to President Jimmy Carter and future White House counsel to Bill Clinton, an éminence grise in Washington's permanent establishment. Cutler and Gerson hammered out a partnering agreement, which turned out to be short-lived, although it lasted long enough for them to hold several unproductive meetings with senior State and Justice Department officials, including Undersecretary of State for Global Affairs Tim Wirth and Mark Richards, the veteran principal deputy assistant attorney general in charge of the Criminal Division, who was overseeing the team of Justice Department lawyers and FBI agents assigned to the case. Next he approached Sol Linowitz, a major figure in the Democratic party, a former ambassador, and the American negotiator on the Panama Canal treaty. Linowitz was senior partner in the Washington office of Coudert Brothers, one of the oldest and largest international law firms. Coudert wasn't prepared to join the case, but Linowitz introduced Gerson to a younger partner named Douglas Rosenthal, who besides his law degree had a Ph.D. in political science from Yale and a background in international law as the former chief of the foreign commerce section of the Antitrust Division at the Department of Justice. Rosenthal was attracted to the idea of breaking new ground in human-rights law. If the law stripped foreign governments of sovereign immunity when they negotiated to buy airplanes from American companies, why not also when they blew up airplanes with Americans in them? With his firm's permission, he agreed to act in his personal capacity as Smith's attorney of record and, together with a Coudert associate named Doug Rutzen, to similarly advise Gerson and Zaid on the tricky business of suing a foreign government.

On December 15, 1993, the cause of government accountability took a step forward out of the nineteenth century, with the filing of a suit for $15 million (plus additional unspecified damages) in U.S. District Court for the District of Columbia in the case *Bruce Smith as personal representative of Ingrid Smith, deceased, v. The Socialist People's Libyan Arab Jamahiriya; Libyan External Security Organization; Libyan Arab Airlines et. al.*—the remaining defendants being Megrahi and Fhimah, plus five aliases or variant spellings of their names. About half of its eighty-two paragraphs were taken up with reciting the available information incriminating Libya in the bombing—drawn from the criminal indictments, now more than two years old, plus books, newspaper articles, and the evidence Kreindler and Baumeister had presented in the Pan Am trial. But its crucial section was paragraphs 10 through 18, in which Gerson, Zaid, and Rosenthal laid out the case for asserting jurisdiction over Libya, despite the patent obstacle of sovereign immunity. "The international prohibition of terrorism, particularly when directed against civilian aircraft, is a basic norm of international law known as *jus cogens*," they wrote. "Violation of that *jus cogens* subjects the perpetrator to universal jurisdiction for commission of a crime against humanity." Then, having provided the court with the opportunity to take a principled stand in defense of humanity, they got down to the humble work of constructing an argument on their narrow patch of legal ground:

Because the activities in question in this suit are not within a State's sovereign prerogatives, they must necessarily be deemed to be commercial within the meaning of that term in the Foreign Sovereign Immunities Act. These activities include, but are not limited to, the training and hiring of terrorists to conduct unlawful activities against foreign and domestic nationals. Such training is the same as that provided by a private security company in training private foreign security services. Libya has also accepted remuneration for the training of terrorists . . . Seen in this light, Libya's program of worldwide terrorism constituted commercial activities directed particularly at the United States . . . As such, these activities have a 'substantial connection' to the United States which renders Libya subject to the jurisdiction of the United States Courts over commercial activities in the United States.

And:

The specific bombing of Pan Am Flight 103 occurred aboard an airplane within . . . the 'special aircraft jurisdiction of the United States'. . . . As such, the act occurred within the United States as the confines of the United States are defined in the Foreign Sovereign Immunities Act of 1976.

In subsequent briefs, they would refine these arguments and add others as they thought of them. The UN Security Council resolutions calling on Libya to pay compensation had more than the force of an ordinary resolution, they argued; when the Council "decides" something under Chapter VII of the UN Charter, it becomes binding on all member countries, and creates a private right of action in their courts. They cited a 1992 letter from Libyan foreign minister Ibrahim Bishari (actual title: "Secretary of the People's Committee for Foreign Liaison and International Cooperation") to the UN secretary-general. "Despite the fact that discussion of the question of compensation is premature," Bishari wrote, "since it would only follow from a civil judgment based on a criminal judgment, Libya guarantees the payment of any compensation that might be incurred by the responsibility of the two suspects who are its nationals in the event that they were unable to pay." The letter was part of Libya's effort to head off further economic sanctions, but Gerson and Zaid argued that it amounted to an implicit acceptance of jurisdiction by a foreign court—or, to put it another way, a waiver of sovereign immunity.

There were fifteen judges in federal district court in the District of Columbia, and cases as they came in were assigned to them in strict rotation. When Zaid showed up with the complaint at the court, the clerk stamped the papers and told him that in a few days he would get a notice of the case's docket number and the name of the judge to whom it had been assigned. When the notice came, he rushed to call Gerson. "We've got Sporkin!" he exclaimed gleefully.

If Gerson had been able to pick a judge, Stanley Sporkin would have been his first and only choice. Sporkin, crusty and outspoken, was acquainted with Gerson, although by no means such a close friend that he would feel compelled to recuse himself. He had been a famously tough chief of enforcement at the Securities and Exchange Commission in the 1970s, then general counsel to the Central Intelligence Agency under William Casey, where he had a record as a staunch opponent of terrorism. When he'd joined the bench in 1985, he had recommended Gerson as his successor at the CIA. On his retirement as a judge fifteen years later, a laudatory profile in the *Washington Post* observed that "his critics said he stretched the law to come up with his desired solution." But that's exactly what Gerson thought should happen here. In fact, just a year earlier, Sporkin had handed a victory to an American citizen suing a foreign government that had claimed immunity under the 1976 Foreign Sovereign Immunities Act. Gerson knew the case—*Princz v. Federal Republic of Germany*—and concluded that Sporkin's ruling was the best possible augury for *Smith v. Libya*. In the eighteen months since Smith had walked in his door at Hughes Hubbard & Reed, this was the biggest stroke of luck he'd had yet.

Hugo Princz was an elderly New Jersey man with one of those extraordinary histories of misfortune unique to the twentieth century. His father, an American citizen, had been a businessman living and working in Czechoslovakia at the outbreak of World War II. In 1942, a few months after America entered the war, the teenage Princz and his parents, brothers, and sister were arrested by the puppet Slovak forces and turned over to the German SS, who shipped them to a concentration camp in Poland. Most of the Americans captured by the Germans in this way were turned over to the Red Cross for repatriation, but the Princz family had the misfortune to be Jewish. His parents and sister disappeared, most likely into the gas chambers at Treblinka. Princz, along with his two brothers, was sent to the Birkenau slave-labor camp, where they were put to work building a factory for the German chemicals cartel I. G. Farben. His brothers were injured and sent to the hospital, where they starved to death, but Princz survived to be liberated by American troops. He had "USA" stenciled on his uniform, so the GIs took him to an American military hospital instead of a displaced-persons camp. After a futile search through the ruins of central Europe for his family, he returned to the United States.

But his good fortune came at a price, because he fell through the cracks of the system Germany set up in 1954 to compensate the victims of Nazi war crimes. Technically, the reparations were intended for German nationals or for "displaced persons"—refugees from countries occupied after the war by the Soviet Union. Additionally, Germany had entered into bilateral agreements with certain countries to compensate their citizens. But Princz fit into none of these categories. Unaware that any American civilians had been imprisoned (although more than 100 Jewish GIs captured in the Battle of the Bulge ended up in Nazi concentration camps), Germany made no explicit provision to compensate them. Nor did it recognize any implied obligation; when Princz filed a claim in 1955, they refused to make an exception.

In the face of legal appeals, political pressure, and American diplomatic intervention, Germany steadfastly maintained its refusal for decades after. By the time Princz's lawyer, Steven R. Perles, appeared before Sporkin in 1992, the man had spent thirty-seven years trying to collect a pension that would have amounted to around $500 a month. In upholding Princz's right to sue in American courts, Sporkin ringingly declared that "the Court cannot believe that, in enacting the Foreign Sovereign Immunities Act, Congress . . . intended to bar a U.S. citizen from seeking redress against a nation standing in the shoes of his or her would-be butcher . . . The Court cannot permit such a nation, which at the time these barbaric acts were committed neither recognized nor respected U.S. or international law, to now block the legitimate claims of a U.S. citizen by asserting U.S. law to evade its responsibilities." Gerson himself couldn't have written a better précis of the argument he intended to make against Libya.

Gerson paid one of his foreign students to translate the twenty-eight-page complaint into Arabic, and Zaid mailed copies off to the Libyan authorities. He also gave copies to the State Department to pass along to Belgium, whose embassy represented "American interests" in Tripoli. And then they waited, anxiously, for Libya to reply. The summons set a deadline for Libya to respond within sixty days. Weeks went by. Finally they got a letter from a lawyer in Paris—a distinguished, courtly practitioner named Abdelhay Sefrioui, who announced himself as Libya's lawyer in the matter. He said he was trying to hire an American firm to handle the case in Washington, but was having trouble finding one to take it on. He requested an extension of the sixty-day deadline.

Here, it seemed, was another lucky break. Libya could have just ignored them. Then Gerson and Zaid would have needed only to demonstrate a reasonable basis for their suit to win an easy, but hollow, victory. Hollow because Libya's guilt would not be tested and proven in open court, but simply assumed as a procedural matter, which would hardly constitute the ringing condemnation of Kaddafi they were seeking. And hollow also, as Rosenthal dourly informed them, because a default judgment—as opposed to a contested one—would be difficult to enforce in most other countries. This meant they were unlikely ever to collect any money.

On strictly procedural grounds, it appeared, Libya might have been well advised to do nothing. But Libya also had political considerations. They wanted the sanctions lifted, and thumbing their nose at the U.S. courts wasn't going to advance that agenda. The Libyans weren't seeking to avoid paying compensation; they had spent the past year desperately trying to find a family member who *would* take their money (under conditions of Libya's choosing). Whether to avoid giving the United States an excuse to tighten the sanctions, or because they saw the suit as a way to open negotiations, or simply because they took the word of their lawyers that the Foreign Sovereign Immunities Act would protect them, Libya elected to answer the summons. At this stage, anyway, they showed up not to argue the facts, but merely to contest the court's jurisdiction, on the same basis that Germany had used to fight Princz: that America's own laws gave them immunity from being sued. But if this was a tactical victory for Gerson and Zaid, it was also the harbinger of a drawn-out struggle.

It took six months—until July 1994—for Libya to hire an American law firm, and by the end of that time Sporkin was threatening to appoint lawyers himself if necessary. He was so grateful, in fact, that he thanked the lawyer, Daniel Grove of Chicago-based Keck, Mahin & Cate, just for showing up. "I don't know if people understand our legal system, but it really depends upon lawyers like yourself to take on causes," Sporkin said at a July 21 hearing. "And sometimes some of the parties might not be the most popular people, but that's been the history of the legal profession." He was quite right about that. Keck,

Mahin & Cate was not the most obvious choice in terms of Washington connections or international experience, but among its Washington partners was a lawyer named Victoria Reggie, the wife of Sen. Ted Kennedy of Massachusetts. Kennedy, besides being one of the most powerful men in the Senate, was a conspicuous champion of the Pan Am 103 families. Kaddafi never quite figured out that the United States of America was governed on different principles than those of clan and family loyalty, which ruled most desert Arab states. Shortly before Grove made his appearance, Reggie announced her resignation from the firm as "an act of conscience." She was followed out the door by another Keck, Mahin partner—Geraldine A. Ferraro, the Democratic candidate for vice president in 1984.

Gerson and Zaid had always hoped to broaden the suit beyond the death of Ingrid Smith. They believed in their case on so many levels: as a way to punish a despicable act; to make a larger point about holding governments accountable; to compensate people they had come to know and care about; and as a vehicle to make money for themselves, although for two lawyers in Washington in the 1990s there certainly were easier and faster ways to do that. "Look, if I ever get rich from this case, that's fine with me," Zaid said, years later. "I'm a lawyer; this is what I do. But if I never make a penny at it, that's fine too, and it will still have been worth it." They considered approaching other family members. Zaid was still going to meetings with the family members, and had become close to many of them. From time to time, as he was talking to some of the parents of the college students, the thought would creep up on the parents that Zaid was just the age their children would have been, had they lived. A fine young man, a lawyer. How proud his parents must be of him. He could see in their eyes what they were thinking. The moment would always pass without comment. Zaid was confident some of them would be interested in joining the suit, at least the ones who didn't get up and walk out of the room when they heard the words "Bruce Smith." But that would take time, and as 1994 wore on they came to realize that time—in the form of a statute of limitations on filing complaints for damages—was running out. Like everything else about the case, the question of which statute of limitations applied was open to interpretation. But eventually they concluded that to withstand any challenge, the suits would have to be filed by November 1994—three years from the date of the indictments of Fhimah and Megrahi. Any of the family members who did not file suit against Libya before then might lose the chance forever.

Paul Hudson, who had briefly been Gerson's client at Hughes Hubbard & Reed, had switched (amicably) to Richard Emery, a well-known New York civil-liberties lawyer. Emery filed suit against Libya in early 1994, but no one else followed him. Rather than attempt to sign up clients piecemeal, in early June Gerson, Zaid, and Rosenthal filed an amended complaint with the court. The plaintiff was now identified as "Bruce Smith as personal representative of Ingrid Smith, deceased, and on behalf of all others similarly situated." In other words, they were filing as representatives of a class, consisting of the family members of all the Pan Am 103 passengers and crew members—a group they estimated to number at least 700. Class action suits do not require the initial assent of every member of the class (as millions of Americans finding themselves unwitting plaintiffs against car-rental companies or appliance manufacturers have discovered). The members of the class must be allowed the opportunity to opt out of the suit, and the Pan Am plaintiffs would be offered that choice. For now, though, this maneuver would stop the clock on the statute of limitations. To cover the potential new army of plaintiffs, the damages they sought had increased by a factor of 200. They were now suing Libya for $3 billion.

That brought a swift reaction, not from Libya but from a totally unexpected direction. To Lee Kreindler, this was another instance of Gerson screwing up his carefully laid plans. Kreindler had first heard about Smith's lawsuit when it was originally filed in December, from a reporter from the *Wall Street Journal*. He dismissed it then, stating, "This raises more questions with me than it answers . . . None of the families that I know of anywhere support what [Gerson and Zaid] are trying to do." Now, six months later, his Pan Am clients still hadn't received any money, the case was still on appeal—and here was Gerson, purporting to represent everyone on the airplane. Including Kreindler's own clients! He felt the need to set the judge straight:

"I serve as Lead Counsel and Chairman of the Plaintiffs' Committee in the [Pan Am case], which has now been pending . . . for five and a half years," he wrote Sporkin in late July. "At the inception of the litigation, we looked into the potential liability of several potential defendants. . . . As to Syria, Iran, or, as it turned out, Libya, we concluded that there was no way, under the Federal [sic] Sovereign Immunities Act, or otherwise, to successfully sue in the United States. Again we were concerned that any such effort might detract from recovery against Pan Am, Alert, and their insurers." In other words, Kreindler, who was not involved in Smith's suit, was volunteering his opinion to the judge that it wasn't valid. He had researched it himself and concluded that Libya was protected by the FSIA—which, of course, happened to be Libya's position as well.

When they saw this letter, Rosenthal, Zaid, and Gerson considered it a hostile attack. Kreindler's concern that the suit would "detract from recovery against Pan Am" struck them as disingenuous. Detract how? The Pan Am suit was now before the appellate court. Kreindler's colleague on the plaintiffs' committee, Nicholas Gilman, explained to Sporkin that "the judges in the Second Circuit are human beings . . . let's say there is a $10 million recovery against Libya. . . . [They will say] let's make a decision based on the merits of what we think these people should recover. They're not going to recover twice for the same event." That was the same fear Kreindler had raised about Gerson's op-ed article in the *New York Times* back in 1992, when the case was about to go to the jury. But the jury had handed down multi-million-dollar verdicts anyway. If it was so obvious to Kreindler that Libya couldn't be successfully sued in American courts, surely the judges on the Second Circuit were capable of coming to the same conclusion. In that case nothing would "detract from recovery against Pan Am." On the other hand, if Kreindler was wrong and the families did successfully sue Libya, then his clients would be ahead of the game. Even if there was an offsetting reduction in what they received from Pan Am's insurance companies, they couldn't wind up with any *less* money. And they would have the satisfaction that some of it came out of Kaddafi's pockets. The one who might wind up with less, though, was Kreindler, whose fees (and reputation) would be based on what his clients collected against Pan Am and its insurers, and not against Libya.

Kreindler followed his letter with an appearance in Sporkin's courtroom to oppose the class-action designation in person. And just in case he couldn't defeat it, he sought to control it. He wrote to the federal panel on multi-district litigation (MDL), an obscure judicial office that attempts to consolidate lawsuits filed in different venues for the sake of efficiency. The hundreds of Lockerbie cases against Pan Am had been consolidated into an action collectively known as MDL 799. Kreindler informed the panel of the existence of the *Smith* suit as a potential "tag-along" to MDL 799, which could bring it under the control of his plaintiffs' committee—and up to Platt's courtroom in New York.

His intervention was greeted coldly by Sporkin. The judge made it plain he didn't want the case transferred out of his court. In early July, he had been dealt a wounding reversal by the D.C. Circuit Court of Appeals in the *Princz* case—the opinion Gerson had so admired, allowing Princz to sue Germany for Holocaust reparations. Writing for a two-to-one majority, Judge Douglas Ginsburg took the narrowest possible view of the exceptions to foreign sovereign immunity in the FSIA. Enslavement did not, in Ginsburg's view, constitute a commercial activity having a "direct effect in the United States." The key word was "direct." Princz had been conscripted to construct a munitions plant. "Many events and actors necessarily intervened between any work that Mr. Princz performed . . . and any effect felt in the United States," Ginsburg wrote. (Even after his own retirement in 2000, Sporkin could become indignant over Ginsburg's reasoning: "We were fighting a war against them! If they'd taken the bricks and thrown them at American soldiers, would *that* have been a 'direct effect'?") Ginsburg's point, though, seemed to strike uncomfortably close to the heart of the Gerson-Zaid argument that Libya's financial support of terrorists was a "commercial activity" under the FSIA. Nor did Ginsburg think much of the *jus cogens* argument, that Germany's behavior was so abhorrent it amounted to an implied waiver of sovereign immunity. ". . . [A]n implied waiver," he wrote, "depends upon the foreign government's having at some point indicated its amenability to suit. Mr. Princz does not maintain, however, that either the present government of Germany or the predecessor government of the Third Reich actually indicated, even implicitly, a willingness to waive immunity for actions arising out of the Nazi atrocities." Quite right: Hitler never volunteered to be sued for his atrocities, any more than Kaddafi had for his. "Implied waiver" is an artifice, a construct, of the sort often encountered in courtrooms, where certain things are assumed as a matter of law. The driver of the getaway car may not have planned for his accomplice to shoot the bank teller, but the law imputes the intention to him anyway, and charges him with felony murder. "Implied waiver" of sovereign immunity, as Perles argued and as Sporkin ruled, simply meant that immunity was not a right but a privilege, which could be forfeited for egregious conduct far outside the norms recognized by civilized nations. Not an outlandish idea, but one too novel for Ginsburg, whose strict constructionist view led him to an absurdist realm where a Holocaust victim couldn't sue for redress because the Third Reich had neglected to communicate its willingness to be subject to the jurisdiction of American courts.

Sporkin could take heart from a ringing dissent by the third appellate judge, Patricia Wald, who pointed out that the *jus cogens* standard was also the rationale for the Nuremberg war-crimes trials, whose very legitimacy the majority opinion appeared to call into question. "When the Nazis tore off Princz's clothes, exchanged them for a prison uniform and a tattoo, shoved him behind the spiked barbed wire fences of Auschwitz and Dachau and sold him to the German armament industry as fodder for their wartime labor operation, Germany rescinded any claim under international law to immunity from this court's jurisdiction," she wrote. For his part, Sporkin did not mince words about Ginsburg's opinion, which he accused of "trivializ[ing] the Holocaust." (Although the Supreme Court declined to hear an appeal, leaving Ginsburg's opinion in place, Sporkin's indignation was credited with embarrassing the State Department into pressing Princz's claim; in 1995 Germany agreed to pay $2.1 million to Princz and ten other Holocaust survivors. As late as 1992, Perles, the lawyer, knew of only one other person in Princz's situation, but by 1999 more than 200 living

American Holocaust survivors, roughly half of them civilians, were identified and ruled eligible for compensation.)

So when Kreindler showed up to object to the class action, he was facing one very unhappy judge. "You have no intention of pursuing this case," Sporkin admonished him. "You made a decision early on that you did not want to bring these [Libyan] defendants in . . . And now you don't want these plaintiffs to bring this case. Therefore what you've done is you're now using every step you can to throw a monkey wrench into this case. And I tell you I think that what you've done is acted very unethically . . . I believe there's been abuse of process here and possibly an obstruction of justice. And I say that, and I've chosen those words, Mr. Kreindler."

Smith, sitting with his lawyers, leaned over and whispered to Gerson: "Wow. I never knew judges talked like that."

Kreindler stood his ground. "We considered the possibility of suing Libya," he replied. "We have a well-thought-out, well-calculated litigation strategy. We decided it would not serve the interests of our clients to do so . . . We spent a lot of time coming to what we thought were the correct decisions on how to represent virtually every family member in the Lockerbie case."

"Yes," Sporkin retorted. "But you see what you're doing is you told the multi-district panel that this case could be more expeditiously handled up in New York. And what you didn't tell them is the reason you're invoking their jurisdiction is to get it to New York to dismiss the case. And to me that is unconscionable for a lawyer to do. It is absolutely unconscionable."

But the fate of the case was now out of Sporkin's hands. Kreindler promptly informed his clients of his efforts in a twenty-page, single-spaced letter that was meant, in part, to warn them and others, to whom the letter was freely distributed, away from any dealings with Smith and Gerson. "When I first heard about the class action complaint brought by Mr. Gerson," he wrote, "it sounded to me like a cooked up deal to provide a format for more Libyan public relations and it strongly hinted [of] blood money. When one considers that the UN sanctions question will again be on the agenda of the Security

Council this month it sounds more that way." He seemed to imply that Gerson and Smith were somehow in league with Kaddafi by suing him. The charge of seeking "blood money"—a payment offered to the next of kin in expiation of a murder—would be hurled at Smith and his lawyers again and again over the next few years. Understandably, the Pan Am families were inordinately sensitive to any suggestion they could be bought off. As everyone knew, paying compensation to the families was one of the conditions Libya had to meet in order to get the UN Security Council sanctions lifted. If you chose to look at it that way, suing Libya meant accepting the possibility of someday taking its money. Kreindler made it sound as if he opposed the idea out of principle. On the other hand, in the very next sentence he assured his clients that if it were easy, he'd be doing it, too: "You can be sure that when and if Libya announces it will waive sovereign immunity and face the music for legitimate damages or when the Supreme Court or Congress changes the law to permit a suit, we will either enter the action with both feet or start our own action against Libya."

His remarks helped fuel a war of letters and press releases between Smith and some of the other family members. Daniel and Susan Cohen denounced the Smith suit as "another backdoor attempt to broker a money deal with Libya. The [Kaddafi] regime," they wrote, "would pay family members an agreed upon sum while not admitting guilt. In return we would consider the matter closed and shut up and go away. It would be called 'compensation' but it would really be blood money. Gerson has said 'If Libya pays, it sends a message to terrorists.' Yes it does, the message is you can kill Americans and buy your way out of punishment." Smith replied with his own open letter to the families, asserting that "the object of the lawsuit against Libya is to put the Libyan government on trial for putting the bomb on Flight 103. If the U.S. government will not take direct and meaningful action against Libya, the Flight 103 families can." Turning the "blood money" accusation on its head, he wrote: "The lawsuits against Pan Am are for money; the suit against Libya is for justice."

But if Smith hoped to persuade anyone to join him, he was disappointed; no one, save Hudson, was willing to take on another cause while the Pan Am suits were still pending. As for the lawyers, any vindication they may have felt at Sporkin's dressing-down of Kreindler was short-lived. Still hoping to keep the case in his court, Sporkin set aside, for the time being, the class-action motion. Kreindler accordingly withdrew his opposition to having the *Smith* and *Hudson* cases, as individual actions, heard in Washington. But the multi-district litigation machinery, once set in motion, continued on its own. Gerson and Zaid filed briefs opposing the transfer, but their effort proved unsuccessful. They filed a lengthy appeal, and Rosenthal argued in person before a special MDL panel in Jacksonville, Florida. But in September the panel affirmed the order transferring the cases to Judge Platt. Gerson's life was about to become a lot harder—not least because the case would now be heard 200 miles away in a courtroom in Long Island.

It would have been harder still, but for a fortuitous move by Doug Rosenthal, who resigned from Coudert Brothers around that time and joined the Washington office of Sonnenschein, Nath and Rosenthal (the Rosenthal in the firm name was no relation), a major litigating firm based in Chicago. At his old firm, Rosenthal and his colleague Doug Rutzen had been working on the case voluntarily, on their own time. In looking to move, Rosenthal made it clear he wanted to bring the *Smith* case with him, and he wanted his new firm to support it with its own resources. Most of the firms he spoke to weren't interested; not only was the issue controversial, and the payoff remote, but among elite corporate law firms, even as late as the 1990s, there was still something vaguely suspect about representing plaintiffs, no matter how worthy their cause. It smacked of being a troublemaker, and therefore scared away corporate clients, the big money who could be expected to regularly incur legal fees. But the Sonnenschein partners agreed to take Smith's case, contrary to their usual practice, and accept a contingency fee rather than bill by the hour. Smith was out of money by this time. Given the chances of actually winning a judgment, let alone collecting it, and the size of the fee Sonnenschein might expect, that was not much different than taking the case *pro bono*. And Sonnenschein threw their top legal talent at the case, including litigating partner Tim Russell and Carol Elder Bruce, a former Justice Department prosecutor whom Gerson first encountered when she questioned him in the investigation of former attorney general Edwin Meese and his friend, e robert wallach. And, at Gerson's request, his former mentor at Yale, Michael Reisman, also came on board as special counsel to the team. Eventually the hours spent by Rosenthal, his partners and associates and consultants would amount to nearly $3 million.

And now the odds were longer against them, because Sporkin had been replaced by Platt, a much more cautious jurist. They were still fighting the threshold battle of establishing their right to sue under the FSIA, and Libya was still contesting it, although with new lawyers. Keck, Mahin & Cate took the occasion of the transfer to bow out of the case before any more partners resigned. Libya, true to its philosophy of jurisprudence, replaced Keck, Mahin with a lawyer in White Plains, New York, named John R. Bartels Jr. The senior John R. Bartels was a judge in federal district court for the Eastern District of New York. The first words Platt uttered on the record in *Smith v. Libya* were, "Mr. Bartels, does everybody know the obvious, that I know you and your father?"

Zaid thought the change of judges and lawyers called for a change of tactics. He wanted to put less emphasis on the sweeping *jus cogens* theory and more weight on the relatively narrow argument that a U.S.-flagged airliner can be considered American "territory," which would bring the bombing under one of the specific exceptions to sovereign immunity contained in the FSIA. "It's just the sort of argument you want to use when you're trying to make new law," he reasoned. "You want to make it easy for them to decide the case your way, without affecting anything else. The problem with the other approach is that the judge is going to worry he's throwing open the doors for anyone in the world to come to the U.S. and claim his rights were violated by a foreign government." But Rosenthal and Tim Russell, his new partners at Sonnenschein, Nath, disagreed; they felt the U.S.-flag argument was probably foreclosed by the decision in a case called *Amerada Hess v. Argentina*. In that case—involving damage to an oil tanker attacked during the 1982 Falklands War—the Supreme Court defined the territory of the

United States, for FSIA purposes, as meaning . . . well, the territory of the United States. There were cases that seemed to support Zaid's argument as well, and he kept finding them and bringing them up, but unfortunately they were mostly from the nineteenth century. Rosenthal prevailed; the *jus cogens* argument got most of the space in the brief and most of the time in the oral arguments, which took place before Judge Platt in the winter of 1995.

They came in with a sense of foreboding. In the taxi, on the long drive from JFK to Platt's courtroom in Long Island, Gerson fretted over the argument Russell would make that afternoon. He had become increasingly concerned that the *jus cogens* theory meant asking the judge to do something he really didn't understand. It would be different if Sporkin—with his background at the CIA—were trying the case, but what familiarity would Platt have with such exotic concepts in international law? For his part, Russell saw the argument as something they had to get through in order to bring the case before the Court of Appeals, where the judges had the freedom to take a longer view of the underlying issues than a district-court judge. Only Zaid, less than three years out of law school, was confident. "We're going to win this!" he assured Gerson.

The scene in Platt's courtroom did little to hearten them. They waited for hours through a series of droning procedural motions, followed by a hearing for a half dozen manacled illegal aliens charged with drug trafficking. Finally they were called. The defendants went first, since the hearing was technically on their motion to dismiss the case. Bartels attacked the argument that Libya's letter to the UN secretary-general guaranteeing to pay any judgment against Fhimah and Megrahi, amounted to a waiver of immunity. From his questions, Platt seemed ready to agree. Then Bartels got to the meat of his argument: that accepting the *jus cogens* theory would open the American courts to a flood of litigation "over the countless human rights cases that might well be brought by the victims of all the ruthless military juntas and presidents for life and multiple dictators of the world, of Idi Amin and Mao Tse Tung. Such an expansive reading," he went on, "might place an enormous stress not only on our courts, but more to the immediate point our nation's diplomatic relations with any number of foreign nations."

When it was Russell's turn to argue, the judge revealed what was bothering him about *jus cogens*.

"What," Platt asked, "of an act of terrorism by the United States Government in a sense of really horrendous acts against its own citizens, would you say that would be a waiver of their sovereign immunity doctrine here?"

The obvious answer, consistent with the position they were taking, was *Yes, any government that practices terrorism should be held accountable for it*. But Russell saw trouble down that path and tried to sidestep the question. "We don't have to reach [that point]," he responded. Unfortunately Platt refused to drop the issue. Out of the blue came a question about Hiroshima:

"What about our act of dropping the atom bomb on the Japanese? . . . At least the current view of those people who were alive, like I was at the time that it happened, was that it was a horrendous act of terrorist quality, if you will."

People kept bringing up Hiroshima to Russell, and it always drove him nuts. Hiroshima, he would explain, was a legitimate military attack, carried out by uniformed combatants in the course of a declared war. It had nothing to do with smuggling a bomb on board an airplane, an act that had been specifically condemned by the UN Security Council. But Platt put himself in Libya's shoes, for the sake of argument. "Weren't [they] conducting an undeclared war against us[?]" And wasn't the bombing of Pan Am 103 "a far less heinous crime than dropping the bomb on Hiroshima?"

In other words, he seemed to be saying to Russell, who am I to judge such weighty matters of state and draw these distinctions? Russell—a brilliant litigator in his own field of commercial contracts but without a background in public international law—might have responded that of course all these questions belong in a court of law. The United States does not commit acts of terrorism as a matter of policy, but if credible charges are made it should have to answer, no less than Libya, and these are indeed issues that any federal judge should be prepared to grapple with. But by allowing himself to be drawn into a lengthy exchange on the nature of war and terrorism, he ate up precious time. Platt, who had set aside an hour for the case, was not inclined to extend the proceedings past four o'clock. So when it was Reisman's turn to explain why the UN Security Council resolution had created a private right of action, he had less than two minutes for this complex argument. Platt called a halt to the argument by acknowledging that his opinion wasn't going to be the final word anyway: "I don't want any further papers on this. I have enough. This case is not going to stop here. Whatever the result it is going to end up in the Court of Appeals, and probably in the Supreme Court."

It is never easy to predict how a court will rule by what transpires in the courtroom. Often a judge will play devil's advocate, or pose questions merely to test theories. Still, as they walked out of the courtroom that day, Russell, Gerson, and their colleagues couldn't shake the feeling that Platt had already made up his mind, and that it wasn't in Smith's favor.

In May, Platt rendered his verdict in the two cases before him, *Smith* and *Hudson v. Libya*. He dismissed the complaints. The judge rejected the argument that the plane was American territory—citing *Amerada Hess*—and rejected the notion that blowing up an airplane constitutes an "implied waiver" of sovereign immunity, relying in part on Ginsburg's opinion in *Princz*. "Although Libya's alleged participation, if true, in this tragedy is outrageous and reprehensible and the human suffering involved is heartbreaking, this Court may not rightly obtain jurisdiction over Libya for the purposes of these private rights of action," he concluded. "Libya's alleged terrorist actions do not fall within the enumerated exceptions to the Foreign Sovereign Immunity Act and therefore Libya must be accorded sovereign immunity from suit."

A month or so after Platt's decision, Gerson received a feeler from the ruler of an Arab nation that had kept up good relations with Kaddafi. "We have learnt of the personal interest you have in finding a solution liable to bring the concerned parties in the Lockerbie tragedy out of the present deadlock," the letter began. "In our estimation the deadlock is profitable to none; it serves neither the cause of justice, nor that of the eligible beneficiaries who have a claim to a just and equitable indemnification in reparation of the moral and material prejudice caused by this abominable crime." Gerson was invited for a secret visit to the Arab capital. He understood, of course, that what Kaddafi wanted, an end to sanctions, was hardly in his power to grant—not in anyone's power, actually, short of the president himself. On the advice of a colleague skilled in diplomacy, he resolved to convey only one message: that "if Libya were to do good things, good things are likely to follow."

Before leaving on his trip, he had the lawyers at Sonnenschein, Nath and Rosenthal draft an opinion which gave him—he trusted— the legal cover he needed to meet with a foreign head of state, even for the limited purpose of conveying a message about a private lawsuit. American citizens were not allowed to have commercial contacts with Libya without a special license from the Treasury Department, but the opinion assured him this wouldn't apply to a lawyer pursuing his clients' interests. He was convinced that Kaddafi's only chance to escape his box was through the U.S. courts; no American president could take the heat of negotiating with him otherwise. But if Kaddafi were to offer to settle the families' claims on terms acceptable to them—which meant a sum large enough to be considered punitive— and set up an escrow account in Switzerland for that purpose, the administration might have the cover it needed for a comprehensive settlement, consistent with UN Security Council resolutions. As forcefully as he dared, he urged the ruler sitting across the table from him to make the case to Kaddafi: that he would have to take the first step, and he would have to do it alone, voluntarily, with nothing pledged in return, inasmuch as Gerson represented no one except his own client, and certainly not the U.S. government. The response was noncommittal. "Kaddafi is my brother," he said. "I am not his father. Perhaps it will happen, In sh'allah." But Kaddafi was never heard from.

11

A Cairn at Arlington

Less than a minute before it was blown to pieces on its way to America, Pan Am flight 103 passed above the Corsehill Quarry, Annan, Dumfrieshire. Corsehill is the source of an unusually fine-grained, salmon-pink sandstone that was much sought after by British and American builders in the late nineteenth century. At one time the quarry had a standing order for 250 tons a week from New York City alone, where its stone was used in hotels, offices, and public buildings of all kinds. If the flight had continued on to JFK, it would have passed within a few miles of the Statue of Liberty in New York Harbor. Although the statue itself is a gift of the government of France, it stands on a base of stones from Corsehill Quarry.

Shortly after the bombing of Pan Am 103, the Dumfries and Galloway Regional Council established a fund, the Lockerbie Air Disaster Trust, to receive the donations that poured in from around the world for the victims of the disaster. In the spring of 1989, officials of the trust contacted the Victims of Pan Am 103 family group, offering to supply the cherished sandstone of Corsehill Quarry for a memorial to be built somewhere in the United States. The form they proposed was a cairn, a simple pile of stones used as grave markers by the inhabitants of the British Isles since prehistoric times. *The Oxford English Dictionary* cites the expression *"to add a stone to one's cairn,"* meaning "to do all possible honour to his memory after death." An official of the trust, Donald Bogie, designed it as an unadorned cylinder, approximately eight feet in diameter at the base, tapering slightly as it rose to height of ten and a half feet, to be constructed of 270 stones. On behalf of the family group, Joe Horgan, Bert Ammerman's brother-in-law, accepted the offer, and the stones were duly cut, shipped, and taken to a warehouse Horgan's company owned in Pennsylvania while the group decided what to do with them.

At first they thought the White House might come up with an appropriate site, but the government seemed oddly uninterested in the project. It fell to a committee of the victims group, primarily a woman named Jane Schultz. Schultz was a wealthy, socially prominent woman—her husband, Jack, was a leading-department-store executive—known among the family members as the victim of an extraordinary double tragedy, which she bore with great grace and courage. Her handsome, athletic son, Thomas Britton Schultz, who was a student at Ohio Wesleyan University when he was killed, was her only surviving child; his younger brother had died a decade earlier when he pulled the pin on a live hand grenade that had been left behind in the basement of the family's new home in Connecticut. As soon as she heard about the cairn, she regarded it as an opportunity to channel her grief into a concrete accomplishment. In 1990 she had traveled with her husband to Scotland for the dedication of a small memorial in the churchyard at Tundergarth, where the nose of the airplane had fallen, a few miles from Lockerbie. There she met the mother of a young woman who had boarded the plane in London, but whose body was never recovered from the wreckage. "She was there looking for a place to be buried herself, so she could be near her daughter," Schultz recalls. "She was so terribly, terribly distraught. I just felt I had to do something."

The cairn also became a project close to the heart of Frank Duggan, the McLaughlin Commission family liaison, now functioning as an unpaid adviser and ombudsman for the family members. Duggan volunteered to do the legal work of getting the cairn built, without any idea of what he was getting himself into. Few subjects generate as much emotion as the placement of memorials in the nation's capital. Public statuary in Washington is under the control of both the National Capital Planning Commission and the District of Columbia Commission of Fine Arts. Since its inception nearly ninety years ago, the Fine Arts Commission has been the watchdog over the design of monuments in Washington, helping to preserve it as a city of expansive vistas, broad boulevards, and little squares filled, as Duggan noted when he began driving around to look at them, with "statues of South American generals on horseback, covered in pigeon shit." But the actual authority to erect a monument on federal land in Washington resides with the legislative branch, under the 1986 Commemorative Works Act, passed in response to the "monumental chaos" over Maya Lin's controversial design for the Vietnam Memorial on the Mall.

An act of Congress is needed to erect a monument on Park Service or General Services Administration property in Washington—essentially, all federal land except military installations. On the Mall and the surrounding parkland, only "works of preeminent historical and lasting significance to the nation" are permitted, which seemed to Duggan like a fairly high threshold. Elsewhere in the capital, "military commemorative works honoring a major conflict or military branch" were allowed, along with "nonmilitary commemorative works" of "lasting historical significance" provided "the individuals commemorated have been dead at least 25 years." That provision, intended to let emotions cool before the bronze is poured, would appear to rule out a memorial to Pan Am 103 before the year 2013, unless Congress approved an exception. Duggan did not consider this an insurmountable obstacle.

The large concrete plaza outside Federal Aviation Administration headquarters on Constitution Avenue caught his eye. Countless tourists streamed by, and each day hundreds of people with the responsibility of keeping airline passengers safe would have to walk past this reminder of what happens if they don't do their jobs right. He would need the backing of the GSA, which controlled the parcel, and he would have to get a bill through Congress, but he was a lobbyist; he'd done it before. And so, of course, had the families.

To his surprise, though, the family members he consulted rejected the location out of hand. They were appalled, almost offended. They did not want a memorial in front of the FAA; they didn't want to set foot near the place at all. They didn't want a tourist cynosure; they wanted a place where they could mourn. A cemetery would be particularly appropriate, Schultz advised him, for those whose relatives' remains were never returned, and who therefore didn't have a gravesite to visit. But not tucked away in the countryside; it should be in a conspicuous location where it would serve to remind politicians with short memories that we are all together in the fight against terrorism, that the families' tragedy was also America's.

There was really only one such place in the country. Duggan took them across the Potomac to Arlington National Cemetery. Here, alongside the cobblestoned tree-lined road leading to the main gate, stood memorials to the Spanish-American War and to the glorious histories of individual military units. It struck Duggan as a dignified and fitting place for a monument to the victims of what amounted to an undeclared war against America. But the family members wanted the cairn *inside* Arlington. This time Duggan thought they were overreaching. There was, as far as he knew, only one requirement to be buried at Arlington, but it was an almost ironclad one: you had to be a veteran of the United States military. Exceptions were made for former presidents, in recognition of their rank of commander in chief, and a handful of civilians with quasi-military credentials, including CIA agents who had died in the line of duty. Among them was Mathew Gannon, who had been returning to the United States from Beirut aboard Pan Am 103. There was a monument for the astronauts who died in the explosion of the space shuttle *Challenger*, but the civilians aboard had volunteered for a potentially dangerous mission for their country. The great majority of Pan Am victims were just people who happened to be on the wrong airplane at the wrong time, and they were from twenty countries besides the United States. Why not, Duggan thought, try for something simple like Westminster Abbey?

As he looked into it further, though, he realized that as military property, Arlington did not fall under the twenty-five-year rule of the Commemorative Works Act. Furthermore, erecting a monument there would require only a congressional "joint resolution," which the leadership could arrange to pass by unanimous consent—rather than an act of Congress, which amounted to passing a bill into law and ordinarily required committee hearings, roll-call votes, and conference reports. Of course, it would still require the cooperation, or at least neutrality, of the military and the administration. On August 17, 1992, Schultz, on behalf of the Victims of Pan Am 103, wrote to the Secretary of the Army, Michael P. W. Stone, setting out her case:

> The cairn has been presented to the people of the United States from the people of Scotland, a gift with so much love, respect and historical significance. The destruction of Pan Am 103 represents the largest terrorist attack ever committed against American citizens and hopefully history will record this as the high-water mark of terrorism. It is most appropriate that Arlington Cemetery be chosen as a place of reverence and remembrance.

Stone passed the letter on to the superintendent of Arlington, a career civil servant named John C. Metzler Jr. Metzler, whose father had held the same post from 1951 to 1972, had literally grown up in Arlington, in the same house on the grounds he lives in now. He had played hide-and-seek in the adjoining wooded areas and among the monuments with the sons of soldiers in nearby Fort Myer. But always, he emphasized, with respect for the fact that "everyone buried here has a tremendous story, and has contributed to our freedom and the freedom of the world." In particular there were his heroes: people like Gen. John J. Pershing, who commanded the American forces in World War I; Gen. Maxwell Taylor of World War II fame; or Gen. Jimmy Doolittle, who led the famous bombing raid on Tokyo soon after Pearl Harbor. That roster did not, in his estimation, include civilians whose sacrifice, however great and tragic, was inadvertent.

On September 10, on the advice of Metzler, Stone responded to Schultz. His letter was sympathetic but firm:

> The Cemetery was established as a permanent national shrine to the honored dead of the Armed Forces of the United States . . .

While some of the Pan Am 103 victims were active-duty military and dependents, the flight had no direct military connection . . . While I have deep appreciation and compassion for your endeavor, I cannot in good conscience support your request for a cairn within the Cemetery itself.

Metzler, meanwhile, had been scouring Washington for alternative sites, and in December he wrote to the assistant secretary of the army for civil works, informing him of his progress. He had been in touch with the former superintendent of Rock Creek Cemetery, the oldest burying ground in Washington, to explore the possibility of erecting a monument there. He had looked into Washington National Cathedral and received an encouraging reply from officials there. "No government or regulatory approval" would be needed, he added pointedly. Duggan brought up these alternatives at a meeting with the family members, who rejected them out of hand. Schultz made one more appeal to Stone, and backed it with an impassioned letter to Bush himself. The bombing of Pan Am 103, she reminded him, had overhung his administration from the very beginning; now that it was ending, he could close the book on it by approving the memorial for its victims. Just a few days before Clinton's inauguration, a Bush aide called her to say the request had been turned down.

"He deserved to lose the election," she replied bitterly.

Now a new administration was in place, though. In early spring of 1993 the family members had their first meeting with top Clinton officials, including Anthony Lake, the national security adviser. They went in with a three-page agenda running to twenty-nine items, including an oil embargo ("set date of 30–60 days hence"); seizing the Libyan assets frozen by presidential proclamation and distributing a portion of them to the families; invading Libya with Delta Force commandos to capture Fhimah and Megrahi for trial; and a demand for "compensation and reparations from Libya of $23 billion." At the end of the meeting, Lake remarked that he was surprised that the subject of the cairn hadn't come up. He volunteered the information that Clinton would not oppose a congressional resolution, but they would have to get it passed without help from the White House, and raise the money to build it themselves.

The administration had gotten off on the wrong foot with the military over the issue of allowing homosexuals into the ranks, and it wasn't about to run the risk of offending it again. Nevertheless, that was far more encouragement than they'd received from Bush.

On this, and other issues related to Pan Am 103, Lake was to play a major role, meeting with the family members "five to ten times . . . basically, whenever they wanted it," he says. On no other issue did he regularly meet with private citizens outside the administration. Even Dan and Susan Cohen, who disdain most government officials on principle, concede in their book that the Clinton administration was reasonably accessible to the families. They themselves—by their own admission, impossible people to deal with—were included in many White House meetings, even though they represented no organization; Bush's people, by contrast, preferred dealing just with the leaders of the family groups. Responding to a letter from the Cohens during the campaign, Clinton had expressed the opinion that " . . . the United States should make it clear that if [the suspects] are not turned over, it will press the United Nations to broaden the sanctions to include an oil embargo." A Clinton administration official who worked on the issue later concluded, though, that the families were just using the campaign to put pressure on Bush. "As soon as we came in," he recalled, "we became the target and they were asking us for things that were never going to happen."

High on the list of those things was an oil boycott. On April 8, 1993, Ambassador to the United Nations Madeleine Albright announced that "the United States will consider an oil embargo as one means of stiffening the present sanctions regime." A month later, Lake wrote to Cummock that "we are determined to seek tougher sanctions, including oil, if Libya remains intransigent." Yet Libya did remain intransigent, and despite pressure from the families and from Kennedy, Lautenberg, and other powerful senators, it was never seriously attempted.

To some of the family members—such as Peter and Suse Lowenstein—the cairn came to be seen as a sop, a substitute for concrete action against Kaddafi. Suse was the sculptor of the *Dark Elegy* series of figures, so she would not be one to doubt the power inherent in art. But, as they saw it, a monument in a cemetery is something you build when the war is over, and they were still very much fighting. "Our feeling was, you don't build a monument to injustice, which in effect this was," says Peter Lowenstein. "We think it contributed to delaying the criminal trial, and the case has been weakened by the delay. The government could say, okay, we've given them the hallowed ground at Arlington, that should keep them quiet for a while. And for some of the family members, it did. As far as they're concerned, their job is done. I find that amazing."

This is an accusation that Lake deeply resents, and many of the other family members reject. To erect a cairn in Arlington meant elevating their private grief to a matter of national concern. The lines between civilians and combatants had been erased—not by them, but by an act of international terrorism. The preceding decade had blurred the distinctions between heroes and victims, between those who died in battle and those who just had the misfortune to be in harm's way. Where once there had been separate realms of public and private interest, now they were intermingling, joined in the common purpose of assuring the dignity and honor and well-being of all Americans. In fighting for the cairn at Arlington, the families finally achieved, on November 24, 1993, the statement they'd been hoping to hear from the government for nearly five years. It came in the fifth clause of a joint resolution of the 103rd Congress, "to authorize the placement of a memorial cairn in Arlington National Cemetery, Arlington, Virginia, to honor the 270 victims of the terrorist bombing of Pan Am Flight 103," and said, starkly

Whereas the terrorist bombing of Flight 103 was unquestionably an attack on the United States;

An attack on the United States! That language, like that of the rest of the resolution itself, was largely written by Schultz, Vargo, and Jeri Kolesar, an aide to Lautenberg, and would have been cleared by the Senate's legislative counsel. It was unusually strong wording for a Sense of the Congress resolution, and the speed with which it passed caught the Army by surprise. The next day Metzler received an unexpected summons to the Old Executive Office Building adjacent to the White House. He was ushered into a conference room where Duggan, Schultz, and other family members were waiting. Richard Canas, an assistant to the president and a member of the National Security Council staff, produced a copy of the congressional resolution, passed unanimously and signed by Speaker of the House Tom Foley and Robert Byrd, president pro tem of the Senate. "President Clinton," he informed Metzler, "has no objection to seeing this happen." The clear implication was that President Clinton didn't want anyone else to have an objection, either. "You could hear the guy's sphincter squishing," Duggan recalls gleefully. Metzler took his orders like a good soldier, or bureaucrat, and agreed he would do his best to make it happen.

The resolution referred to "a small, vacant plot of land, unsuitable for gravesites [which] has been located in Arlington National Cemetery." Duggan had located it, with the help of a hunting buddy named Bobby Langston, who was high up in the National Park Service Police. Langston had told him that on a hill in the back reaches of the cemetery was a small administration building that was in the process of being turned over to the Park Service. The building faced a kidney-shaped area between two drives, comprising about a quarter of an acre and including three large, handsome oak trees. Duggan and Schultz drove out to see it and realized it would be ideal for the memorial. Equally important, taking into consideration that Arlington was projected to run out of burial space in another generation, it was not suitable for graves; Duggan obtained a map that showed water and utility lines a few feet underground. It was also on one of the highest points in Arlington, and an area that was a particular favorite of Metzler's from his years growing up there, near the equestrian statue of Maj. Gen. Philip Kearney, New Jersey's most decorated war hero, and the old amphitheater of the Grand Army of the Republic that forms the arc above the John F. Kennedy gravesite. Not far away, facing the Potomac and downtown Washington, was the tall mast that had supported the crow's nest of the battleship *Maine*, destroyed by a mysterious explosion in Havana harbor in 1898. The cause of the blast, in which 260 seamen died, was never conclusively established, but the incident helped spark the Spanish-American War. Here was history you could see and almost touch from Metzler's own doorstep. And close to the center of these great monuments, on the high plain of Arlington, was the spot the Pan Am 103 families had chosen for their memorial, a red sandstone cylinder that to Metzler's eye had no place among the heroic bronze statuary and the fields of neat white crosses dotting these rolling hills. But swallowing his feelings, Metzler went to work on the project. He informed the Fine Arts Commission that the Army would no longer object to the design of the Pan Am 103 memorial or to the site chosen for it.

On the fifth anniversary of the bombing, December 21, 1993, Clinton presided over a groundbreaking ceremony for the cairn attended by many of the family members. Cummock came up to Washington for the event with her children. Her eight-year-old daughter, Ashley, had had an exchange of letters with Clinton earlier that year, prompted by Hurricane Andrew. In 1992, Andrew had barreled through southern Florida and torn the roof off Cummock's house, along with thousands of others. For a class project on "shelter," Ashley had chosen to make a model of the White House, and Cummock—who had a penchant for introducing her children to important people—had carried it to Washington for a meeting with Lake and delivered it to the White House in person. Clinton wrote back, thanking her ("I can tell from your letter that you have a very big heart, and I think that big heart will help you keep a sense of hope and faith"), but he never made the connection to the Cummock who died in the bombing. At the groundbreaking, Ashley walked up to Clinton and introduced herself, and Clinton asked what she was doing there.

"My father died on Pan Am 103," she told him.

And as Clinton bent down toward her, he started to tear up, and she patted him on the back and said reassuringly, "Yes, it's a sad thing."

Clinton's speech picked up the stirring language of the congressional resolution:

I say to you that our nation will never stop pursuing justice against [the bombers]; for the attack on Pan Am 103 was an attack not only on the individuals from twenty-one different countries who were aboard that aircraft, it was an attack on America.

It was a powerful moment, especially for those who had worked so hard to reach that point. "When he said that," Duggan recalled, "I stood up and cheered with all the rest of them. Even though I knew the son of a bitch didn't mean a word of it."

There was still nearly two years of work to do on the cairn. The Commission of Fine Arts would have to approve its design, its exact placement on the plot, and the wording of the inscription, a process involving numerous meetings and exchanges of architectural drawings. An early design called for inscribing the names of the victims on a low berm adjacent to the cairn, echoing the Vietnam Veterans Memorial on the Mall, but the commission opposed tampering with the geography of the site, and so it was decided the names would go on a granite ring around the base. A more serious conflict arose over the inscription. The families insisted it include the phrase "terrorist bombing," over the objections of the commission, which seemed to regard that graphic, stark phrase as out of keeping with the elegiac tone of the surrounding monuments. This required the intervention of the new secretary of the army, Togo West. Schultz explained to West why that phrase was so important to the families. Airplanes crash all the time, and the victims are soon forgotten by history; the fact of the bombing was what made this particular disaster worthy of Arlington. The design of the cairn itself, with its somber, brooding power, was left essentially unchanged from what was envisioned by the original Scottish architects. A woman named Deirdre Fortune, whose husband, Robert, had been on the flight, arranged for her employer, the architects Haines Lundberg Waehler, to do all the drawings for the Fine Arts Commission *pro bono*. Schultz helped organize a fund-raising drive that eventually collected over $300,000; the lawyers on the plaintiffs' committee made sure to contribute generously.

The cairn was built over six weeks in the summer of 1995 by Frank Klein, who owned a construction company in New Jersey. Klein's daughter, Patricia Ann, had been on board Pan Am 103, returning, as her page in *On Eagles' Wings* notes poignantly, from a visit to comfort an ailing nun, a longtime family friend. Klein didn't build the cairn in the sense that his company built buildings; he constructed it himself, with his hands and with a single stonemason he chose for the job. On the day before the cairn was dedicated in November 1995, Schultz went up there for a quiet moment, just with Lake and with Richard Clarke, the NSC's expert on counter-terrorism. It was the first time she was going to see the inscription with Tom's name on it, and she didn't want to be alone. It was a crisp fall morning, and the three of them stood quietly for a few minutes as the shadows of clouds chased across the hills, appreciating a job well done.

The cairn occupied a unique niche in Washington—a privately financed memorial on public property, a place of mourning and a national symbol. Misunderstanding inevitably arose from that duality. Among the victims was Maria Nieves de Larracoechea, the only Pan Am flight attendant who was a citizen of Spain. On behalf of her family, her sister demanded that Nieves's name be left off the monument. And not just her name, but the stone representing her—in other words, that the cairn be constructed of 269 stones, leaving one space empty. In light of "the hypocrisy of the U.S. administrations, Republican and Democrat, in manipulating the truth and obstructing justice, while inundating the public with endless rhetoric and sympathy," the lawyer wrote, Nieves's family "finds unbearable the public and permanent ignominy of being 'memorialized' at the very cemetery that serves to glorify members of the U.S. government, particularly the military." The demand was rejected. The names of the victims were now public property. The 270 victims had entered history together, however unwillingly, so that their names would now be inscribed in a granite ring around the base of the cairn—the soldiers and the babies and the husbands and sons and daughters, joined forever.

In its mingling of private and public concerns, the cairn symbolized the larger struggle of the Pan Am families for justice against Libya. They had no way of knowing, but their efforts were about to be overtaken by history. Two great trends of the end of the twentieth century, globalization and privatization, were coming together to end the monopoly of sovereign states on international justice. As totalitarian governments were beginning to discover, instantaneous worldwide communications handed unprecedented power to private citizens, who with a laptop could command a global audience larger than a million-watt broadcast transmitter. At the same time functions long considered the prerogative of national governments, from the delivery of mail to the administration of prisons, were increasingly being privatized. Private citizens, or their lawyers, were assuming police functions, such as the regulation of hazardous products, imposing their own form of accountability on tobacco companies and auto manufacturers.

In principle, therefore, why not add state-sponsored murder to the list? And pursue the perpetrators without distinguishing between ordinary criminals and agents of the state, as they themselves made no distinction in who was targeted by their bombs? To at least some of those who listened to Clinton's speech that December day, it was apparent that despite the brave words America actually had no intentions of responding to the attack represented by the bomb on board Pan Am 103, beyond what it had already done in the form of economic and diplomatic sanctions. The government was good at giving speeches and fighting wars, but all of Clinton's eloquence couldn't bring Kaddafi to justice, and all of America's missiles were useless without the will to use them. That left the families to pursue matters on their own, and the only venue for that seemed to be the courts.

Yet the courts weren't ready for this challenge. Few judges understood the role they could play in transforming public policy on an international scale. Sporkin and Wald did, as their rulings in *Princz* proved, but others, like Ginsburg and Platt, said, show us where our jurisdiction lies—not by implication, not by invoking universal principles, but precisely, explicitly, by the "black letter" of the law alone. But even as Gerson and Zaid were trying to squeeze *Smith v. Libya* through the needle's eye of the FSIA, others were trying to expand the exceptions to sovereign immunity by amending the act itself. Most of this work was being done by the lawyers for Nelson (the American engineer tortured in Saudi Arabia) and Princz (the American Holocaust survivor trying to collect compensation from Germany). A bill was introduced in the House in 1993 to deny sovereign immunity in cases

> . . . in which money damages are sought against a foreign state for personal injury or death of a United States citizen occurring in such foreign state and caused by the torture or extrajudicial killing of that citizen by such foreign state . . .

That was a provision tailor-made for Nelson. Even if it had passed, though, it wouldn't have done much good for the Pan Am 103 families, since the wording required that the act (blowing up an airplane) take place within the borders of the guilty state (Libya). Also, it wouldn't have helped Bruce Smith at all, since it only covered attacks on American citizens, and his wife, of course, had been English. But although it was too narrow for Gerson and Zaid's purposes, it was far too broad for many of the other interested parties, including the State Department, which was looking after both its own interests and the concerns of foreign governments with whom the United States had sensitive relations. Saudi Arabia obviously would not be pleased. Less obviously, Israel had reservations about setting a precedent for holding foreign governments accountable for "torture or extrajudicial killing." Unlike Saudi Arabia, Israel was a democracy with an independent judicial system, but it also was fighting Palestinian guerrillas in the West Bank and Gaza Strip, and its security forces did what they had to do. And the State Department for its own reasons opposed efforts to restrict sovereign immunity, which was, after all, a two-way street. When Nelson's case against Saudi Arabia reached the Supreme Court—not on the merits, just on the question of American jurisdiction—the State Department's lawyers were right there alongside the Saudis, arguing, successfully, that his case should be dismissed. So while the House bill and a similar measure introduced in the Senate went nowhere, Princz's lawyers began lobbying for a much narrower bill, which would specifically assist American citizens suing the Federal Republic of Germany over acts of genocide "occurring in the predecessor states of the Federal Republic of Germany." That version finally passed the House—

unanimously—in 1994, and even though it never became law, it had the desired effect of putting pressure on Germany to settle with Princz.

But beginning in 1994, around the time the *Smith* and *Hudson* suits were transferred up to New York, Gerson and Zaid began to consider more seriously the possibility of changing the law. Gerson was at the Supreme Court the day it ruled against Nelson, and he passed him later in the corridors, looking defeated and haggard; he didn't want the same fate to befall Smith. In June, he and Zaid wrote an impassioned, six-page, single-spaced letter to Sen. Howell Heflin (D–Ala.), chairman of the Subcommittee on Courts and Administrative Practice, urging him to support a bill amending the FSIA to allow suits for civil damages against state sponsors of terrorism.

To go over basics, because basics are what this revision is all about, justice requires in cases such as Pan Am 103 the punishment of the perpetrator. But criminal punishment—assuming it is a realistic prospect—is by no means the sole remedy. . . . To [deny the right to sue] twice punishes those victimized; first by the terrorists who caused the harm, and secondly by the country that, after having failed to protect them from harm, precluded them from the opportunity to seek punishment of the perpetrators, often by the only means available in these situations: civil damages.

Nelson's lawyer—Len Garment, the pugnacious former White House counsel to Richard Nixon—was doing the same thing, working through the influential Sen. Arlen Specter (R–Pa.). Gerson and Zaid decided to join forces with Garment and try to assure that whatever came out at the end met their needs as well as Nelson's. Zaid worked closely with Specter's aide Richard Hertling, and when Specter introduced his version of the bill in 1994 it showed the effects of Zaid's tinkering. Specter's bill was loosely based on the 1993 House bill, but contained some crucial changes. Besides "torture and extrajudicial killing" the bill now explicitly recognized "*aircraft sabotage*, hostage taking, or genocide" [italics added] as acts not covered by sovereign immunity. It dropped the requirement that the torture or killing had to occur within the borders of the state being sued. It retained the provision that the victim had to be an American citizen, but Zaid assumed he could fix that technicality when the time came; Smith himself was an American, even if his wife wasn't, and it would just be a matter of adding a few words to cover that particular circumstance.

The 1994 bill contained a couple of other provisions worth noting. It allowed suits to be brought for acts up to ten years in the past (except in cases of genocide)—in other words, it was retroactive. You cannot, of course, make something a crime in retrospect, at least in the United States. The courts have held that applying criminal law retroactively is a violation of the Constitution's guarantees of due process, but they have never applied that standard to laws affecting civil claims. A crime is a social construct, defined by statute, but a tort is a wrong, eternal and universal; it stands on its own. If all the laws against murder were to be repealed tomorrow, it wouldn't change what was owed by the killers to the sons and daughters of the people killed.

The other new provision in the 1994 bill required that anyone bringing a lawsuit under the act must have "exhausted adequate and available remedies" in foreign courts and "afforded the foreign state an opportunity to arbitrate the claim before an international tribunal . . ." This was meant to appease opponents, in particular a Florida congressman named Bill McCollum, who was emerging as the chief congressional skeptic of FSIA reform. (He eventually dropped his objections and ended up supporting the measures sought by the family members.) "McCollum was a conservative Republican, pro-military, anti–big government, the kind of guy we thought would be on our side," Zaid says. "But he had a couple of staffers who considered themselves terrorism experts, and they were dead set against putting any of this in the hands of private citizens. Their attitude was, let the pros handle it. So we put in this language, basically, to mollify them by setting up an additional obstacle for plaintiffs. The way it was written, it wasn't that great, but we figured we'd end up with something we could live with."

But the State Department was having none of it. In June, the Senate Subcomittee on Courts and Administrative Practice held a hearing on the bill. Among those testifying for it were Abe Sofaer—now no longer representing Libya, but consulting with Garment on *Nelson v. Saudi Arabia*—Hugo Princz, the former Auschwitz inmate; and two Americans who had been held hostage in Beirut, Joseph Cicippio and David Jacobsen. The State Department sent its deputy legal adviser, Jamison Borek, to voice its "serious concerns":

> Current U.S. law allows the U.S. government to fine-tune the application of sanctions against state sponsors of terrorism, increasing them or decreasing them in the national interest. In addition, the U.S. government coordinates closely with other nations at the U.N. and elsewhere on the imposition of sanctions . . . The possibility of civil suits and potential judgments against state sponsors of terrorism would inject a new unpredictable element in these very delicate relationships. Such proceedings could in some instance interfere with U.S. counter-terrorism objectives. They could also raise difficult issues involving sensitive intelligence and national-security information.

The part about intelligence and national security was the H-bomb of congressional testimony, with the potential to wipe out civilian opposition in a single phrase. In fact, Borek's testimony would later be cited in a brief by Libya's lawyers as they sought to throw the Pan Am lawsuits out of court. Assistant Secretary of State Wendy R. Sherman followed up with a letter to senators elaborating on the department's concerns. "States are sensitive to allegations of deliberate governmental wrongdoing," she wrote. "They would likely view with particular concern any effort to have such allegations adjudicated in our courts. . . . The amendment also presents potential reciprocity problems . . . Many actions undertaken by the U.S. government—e.g. application of the death penalty and detention of excludable aliens—reflect policies that are controversial abroad. While these matters may be subject to review in the U.S. courts, we would not wish to have such policies judged in foreign courts." Gerson asked Nicholas Kittrie, a law professor at American University and authority on international criminal law, to reply to the State Department's objections. Kittrie, citing Judge Wald's dissenting opinion in the *Princz* case, argued that the bill "would not extend the jurisdiction of U.S. Courts beyond accepted international practice. State sponsorship of genocide, torture, extrajudicial killing, hostage-taking and aircraft sabotage violates currently accepted norms of international law . . ." As for the danger of the U.S. government being sued in foreign courts, he made the common-sense observation that anyone who had a choice in the matter would prefer to sue in American courts, where damages for injuries and death were so much higher than anywhere else in the world. "The prospects of foreign litigants pursuing actions against the United States in foreign courts," he wrote, ". . . is minimal at best."

Zaid still felt the legislation had a good chance of passing in 1994, but in the face of opposition in Congress and from the Clinton administration, the year ended with no action. A new Congress took office in 1995, meaning the bills would have to be introduced again in each house and the process begun from scratch. But this was the first Republican Congress in a generation, and its agenda was dominated by the GOP's "Contract With America" to the exclusion of almost everything else—certainly an obscure and controversial amendment to a law most legislators had barely heard of. Zaid kept up his correspondence with Hertling, suggesting further changes in the bill, but it wasn't going to matter how good it was if it couldn't be passed. Then, far away from Washington, something happened in the spring of 1995 that had nothing to do with Pan Am 103 but profoundly affected what Gerson, Zaid, and Smith were trying to accomplish. It was another bomb explosion, in a truck outside a federal office building in Oklahoma City.

12

Oklahoma

When the Oklahoma City bomb went off, Victoria Cummock was on the phone with an official in the Department of Transportation, discussing a familiar topic, anti-terrorist measures. It was more than six years since Pan Am 103, and she was still dealing with the consequences every day. Her children had needed intensive counseling and therapy. "Ashley would tell her dolls: 'You've been a bad girl, your daddy will be taken away forever.' What am I supposed to tell her? Is she working out her feelings in a positive way? At the beach the boys would play Air Disaster with their GI Joes, dropping them from toy airplanes and burying the bodies, and the other mothers would say, *come here, darling, play over here!*" She had endured grief in all its manifestations, including the experience, common yet still shocking when it happens, of anger at her husband for his desertion, leaving her with three young children and the rest of her life to get through. This feeling was particularly strong after Hurricane Andrew. Thanks a lot, John, for leaving me with three kids in a house trailer, she thought. Not long after, she flew to Scotland for a memorial ceremony at which the family members were presented to Queen Elizabeth II. The queen, whose residence at Windsor Castle had just suffered a disastrous fire, found common ground with Cummock.

"Are you the American woman whose home was ravished by Hurricane Andrew?" she asked.

"Yes, Your Majesty," Cummock replied. "But there were many houses damaged much worse. People lost all their belongings, their photographs and memories."

"Well, I suppose that's another character-building experience, isn't it?"

The widespread assumption that tragedy is invariably ennobling never fails to surprise Cummock when she encounters it.

"With all due respect, Your Majesty, I'm trying to stay out of harm's way for a while."

Over the next couple of days the dimensions of the disaster in Oklahoma became clear: 168 people dead, including 19 children; hundreds injured or maimed. Cummock put in a call to White House aide Bruce Lindsey to offer some thoughts on how the White House ought to respond, based on her own experience of sitting by the phone for days waiting to hear from someone in the government. "It's so important to say the right things, Bruce," she told him.

A few hours later the White House called back.

"I was just in a meeting with the president," Lindsey told her. "I told him what you told me, and he would like to use it in his speech in Oklahoma City. Can you give it to me in writing?"

"I'd be happy to, but I'm about to take my kids to a soccer game, so I'll just do it when I get back, okay?"

Of course it wasn't okay.

"Can't you just dictate it to someone?" Lindsey demanded.

"Dictate it to who? Don't you understand? It's just me here!"

She found a friend to drive her sons to their game and sat down at her desk. She put her feelings of six years earlier into a two-page letter, along with what she'd hoped to hear from the government, but didn't. "As an American, I was stunned by the unspecific and general rhetoric that I heard from the White House, which left me feeling that no one shared in our grief, understood our anguish, or cared about the murder of my husband," she wrote. At a prayer service the next day at the Oklahoma State Fair Arena, Clinton spoke to a crowd of 20,000 about the grief of those who lost loved ones in the bombing.

Our words seem small beside the loss you have endured. But I found a few I wanted to share today. I've received a lot of letters in these last terrible days. One stood out because it came from a young widow and a mother of three whose own husband was murdered with over 200 other Americans when Pan Am 103 was shot down. Here is what that woman said I should say to you today:

"The anger you feel is valid, but you must not allow yourselves to be consumed by it. The hurt you feel must not be allowed to turn into hate, but instead into the search for justice. The loss you feel must not paralyze your own lives. Instead, you must try to pay tribute to your loved ones by continuing to do all the things they left undone, thus ensuring they did not die in vain."

The next day, Clinton himself called to thank Cummock for her suggestions. He asked if there was anything else he could do to help.

"How are the families doing?" she asked.

"The families?" Clinton responded in surprise. "I guess they're being taken care of."

"I want to help," Cummock said.

In Oklahoma City, as at Lockerbie, hundreds of people were waiting to learn the fates of people they loved. Actually, most already knew. There was a list of people who got on board Pan Am 103, and everyone on it was dead. Similarly, there was a list of people who were known to have been in the Murrah building and who didn't turn up alive after the bombing. After the first two days it was pretty clear that all of them were probably dead, too. Nevertheless the names had to be matched up with bodies. One of those waiting was a woman named Diane Leonard, a petite, dark-haired woman with a husband, Don, and three grown stepsons she'd helped raise from the time they were toddlers. In her job she traveled the state as a sales representative for a stationery company, but she was looking forward to the end of the year, when her husband was planning to retire. He was a Secret Service agent, and he had an office on the ninth floor of the Alfred P. Murrah Federal Building.

Leonard was in Tulsa on business on the morning of April 19, and for one reason or another she didn't hear about the bombing until the early afternoon, five hours after it happened. "I went in to see a customer," she recalls. "She looked surprised to see me and said, did you hear about the explosion? She told me the name of the building. I figured it was a minor gas explosion. I knew my husband had all kinds of training and felt he could take care of himself, so I said, let's just finish our business and then I'll go home." She was reacting just like Cummock, who was the calmest person in the house when John's boss came to tell her he had been on Pan Am 103. "But she kept insisting that I call someone. I called the Secret Service office in Oklahoma City, but there was no answer, and I called the office in Tulsa and they said, well, six of our people are missing, but we don't know which ones. Of course, they did know. I called the house, reached one of the boys and they told me Don was missing. I jumped in the car and drove home, 100 miles, it took me exactly an hour."

On the drive home she heard a newscaster say they were bringing 200 body bags to the scene. And she said out loud, Oh, God, please, not another body bag. She was thinking of her mother, who had committed suicide in her garage a few years earlier and been carried out in a body bag. When Leonard got home, she turned on the television and the first thing she saw was the building, as everyone now remembers it, half blown to pieces and on the verge of collapse, and she thought well, that doesn't look so bad, it's just the glass in front that's gone. Leonard and Cummock, two intelligent, rational women, followed precisely the same course of denial. Their husbands were big strong men; they were expected to survive. By contrast, the parents who lost children aboard Pan Am 103 seemed to grasp the worst from the very first moment. In their mind's eye they saw not strapping college students but babies, tiny and vulnerable.

Don Leonard did come out in a body bag, and when Diane asked about his condition, the Secret Service agents who were assigned to be with her around the clock from the day of the bombing until the funeral looked away and said only, "Well, his upper body was crushed." When she told the mortician she wanted to see the body, he looked stricken. "You don't want that, Mrs. Leonard," he whispered. She insisted. "I'll unzip it from the bottom," he said finally, "and you tell me when you want me to stop." Slowly the zipper made its way to the top. Leonard never looked away from the sight of this man who had loved her, crushed and mangled almost beyond recognition. She has been told since that her words were, well, at least he didn't suffer. "I'm glad I saw Don," she says calmly. "There are many families who have lost loved ones in the bombing and have suffered terribly about not having viewed the bodies. I know people are trying to spare them when they advise them not to look, but they're taking away a tiny window of time to be with their loved ones.

"I had never before seen anything like what I saw. It was painful to know my husband had suffered so much damage, but it was not repulsive. A family member sees a body through the eyes of love. It's not the same as a stranger. I did not look at my mother's body after she died and I have had many nightmares since then. But I have not had a nightmare about my husband, not once since I saw him."

About three weeks after the bombing, Leonard went to a small meeting in a church with the attorney general of Oklahoma, Drew Edmondson, and a handful of family members, mostly relatives of the Secret Service employees who had been killed. The meeting was prompted by a man she knew only vaguely, Glenn Seidl, who worked as a plumber and lived down a dirt road near Shawnee, thirty-five miles from Oklahoma City. He lived just off Waco Road, a fact that would come to seem like a grim coincidence as the motives of the accused bomber became clear. Seidl was laconic and tended to keep to himself, the last person you'd expect to organize a meeting like this, but he'd had a pretty wife named Kathy Lynn, who had worked for the Secret Service, and a sweet-faced young son named Clint, whose photograph, creased and smudged, was recovered from Kathy's desk and returned to him before the building was demolished.

Like most of the Oklahoma City relatives, Seidl had spent the weeks after the bombing in a fog of grief. But on May 1, not long after

Kathy's funeral, he saw something on the television news that touched off a burst of anger. It concerned a request for a stay of execution by one Roger Dale Stafford. The story struck Seidl because he remembered the Stafford case from more than a decade earlier. Almost everyone in Oklahoma City did; Stafford was probably the most notorious criminal in the state in the decades between Pretty Boy Floyd and Timothy McVeigh. He'd been convicted of nine murders—a husband, wife, and their twelve-year-old son who were ambushed in a roadside stickup, and six restaurant workers who'd been herded into a freezer and executed in a $1,500 robbery. What shocked Seidl was that Stafford was still alive in 1995. He'd been arrested, convicted, and sentenced to death on one set of murders in 1979, and then again in 1980. A chronology compiled by the *Daily Oklahoman* showed that his case had been up to the Supreme Court at least five times, on a wide and imaginative variety of procedural claims including ineffective counsel, unconstitutionally vague instructions to the jury, and the use of hypnosis on a witness. Under the law at the time, his lawyers were permitted to raise each of these issues in turn—first in state appellate courts and the state's supreme court and then, through the mechanism known as a habeas corpus appeal, in federal district court, federal appeals court, and the Supreme Court. In recent years the U.S. Supreme Court had begun cutting short some of the most time-consuming practices, but even so the proceedings on each individual appeal could eat up years—and then, after state officials had set a new execution date, the process would start all over again with a new claim. Along the way Stafford had been married in prison—twice, after one wife received an annulment on the grounds that he'd falsely assured her he would soon be free—and he had gained twenty-five pounds.

To Seidl, Stafford's sixteen years on death row seemed to be making a mockery of the law—"like rubbin' dirt in the families' faces," he felt. In the heat of his anger he couldn't imagine waiting that long—even worse, sitting through so many appeals—for justice to be carried out on his wife's murderer. "My biggest fear," he told a local newspaper, "is that these people that are responsible for this crime will outlive me." It was not in Seidl's ken to pick up the phone and call the White House.

Unlike the Pan Am victims, who included some prominent and wealthy citizens close to the centers of national power, the people who died in Oklahoma were mostly ordinary civil servants and their children. The closest Seidl had to a contact in the government was his sister-in-law, Wanda Fincher, who had a clerical job in Edmondson's office. He called her to ask how someone like Stafford could have evaded his sentence for so long and whether the same thing was likely to happen to the Oklahoma City bomber.

Fincher put him in touch with Richard Wintory, one of Edmondson's chief aides. Edmondson had long sought to reform the handling of death-sentence appeals in Oklahoma. The average stay on death row in the state penitentiary was twelve years, which struck many observers as a perversion of the great principle embodied in the common-law writ of habeas corpus. A bedrock of American jurisprudence, its original purpose was to provide protection against illegal imprisonment by requiring authorities to literally produce the body of a prisoner. Under the U.S. Constitution the writ could not be suspended except when "the public safety may require it" in cases of rebellion or invasion. The principle was also embodied in state laws. Over the years bills to streamline criminal appeals had been introduced, debated, and sometimes even passed in the Oklahoma legislature, but never by both houses in the same session; it seemed to the frustrated lawyers in Emondson's office that the legislators had arranged things so that each of them could cast a vote for reform in turn, without anyone ever taking responsibility for actual passage of a law.

But, Wintory explained to Seidl, the bombing of the Murrah building was a federal crime, and thus federal habeas corpus law would apply. If he were serious about the issue, he would have to lobby for reform in Washington. Perhaps a meeting with the other family members would be a way to start. He offered the help of the Oklahoma attorney general's office.

Stafford's case soon became a rallying cry for the Oklahoma City families, even after Stafford himself was executed on July 1, following a final meal of six foot-long hot dogs with chili and cheese. On his last day judges rejected several additional requests for a stay, including one

premised on the fairly desperate argument that the many postpone-
ments in his execution—which, of course, he himself had sought—
themselves constituted cruel and unusual punishment. His lawyer was
Stephen Jones, who would soon become nationally known for representing McVeigh. Of course, some of the relatives of the bombing victims were opposed to the death penalty on principle, and others might
have felt that no cost in time and money was too high to pay when a citizen's constitutional safeguards were at issue. But Stafford's never-
ending, taxpayer-funded manipulation of the rules to evade his
sentence made him, in Edmondson's words, "a poster boy for habeas
corpus reform." And if that was true of Stafford, who at bottom was
just a stickup man whose crimes had gotten out of hand, it was even
more painful to imagine that fifteen years later society would still be
trying to exact justice on someone who had deliberately slaughtered
168 strangers in an armed attack on the United States government.

Long before McVeigh's trial and sentencing, the husbands and
wives of the people he killed made up their minds they wouldn't still be
waiting for the courts to finish their business with him in 2010.
Edmondson, knowing that political power flows to those who can
command the media, realized that the national outpouring of sympathy for the families of the victims could be harnessed to achieve in
Washington the changes that had been stymied in Oklahoma City.
With the understanding that the idea originated with the family members, so he could never be accused of taking political advantage of their
tragedy, he agreed to advise them on lobbying Congress for changes in
the federal habeas corpus law. Without even incorporating as an organization, without a name or a formal leadership, they agreed to begin
meeting regularly on tactics.

And there was now a bill to lobby for. In fact, the new Republican
majority in the House had made restricting habeas corpus a priority
even before Oklahoma City. Legislation was introduced on January 30
and passed barely more than a week later. In their first few months of
power, Newt Gingrich's minions were taking no prisoners; the House
summarily voted down an amendment that would have allowed defendants to present new factual evidence that might prove their actual

innocence, as distinguished from the endless procedural appeals that had kept Stafford alive so long. The Senate, however, was less inclined to speed up the march to the death chamber, and it took no action on the House-passed bill—until McVeigh inadvertently touched off an explosion of antiterrorism legislation. Bodies were still being retrieved from the wreckage of the Murrah Building on April 24 when Sen. Orrin Hatch introduced the 25,000-word "Comprehensive Terrorism Prevention Act of 1995." It combined elements of the House bill with antiterrorism proposals made by the Clinton administration in response to the 1993 World Trade Center bombing. By requiring defendants to bundle their legal challenges rather than string them out serially, and limiting the freedom of federal judges to consider certain issues already decided in state courts, the bill was meant to "stop the frivolous appeals that are driving people nuts," Hatch explained succinctly. Other sections mandated "Enhanced Penalties for Use of Explosives or Arson," "Opposition to Assistance by International Financial Institutions to Terrorist States," and "Removal of Alien Terrorists." It appeared to Zaid that, in their haste to get a bill to the floor, Hatch's people had incorporated every "antiterrorism" measure they could find. On the first day of hearings, he showed up to see what he could learn and he ran into Michael Kraft of the State Department's counterterrorism office.

"I'll bet you're happy about this," Kraft said. Zaid had no idea what he meant until Kraft showed him a section deep inside the bill titled "Jurisdiction of United States Courts Over Acts of International Terrorism." As Zaid read it, his eyes widened: not only had the drafters expanded the FSIA exemption, they had done it in three different sections, all purporting to do the same thing—but, unfortunately, in mutually incompatible language reflecting the various versions of the amendment that had been introduced over the past eighteen months. He'd have his work cut out for him again—but from nowhere a month earlier his hopes had now been resurrected, through the unlikely intercession of Timothy McVeigh.

"You're not gonna believe this . . ." he told Gerson when he got back to the office.

* * *

Three days after her conversation with Clinton, Cummock found a teacher at her children's school who agreed to stay with Christopher, Matthew, and Ashley, and she flew off to Oklahoma City. For her to be allowed to work on the disaster-relief efforts required not just the intervention of the White House but the personal approval of the president of the Red Cross, who was, fortuitously, Bob Dole's wife, Elizabeth Dole. It was unprecedented for a volunteer whose only credential was her connection to another disaster to be allowed into the death notification center, where the families of the missing waited to hear that their bodies had been found. The work otherwise was restricted to trained disaster-relief professionals and the occasional television star, politician, or football player. According to a long *Miami Herald* profile written soon after Cummock's return to Florida, Cummock showed up the same day as the actress Kirstie Alley. "When we saw Victoria," one of the center's directors recalled, "we thought we had another Kirstie Alley. Only we weren't sure what show she was on."

Anyone coming into contact with the families was required to undergo several hours of interviews by Red Cross and law-enforcement officials, in part to weed out people whose agenda was to hand out political tracts or spiritual advice. For her part, Cummock got a very strange look from the FBI agent to whom she gave her profession as "interior decorator"—what do you plan to do, he responded, redecorate the Murrah building? The interviewers asked Cummock what she planned to say to the families. "I will tell them," Cummock said, "the waiting is the worst part. If someone is alive and in the hospital, you know what to do, if they're dead you know what to do, but sitting and waiting is unbearable. Everyone around you is saying, this is day seven, wake up, but when you're in shock, day one and day seven are the same." One of her distinctive contributions was to expunge euphemisms from the discussions with family members. She was the first person to use the word "murder," instead of "incident" or even "tragedy." "We had 350 mental-health professionals, and Victoria taught us all something," the director of the center told the *Herald*.

Cummock describes disaster-relief work as the hardest thing she's ever had to do in her life, apart from telling her own children about John. To any of the family members who asked, she described her own experiences as "a million minutes of pain." Nothing but the minute of acute pain and the anguish that the next minute would be the same way." She met a man whose mother had died in the bombing, and who wanted to be the first one to sue. "He wanted to sue everyone," she says. "He asked about us and I had to explain, we don't even have our suspects yet . . . and he was incredulous." She stayed in Oklahoma City just short of two weeks. Back in Miami, she thought there was more she could do. She would, she told friends, begin writing and speaking on how to help families cope with mass disasters. Overhead, although she didn't give it a thought at the time, a start-up airline called ValuJet was flying in and out of Miami International Airport, on routes that took it over the Everglades just a few miles from her home.

Meanwhile, in Washington, the anti-terrorism bill was quickly engulfed by the ferocious partisanship that had come to characterize the politics of the mid-1990s. The Democrats in the Senate by themselves introduced sixty-seven amendments, the Republicans nearly half that number, as both sides maneuvered to shape the bill and to take credit for getting it passed while escaping blame for the delays. Sen. Dianne Feinstein of California put in an amendment promoting the use of chemical tracers in explosives, to help authorities track their sales; it passed only after the Republicans insisted on excluding black powder, which was the explosive most commonly used in homemade bombs. (Another amendment, in time-honored congressional fashion, renamed a building on Ellsworth Air Force base in South Dakota; if Congress were to pass a resolution hailing the Second Coming, it would likely have in it somewhere a $50,000 appropriation to fix a bridge in West Virginia.) To help break the deadlock, Hatch called a press conference and flew in a number of injured victims and family members from Oklahoma City, including Diane Leonard. "We cannot allow anyone to commit a crime of this magnitude and make a mockery of our criminal justice system by remaining on death row for so many years," she said.

On June 7, the bill—by now up to 30,000 words—passed on a vote of ninety-one to eight. The final version showed Zaid's fine hand at work in the section on foreign immunity. The language in the earlier bill about "exhaust[ing] adequate and available remedies" in foreign courts was gone. "It couldn't have even passed the smell test," Zaid says disdainfully; "you're going to tell someone, yes, you can sue Iran, but first you have to go over there and sue in their courts?" It did retain a companion provision requiring that "the claimant must first afford the foreign state a reasonable opportunity to arbitrate the claim in accordance with accepted international rules of arbitration," but Gerson and Zaid didn't think that would have much practical effect on them. Why would Kaddafi submit to arbitration over a murder he insists he didn't commit? The requirement in the earlier version that the victim had to be an American, which would have excluded Smith because his wife was English, was now cleverly worded to require that "the individual bringing the claim" had to be an American—in other words, Smith himself.

The bill also contained a significant concession to the State Department in exchange for their agreement to drop their opposition to its passage. In the new version, exceptions to sovereign immunity now covered only the foreign states "designated as a state sponsor of terrorism." There were seven at the time: Iran, Iraq, Libya, Cuba, Sudan, North Korea, and Syria. Zaid and Gerson accepted this change with the greatest reluctance. As international lawyers with a concern for human rights, they preferred giving the bill the broadest possible coverage; was the life of an American citizen any less valuable if he happened to be a victim of terrorism sponsored by a state not on the list? And when their ally, Garment, found out about it, he gave a bellow of outrage that could have been heard in Riyadh; if the law passed in that form it would have rendered the whole exercise useless for his client, Nelson. Garment argued that the terrorism list was a crude device for determining jurisdiction. Accountability for terror should flow from the act itself, not membership on a list, which was, ultimately, a product of politics, not jurisprudence.

In fact, Gerson tended to agree with him. And this was not just an abstract issue; Gerson quickly perceived that there were constitutional problems with the State Department's approach. A clever lawyer could argue that it took away from the judicial branch of government what lay within its sole domain—the determination of factual questions with legal consequences—and turned it over to the State Department, an arm of the executive branch. Presumably Libya's lawyers would be able to figure this out as well. It galled him to think of Libya cloaking itself in the protections of the U.S. Constitution—on an issue as fundamental as the separation of powers, no less—especially since it might mean that even after changing the law, he would have to fight to establish that the jurisdiction it purportedly granted was legal under the Constitution.

On the other hand, as Gerson and Zaid were well aware, this change would vastly improve the chances of getting the FSIA amendment passed for the benefit of their client. "Obviously," Zaid had written to a Senate staffer in May, "the more narrow an FSIA exception is the more likely it will pass." The change would mollify not just the State Department but other countries as well, including some, such as Israel, which were potent forces themselves in Congress. The politics of it dictated the decision, reluctantly, to jettison Garment. If the bill was going to pass at all, they concluded, it would be in the form acceptable to the State Department, and that's what they would concentrate on. And as Zaid read the *Washington Post* story about the passage of the Senate bill, he was relieved to see that it made no mention whatsoever about sovereign immunity or suing foreign governments. The less attention this got, he thought, the better.

The *Post* also reported that the House would begin work on a similar bill the following week, sponsored by Rep. Henry Hyde, the powerful Judiciary Committee chairman, "virtually ensuring enactment . . . probably this summer." The news was not lost on the Pan Am families. Cummock had already expressed interest in joining the Smith case once she settled with Pan Am. In June, Gerson asked Frank Duggan whether he thought the family members would support a suit against Libya. George Williams—at that time president of Victims of Pan Am 103—polled the members of his board. A year earlier, when *Smith* first came up as a potential class action, the victims group had opposed the idea, but now, Duggan reported back to Gerson, the board was unanimously in favor, even if they hadn't yet begun to think in concrete terms about how much money they would seek. There were some—notably Dan and Susan Cohen—who would fight the idea almost to the end, although even they eventually, with great reluctance, joined in the suit. "Since the majority will still consider monetary compensation 'blood money,'" Duggan wrote, "the award must be punitive as well as compensatory and be large enough to discourage any government from ever contemplating support for another terrorist act. The families have not made their political effort for money, rather they have made it for justice and to leave some legacy in the names of their lost loved ones."

But the assumption that the bill would pass the House as quickly as it had the Senate was wrong. Despite Hyde's backing, the bill ran into trouble from both sides of the political spectrum. Liberals opposed measures to speed up the death penalty, while the right wing of Hyde's own party rebelled over the bill's antiterrorism provisions, including enhanced wiretap authority for the FBI and restrictions on armor-piercing ammunition. In a development that would have surprised anyone old enough to remember the 1970s, it was conservatives, led by Gingrich's Georgia protégé Rep. Bob Barr, who fought the expansion of police power by the federal government. They were encouraged by a fierce lobbying campaign under the direction of the National Rifle Association. Their suspicions ran so deep they managed to eliminate a provision that would have permitted the Army to conduct law-enforcement operations against terrorists armed with nuclear weapons.

In early November the families gathered again at Arlington to dedicate the now-completed cairn. Clinton spoke again, but the story in *Congressional Quarterly* called the event a "dubious milestone" in the struggle against terrorism. "It is clear," *CQ* wrote, "that the Pan Am tragedy has lost some of its political resonance . . . Libya has barely earned a mention in the GOP-backed foreign-policy bills making their way through Congress." Lowenstein, Ammerman, and a handful of other family members skipped the dedication, meeting instead with

Attorney General Janet Reno. On the assumption, which appeared reasonable at the time, that there would never be a criminal trial of the suspects, they tried to convince her to release the evidence against Megrahi and Fhimah, to put it on the public record. "She didn't want to hear about releasing the evidence," Lowenstein says. "It was a very cold meeting." Finally, after much arduous compromise with his rebellious freshmen, Hyde scheduled a vote for the week of December 18. But when whips reported that nearly 100 Republicans were still opposed or undecided, he pulled the bill, acknowledging that "the votes aren't there."

A few weeks earlier, however, a meeting had taken place that would change the political calculus—a meeting between the two widows, Diane Leonard and Victoria Cummock. They hadn't met when Cummock went to Oklahoma City, because as a law-enforcement family member Leonard didn't have to go to the family center; she was cared for by two agents in her own home. In November, the law-enforcement families were flown to Miami for a celebrity party to raise money for a scholarship fund. "They were arriving the day before Thanksgiving, and nobody wanted to have Thanksgiving dinner in the hotel," Cummock says. "So I invited them all to my house, with their escorts. I had 143 people for Thanksgiving on less than twenty-four hours' notice. I didn't even know how many turkeys you need for 143 people. I called up seven friends and had them each make an extra turkey." Glenn Seidl came with his son, Clint. He and Leonard were talking about the discouraging news out of Washington when Leonard's eye fell on Cummock's souvenirs, including photographs of herself with Dole, Bush, and Clinton. "Come here and look at this," Leonard said. "We ought to talk to her about what we're doing."

That marked the beginning of an informal alliance among those whose lives had been touched by these two immense crimes—between Leonard, Seidl, and their allies in Oklahoma, who wanted to see McVeigh die, and Cummock, Bruce Smith, and the others who wanted to make Libya pay. In the winter of 1996 about a dozen Oklahoma City family members made a lobbying trip to Washington. Cummock joined them and hosted a dinner at the Hay-Adams, one of the capital's most impressively wainscoted and upholstered power-dining settings. "That was Vickie, cleverly cementing relations with the Oklahoma families so they could join forces in lobbying," says Gerald Adams, one of Edmondson's aides. "It was pretty impressive, especially for some of these people who had never been to Washington before, who might never have flown on an airplane before." Cummock "held it all together," he says. "She, and Diane Leonard. But Vickie had a long view of the legislative process. She saw early on how her interest could be merged with those of the Oklahoma City families. She's this beautiful, wealthy, sophisticated woman and as sincere as anyone they'd ever known in their lives." Over the coming months Cummock and Leonard would speak frequently, sharing notes about their lobbying efforts for the stalled House bill. They had "a common experience of grief and loss," says Adams. "But the Pan Am families were way ahead of us in terms of lobbying. They really knew what they were doing."

An accident of politics had thrown them together. The two issues they cared about were linked only because they happened to be part of the same "counter-terrorism" bill. In fact, habeas corpus reform was more properly considered an anticrime measure; there was only one McVeigh, but hundreds, or thousands, of ordinary state prisoners whose appeals would be curtailed under the bill. Besides, terrorists are generally prepared to die for their cause—as McVeigh himself was, at least until the FBI's bungling gave him a second opportunity to embarrass the government by seeking a stay just before his first scheduled execution date. Leonard, Seidl, and their allies took pains to say they were fighting not just for themselves but on behalf of all victims of violent crime, and so they were. Ironically they began their involvement by seeking to speed the execution of someone who was ready to die anyway.

Moreover, the two groups were vastly different in their political outlook. The Pan Am 103 families felt betrayed by the system, by giant corporations, bureaucrats, and politicians. The Oklahoma City families mostly just blamed McVeigh. In the wake of the bombing there were plenty of lawyers eager to sue the government, which, after all, had arguably failed to provide adequate security at the Murrah building, but they didn't find many takers. "The view of the people that we dealt with," says Edmondson, "was that there had already been an attack on the government. A lawsuit would just be another attack. A woman who was injured in the bombing stood up at a meeting in which the 'government' was denounced and said, 'The government? Who is the government? I'm the government.'"

Finally, in late winter of 1996, the House took up the measure again, after Barr won additional concessions, further weakening the federal law-enforcement provisions the administration had sought. Hyde called a Capitol Hill press conference to rally support for the bill, highlighting its remaining counter-terrorism provisions, in particular the FSIA amendments. He was supported by victims sure to generate sympathy and support. Some of them were likely to benefit from the changes, including the Pan Am 103 families; the Beirut hostages, Cicippio and Jacobsen, who had been held captive by Iranian-backed guerrillas; and a New Jersey man named Stephen Flatow, whose daughter had been killed in Gaza by terrorists also linked to Iran. Others had no direct stake in changing the FSIA, but came anyway: the daughter of Leon Klinghoffer, the American Jew killed in the *Achille Lauro* hijacking, whose efforts to hold the PLO accountable in U.S. courts had failed, and Hans Ephraimson, the leader of the dwindling group of family members of the passengers aboard KAL 007, a tragedy by then thirteen years in the past, who could expect no relief from the new bill because Russia certainly wouldn't be included on the State Department's list. But by far the largest and most potent political presence there that day was that of the Oklahoma City families and the Oklahoma attorney general and his aides, whose concerns had nothing to do with the FSIA or foreign terrorism at all. The bond that Cummock had forged with the Oklahomans—with her own toil and tears during those two dreadful weeks at the family center, and then with the money and effort she devoted to helping them lobby for their cause—was now being repaid.

Gerson and Zaid sat back and watched it unfold, concerned mainly to keep the changes regarding sovereign immunity intact. But even as the bill moved toward passage—congressional leaders had set an informal deadline of April 19, 1996, one year after the Oklahoma City bombing—some in the administration were still fighting a rear-guard action against the FSIA amendments. One day in March the family leaders were summoned to the office of Randy Beers, a former U.S. Marine officer who was the senior National Security Council official dealing directly with Pan Am 103 matters. Beers offered them a deal: drop their support for the FSIA amendments, and the administration would in effect pay them off, out of funds derived from Libyan assets frozen back in the Reagan administration. Not long before, Clinton had offered to do something similar for the families of four Cuban Americans from the organization Brothers to the Rescue, whose small planes had been shot down by Cuban MIGs while patrolling the Gulf of Mexico for boat people fleeing Castro. In that case, though, there were no strings attached to the offer. Here, the families would have to give up something they badly wanted in exchange for a promise of a payment of uncertain size. It was a promise, moreover, which the administration might not even be able to keep. To distribute the blocked assets would require legislation, and there were other claimants for that money, chiefly businesses, who might oppose a plan to jump the families to the head of the line. Meanwhile, if the families backed down on lobbying for an FSIA amendment, it wouldn't pass, and the families' chance of suing Libya would likely be lost forever. Even for the families who could very much have used the money, it was a bad deal, and Beers himself knew it. He was carrying out a mission. George Williams, a U.S. Marine veteran himself, was disgusted. "I couldn't believe another Marine would do that to us," he said later.

As April 19 approached, the Capitol went into a frenzy of work to iron out the many differences between the House and Senate versions of the bill, now known as the Anti-Terrorism and Effective Death Penalty Act. Garment had managed to get the House bill worded in a way that would have allowed Nelson to sue Saudi Arabia, but the Senate had retained the language that limited sovereign immunity exceptions to the states on the terrorism list—and as Gerson and Zaid had foreseen, the State Department saw to it that the Senate language prevailed. The conference report was adopted on April 19, and the bill signing was set for five days later, April 24, exactly one year after the bill was first introduced. Most of the provisions the administration had originally sought had been stripped from the law, but Clinton was going to sign it anyway. As the conference was finishing its work, Zaid got a call from Randy Scheunemann, Dole's top foreign-policy aide. Dole still was looking out for the Pan Am families, and Scheunemann had been keeping an eye on the FSIA amendments, which otherwise had been almost totally overlooked in the media and in the contentious, emotional floor debates over the death penalty and civil liberties. Scheunemann was calling to tell Zaid that something had been added to the bill in conference, apparently by a staffer. That in itself was not that unusual; staffers did it all the time, usually over minor adjustments or changes in language. The addition was a paragraph headed "Limitation on Discovery," and it read in part,

> . . . the court, upon request of the Attorney General, shall stay any request, demand or order for discovery that the Attorney General certifies will interfere with a criminal investigation or prosecution, or a national security operation, related to the incident that gave rise to the cause of the action, until such time as the Attorney General advises the court that such request, demand or order will no longer so interfere.

The administration had struck again! This time it was the Department of Justice, rather than State, but working to the same end of subverting the FSIA changes, taking away with one hand what the other had granted. For three years the idea had been making its way through Congress; it had been amended, deleted, restored, and rewritten countless times and now, at last, was approaching the president's desk—and it all could be destroyed in fifteen minutes by a staffer who presumably thought he was making a minor, technical change at the behest of the attorney general. Zaid saw instantly that the provision would make the whole exercise meaningless. Pretrial discovery—the process of subpoenaing documents and questioning witnesses under oath—is the food and drink of a lawsuit; stop it and the case dies. If the bill passed in this form, the attorney general could shut it down, at his own discretion, essentially forever. "They wanted to control the process," Scheunemann said later. "So they would go around and construct the most extreme case imaginable, like we're trying to rescue Iranian Jews and this is going to screw that up, and people would say, yes, you've got a point . . . only, if they're against the whole thing from the start, how can you trust them to honestly apply a waiver provision?"

"If we can't change it," Zaid told him, "then let's kill the whole thing. It's worthless. We'll come back and fight another day."

"I'll do what I can," Scheunemann replied, "but I need substitute language. Get back to me by the middle of the afternoon. That's all the time I can give you."

Zaid spoke to Gerson, and they put out emergency calls to the family members to alert them to the danger. But the matter was beyond the reach of lobbying now; no ordinary member could stop the bill once it was headed to the president's desk. Zaid faxed a letter to Hyde's aide, Patrick Murray, alerting him to the problem, and then sat down to work out a substitute to the Justice Department provision. He wanted it to read as much like the Justice Department's amendment as possible, to raise the fewest alarm bells. He began by inserting the word "significantly" before "interfere," so as to raise the burden on the attorney general and then, in a masterstroke of drafting, inserted the phrase "on the United States" after "request, demand, or order for discovery." That entitled the government to withhold information in their own possession, but not to stop discovery against third parties, such as witnesses in Malta or Germany. The government can always refuse to answer a subpoena by citing national security, so Zaid considered that a meaningless concession. Then he added a paragraph requiring the Justice Department to renew its request for a stay after a year, and a "sunset" provision, which automatically voided any stay (subject to certain conditions) after ten years from the time of the incident. Scheunemann took what Zaid had done and ran it by the conference committee— actually, just the most senior members of both parties. He told the other staffers: "Justice doesn't have to know about this. They had their chance to be upfront, and they blew it." He could control the Republican side, he felt, but he was worried about the Democrats; the administration was a Democratic one, after all. Kennedy's aide, Trina Vargo, had given him his word, but he worried anyway.

It was, in fact, too late to alter the conference report itself, so the matter was kept under wraps, until the morning of April 24, when the bill was actually to go to the president to be signed. Just before noon, Hatch, acting on behalf of the Senate leadership, unveiled an obscure legislative maneuver known as an enrolling resolution, typically used to make last-minute technical corrections in a bill. It was passed without amendment or debate, by voice vote in the Senate, and a few minutes later, by unanimous consent in the House.

The families of the victims of various tragedies that inspired the bill had already been summoned to Washington for the signing ceremony set for the White House lawn. Along with others from Oklahoma, Seidl and Leonard were there, and Cummock had flown up with her children. Someone in the administration, had, however, one last humiliation in store for the obstreperous Mrs. Cummock. She was in Dole's office, thanking him for all his help over the years, when she got a call informing her that there was no room for Christopher, Matthew, and Ashley at the bill signing.

"How can that be?" she asked. "It's out of doors."

"Well," the functionary on the other end of the phone informed her, "there aren't enough chairs for everyone."

"They can stand," Cummock replied tartly. She was deeply distressed; her children had been part of her efforts from the very beginning, had put up with her absences and the nights she put in on the telephone and the computer; she even credits Ashley with having encouraged her to go to Oklahoma City to reassure the families there that "they'll be all right, just as we were." And whoever had made this decision probably knew that Cummock wouldn't go without her kids anyway.

"You'll get in," Dole assured her.

"With all due respect, Senator, you're not president yet," she replied.

Even as they spoke, the Senate was preparing the enrolling resolution.

At the White House gate that afternoon, Cummock arrived, with her children, in a press of family members all brandishing tickets. Cummock had no tickets. She spotted Adams of Edmondson's office. The attorney general had been given extra tickets to hand out. "Here," Adams said. "Take four."

On the South Lawn, Cummock stood beside Dole as Clinton signed the bill. There had been so many brushes with disaster along the way that she could hardly believe the administration hadn't somehow double-crossed them again.

"What's he signing?" she whispered to Dole.

"Don't worry," the majority leader replied. "We took care of it this morning."

Bruce Smith also was left off the list for tickets, and he watched the ceremony from outside the gate.

"I didn't mind it all that much," he said later. "I figured we had beaten Slick Willie and he was signing the surrender document and that's what mattered."

The next day's *New York Times* quoted Clinton:

Your endurance and your courage is a lesson to us all. Your vigilance has sharpened our vigilance. Today we renew our fight against those who seek to terrorize us in your names. We send a loud, clear message today all over the world, in your names: America will never surrender to terror."

The story referred to the bill's "new tools for Federal law-enforcement officials to use in fighting terrorism" and to restrictions on appeals by prisoners. It did not mention the FSIA, sovereign immunity, or Libya.

After the bill signing, Cummock arranged, and paid for herself, a reception at the Ritz Carlton Hotel on Sixteenth Street, just two blocks down from Lafayette Park and the White House. The invited guests included all the families from Oklahoma and the attorney general's staff who had been lobbying in Washington, Gerson and Zaid, and the members of Congress and their aides who had helped bring the bill to passage. Randy Beers was also there. None of the other Pan Am family members attended. It was a glorious spring day, and people spilled over through the high French doors into the adjoining garden area chatting happily, drinking champagne, toasting their achievement. They could have been a wedding party, if someone walking down the street chanced to catch a glance at them—anything but the victims of the two greatest crimes against American citizens of the century. Then they went back to their hotel rooms for the night, and climbed into their beds, the wives without husbands, the parents bereft of children, and stared into the darkness and hoped not to dream.

Less than three weeks later, Cummock was at the beach with her children when she got a message on her pager. A ValuJet DC-9 had crashed in the Everglades, killing all 109 passengers and crew. A family center was being organized, and she was being asked to volunteer.

There would, she realized, be no end of widows in the world.

13

Sovereign Immunity Suspended

With the passage of the antiterrorism bill, Gerson and his colleagues could have chosen to drop the existing case of *Smith v. Libya* and file a fresh case under the new law. The amendment, after all, had been drafted specifically to give the courts jurisdiction over the Pan Am 103 bombing, which in theory should have made winning the equivalent of a six-inch putt. On the other hand, there was no compelling reason to do so right then. They had appealed Judge Platt's 1995 decision in Libya's favor to the U.S. Second Circuit Court of Appeals, and the appeal was pending—so why drop a case that they might still win? A win at the appeals court would have vindicated their strategy and rewarded all the work they had put into the case. And from the standpoint of trying to break new ground in human-rights law, it would have been preferable by far to win the original case than a new one brought under the provisions of the 1996 amendment. If the judges accepted their *jus cogens* argument—that egregious acts of terrorism amounted to an implied waiver of sovereign immunity by Libya—it could have set a precedent allowing Americans to sue even if they had the misfortune to be attacked by terrorists who weren't associated with one of the countries on the State Department list.

The other reason to keep the original case going was that they might, in a crowning irony, actually lose under the new law they had worked so hard to pass. The constitutional problems Gerson had identified with the 1996 amendment were still weighing on his mind. If Gerson were representing Libya, the first thing he would say is that the law took a basic prerogative of the judicial branch—determining its own jurisdiction in light of the facts—and turned it over to the executive branch, which compiled the list of state sponsors of terrorism. Libya's lawyers, if they thought of it, would undoubtedly do the same.

"And you know what?" he told Zaid. "They could be right."

He also foresaw a second, narrower line of attack on constitutional grounds, concerning the use of a law passed in 1996 to sue over something that happened in 1988. This was not a problem with the drafting of the amendment itself. The constitutional protection against retroactive application of legislation applied to criminal matters, not civil suits. But, as they had said over and over, the whole point of suing Libya was to punish it. Strictly speaking they were not asking for "punitive" damages, which were not allowed under the FSIA, but the amounts they were seeking were intended to have that effect anyway. With some plausibility, Libya could assert that it was unconstitutional to impose what amounted to a criminal penalty under an *ex post facto* use of the law.

Finally, if they surmounted those hurdles, they might face yet one more problem with the 1996 law. Once the giddy aftermath of the signing was past, the Sonnenschein lawyers looked at what had been wrought and discovered, to their mounting horror, that it might not actually cover Bruce Smith at all. The problem was in the section about citizenship requirements. Congress had not intended to permit anyone anywhere in the world to sue in U.S. courts, although certainly some human-rights lawyers would have been happy to see that happen. The earliest drafts of the Senate bill had required the victim to be an American citizen, which would have excluded Smith, whose wife had been English. Zaid had succeeded in changing that in a later version so that only the person bringing the claim (i.e., Smith himself) had to be

American. But in the crush of last-minute tinkering, someone had evidently raised a concern about the mirror-image situation, in which an American was killed but the suit was brought by his or her foreign-national spouse. In order to protect them, the wording was changed to cover that scenario as well. To be consistent with the rest of the passage, it was necessary to specify the conditions under which jurisdiction would *not* apply:

> "[t]he court shall decline to hear a claim under this paragraph," it now read, ". . . [if] the claimant or victim was not a national of the United States . . ."

Clear enough? It seems impossible that such simple words could possibly lend themselves to more than one reading. But the pitfalls that lurk in double negatives have trapped even greater legal minds than those at work in the U.S. Congress. As Gerson, Rosenthal, and Zaid read it, it seemed like one of those trick drawings that keep flipping between two women and a vase. Did it mean what the drafters had surely intended, that a suit could be brought if *either* the victim or claimant was an American? Or could the courts construe it to mean that *both* the victim and claimant had to be American? In which case, having come so far, *Smith*—the case, not the man—might be fated, like Moses, to die just short of the Promised Land.

Smith, the man, was characteristically fatalistic when Gerson explained why they might actually need another amendment to the law. "They told me they were working on it," he recalls. "I said, yeah, it would be nice if you could get it changed. In the big picture, it wasn't that important, I might not get anything out of it but everybody else could sue the Libyans and that's what I wanted. I obviously could use the money because I spent all my retirement money. But the point was to demonstrate that it's possible for individuals to do something about these terrorists. That's why State and Justice had such a fit."

These arguments for keeping *Smith* alive in the original form did not, of course, preclude Gerson from suing under the new law on behalf of another plaintiff. On May 3, 1996, therefore, less than two weeks after the president signed the antiterrorism bill, Gerson filed a complaint against Libya in the District of Columbia on behalf of Victoria Cummock, citing the new law as the basis for jurisdiction. Unfortunately, Kreindler beat him to it. After vehemently opposing a suit against Libya when Gerson first broached it, and having done nothing to help pass the amendment, he now decided to take advantage of the change in the legal climate. On April 29, four days before *Cummock* was filed, he brought his own suit, in the Eastern District of New York, in the name of his original plaintiff in the Pan Am case. The first case under the law Gerson and Zaid had helped draft and fought so long and hard for would, to their chagrin, go down in history not in the name of Smith but as *Rein et. al. v. Socialist People's Libyan Arab Jamahiriya.*

At least they had reason to be hopeful about their appeal on *Smith*—much more so than they had been about their chances in the Eastern District with Judge Platt. Only a very self-assured district-court judge—like Sporkin, who never shrank from a challenge—would have undertaken to redefine from the bench such a fundamental concept in international law as sovereign immunity. But Appeals Court judges are supposed to have the time and freedom to take on just such a sweeping intellectual exercise. The Smith team believed in their case, in the cogency of their briefs and the innate reasonableness of their arguments. And they had confidence in their own legal skills: Gerson with his years of experience with the Justice Department's appellate litigation unit; Rosenthal with his formidable grasp of international law and the resources of Sonnenschein to call upon; Russell with his powerful litigating skills, honed by the chastening experience of being caught off guard by Platt's insistent questioning about Hiroshima. Zaid, who had been steeped in the case virtually since leaving law school, brought an intensity and depth of conviction to the cause that the older lawyers could only marvel at. And they had even more lawyers helping them. The cover page of their brief listed Douglas Rutzen, who had been a brilliant junior lawyer at Coudert Brothers back when Rosenthal first became involved with the case, and who had continued to work on it even after he joined the International Center for Not-for-Profit Law, helping fledgling democracies draft their new legal codes; Richard Emery, a leading civil-liberties lawyer who was representing Paul Hudson; and Michael Reisman, the Yale scholar who was one of the world's leading academic authorities on international law.

Their brief ran to forty-six pages. It was detailed in its logic and passionate in its writing. Sonnenschein's indefatigable associates had researched every possible case that could bear on the matter, going back to the earliest days of the Republic, when the main issues arising between sovereign nations had to do with ships at sea. The very names of the cases made for a kind of legal poetry: *The Neriede (1815)*, *Murray v. The Schooner Charming Betsy (1804)*, *Monaco v. Mississippi (1934)*, and the obscure but evocative *Kalamazoo Extraction v. Provisional Military Gov't of Socialist Ethiopia (1984)*.

The argument recapitulated the four main points of their case:

- That Libya had implicitly waived sovereign immunity by engaging in "non-sovereign conduct"—that is, a violation of *jus cogens* norms.

- That Libya had explicitly waived immunity by guaranteeing to pay a judgment against Fhimah and Megrahi.

- That sovereign immunity did not apply because the bombing took place on American territory, i.e., an American-flag airliner.

- That the UN Security Council resolutions calling on Libya to make restitution trumped any claim of sovereign immunity. (Technically, that America's participation in the UN Charter, which gave the resolutions force, constituted a "prior international commitment.")

The oral argument, in late March, was one of the very first federal appeals court arguments to be broadcast by Court TV. One of the commentators was Yale law professor Harold Koh, a future assistant secretary of state for human rights. Koh seemed markedly sympathetic to Smith's arguments. Russell himself performed "brilliantly," in Reisman's view, and the questioning—which often gives the best indication of how the judges are thinking—left them feeling confident of their chances. Russell again devoted most of his time to *jus cogens*. He was closely questioned by Chief Judge Jon O. Newman about the meaning of a waiver "by implication," the phrase Congress used in drafting the FSIA in 1976, and left irritatingly undefined:

> "Do you mean that this statute subjects a state to liability in a United States court, whether or not the state intended that it should be subjected to suit?"
>
> "I think the answer is yes, Your Honor."

The argument kept circling back to the word "waiver," which generally refers to a voluntary surrender of a right or claim. As an example, a defendant may waive his right to a jury trial, usually because he thinks he has a better chance before a judge. Pan Am's insurance company had waived its claim to any money Bruce Smith might subsequently recover in another lawsuit, because Smith insisted on it. Those were intentional waivers; the question was whether a waiver "by implication" could be involuntary.

Both sides conceded the obvious: that Libya did not consciously, subjectively intend to be sued in the United States. Bartels, arguing on behalf of Libya, made the obvious point that if Libya really did blow up the airplane—which of course it denied—then "the last place Libya would want to be sued is the United States." But to put it that way just calls attention to the fact that no country would voluntarily give up one of its most important and cherished sovereign prerogatives. If that was the meaning of "implied waiver," then it referred to a situation unlikely ever to arise in this world. Surely Congress must have meant something else by the phrase.

This was a perplexing issue for the judges. In April, Newman and his colleagues on the three-judge panel decided to ask for guidance from the government. On their own initiative, they took the unusual step of writing to the attorney general, requesting "the views of the United States with respect to this appeal." That turned out to be a disaster for Smith. In an *amicus curiae* brief filed on June 12, the Justice and State Departments set forth their views, which were the ones they'd held all along: that the *jus cogens* argument was not supported by the law, and furthermore was a prescription for trouble in American foreign relations. "[G]iven that no state heretofore has recognized such an exception to sovereign immunity, plaintiffs' theory requires the untenable premise that there can be an international law principle that no state supports," they wrote. Citing the majority opinion in *Princz*, in which the Court of Appeals upheld immunity for Germany against an American Holocaust suvivor, the State Department underscored the "strong policy considerations for not expanding jurisdiction of the American courts over foreign governments":

> We think something more nearly express is wanted before we impute to the Congress an intention that the federal courts assume jurisdiction over the countless human rights cases that might well be brought by the victims of all the ruthless military juntas, presidents-for-life, and murderous dictators of the world, from Idi Amin to Mao Zedong. Such an expansive reading . . . would likely place an enormous strain not only upon our courts but . . . upon our country's diplomatic relations with any number of foreign nations. In many if not most cases the outlaw regime would no longer even be in power and our Government would have normal relations with the government of the day — unless disrupted by the courts, that is.

And, in what Gerson considered the cruelest blow of all, the government brief called the court's attention to the recently enacted FSIA amendment: "Unlike the plaintiffs' far-reaching theory of an implied waiver, however, the recent amendments reflect a considered decision to create a limited exception to sovereign immunity under U.S. law. In so doing, Congress specifically rejected a proposal for a more expansive exception to immunity." The government lawyers modestly avoided calling attention to the fact that this choice was forced on Congress in the first place by the administration's opposition to a broader law. The point of the argument was to assure the judges that the families would still have their day in court, so they could skirt the minefield of creating what amounted to new law from the bench. "Many of the plaintiffs," the brief pointed out, "have already sought to reap the benefit of the new amendment."

Gerson felt that the circle had now closed on him: the very FSIA amendment he had fought for was being cited against him. He knew well the constitutional arguments against the amendment, and he suspected that the State Department's lawyers knew them, too. The government was telling the court that they could rule against Smith with a clear conscience because he could sue anyway under the new law. The obvious reply would have been: yes, but the 1996 law was untested and might not stand up to constitutional scrutiny. But he couldn't attack the law he had helped to pass! Not merely as a matter of principle, but because he would have to defend it himself sooner or later, possibly in front of the very same court. If the *Smith* appeal failed, he would be right back in court suing Libya under the revised FSIA. And now he had Cummock and hoped to sign up other clients as well. To attack the law would be to hand Libya's lawyers a roadmap to their defense. That was his dilemma. In his darker moments he wondered, was it just a coincidence that the State Department had insisted on drawing the amendment in a way that left it vulnerable to constitutional challenge?

It took until the end of November for the Court of Appeals to reach its decision. The opinion briskly addressed, and in turn dismissed, each of the four points raised by the Smith team. Looking back to the legislative history of the FSIA, the judges concluded that an "implied waiver" of sovereign immunity was meant to be construed narrowly:

> The appellants vigorously argue that Congress would not have wanted to condone, by insulating from legal redress, such outrageous violations of *jus cogens* as the bombing of a passenger aircraft. The emotional power of that argument is not persuasive for at least two reasons. . . . Congress might well have expected the response to such violations to come from the political branches of the Government, which are not powerless to penalize a foreign state for inter-

national terrorism. Second, when Congress recently amended the FSIA to remove the sovereign immunity of foreign states as a defense to acts of international terrorism, it enacted a carefully crafted provision that abolishes the defense only in precisely defined circumstances. . . .

In the effort to empower individuals to seek redress against outlaw governments, the court—widely considered the most influential in the nation after the Supreme Court and the District of Columbia Court of Appeals—declined to lend a hand. Satisfied that Congress had assured that Smith would eventually get his day in court, the court felt no obligation now to decide the case his way.

The next day, November 27, 1996, Gerson, Rosenthal, and Zaid issued a press release expressing disappointment with the verdict. They pointed out that the same court had allowed a civil suit to proceed against an *individual* charged with war crimes, in a case (*Kadic v. Karadzic*) involving allegations of war crimes in Bosnia. Newman's opinion cited that very case. It was apparent, they said, that to hold accountable individuals who perpetrate terrorism, but not the state sponsors, made no sense in the battle against international terrorism.

The only appeal left was to the Supreme Court. Even to get the Supreme Court to hear the case—almost any case, for that matter—was a long shot, especially after losing twice already. But if they were going to preserve Smith's right to confront the Libyans in court, at some date receding ever further into the future, they had no choice. There was a new Sonnenschein partner on the case, a very smart and prodigiously hard-working former federal prosecutor named Carol Elder Bruce—the same Carol Bruce who, years earlier, had interrogated Gerson over his dealings with Meese's friend, e robert wallach, and the ill-fated Iraqi pipeline project. Bruce had made her reputation in high-visibility federal cases, including the prosecution of two former CIA employees for conspiring to ship explosives to a terrorist camp in Libya. She had joined Sonnenschein's Washington office in late 1995 to head up its white-collar criminal practice, but she was also drawn to the

Smith case and asked to be assigned to it shortly before the Circuit Court argument. While Russell and others were preparing for the oral argument, Bruce eagerly plunged into its legal and factual complexities.

As they all knew, the 1996 law had been less than elegantly drafted, and depending on how the courts read it might prevent Smith from suing because his wife was English. This was a problem that affected not just Smith, but at least two other American family members, plus an unknown number of foreign relatives of Americans who were killed. So the law would have to be amended yet again—but even that might not rescue Smith! The man had a positive gift for being an exception! Bruce called attention to a well-established doctrine that a lawsuit which has been disposed of in the courts cannot be revived by an act of Congress. They couldn't drop their appeal now, but on the other hand if they pursued it to the Supreme Court and lost there, they might be foreclosed forever from refiling a complaint on the same set of facts—unless, *before that happened,* they managed to get a new amendment drafted, introduced, passed, and signed into law.

So back they went to Congress. Rutzen, working closely with Hyde's Judiciary Committee staff, wrote a one-sentence fix to the ambiguous section of the law, which now read: "the court shall decline to hear a claim under this paragraph . . . *if the claimant or victim was not a national of the United States.*" Their proposal would substitute for the second clause: "*. . . if neither the claimant nor victim was a national of the United States.*" (This version won out over one saying "*. . . if both the claimant and the victim were not nationals of the United States.*") Their first opportunity came in September, as Congress worked out the details of an unrelated piece of legislation involving the State Department. An effort to attach their amendment to that legislation failed, and as the end of the year approached, Zaid and Rutzen began writing and calling key congressional staffers, laying the groundwork for another attempt when the new Congress took over in January. "There is no known opposition to this change," they advised them, adding a note of urgency: "In order to prevent Bruce Smith . . . from being forever precluded from seeking accountability from Libya, we must amend the FSIA before the Supreme Court acts on a petition for *certiorari.*"

In fact it was a tiny change, a mere technical correction reinstating what was undoubtedly Congress's original intention—a bill one-sentence long in its entirety—and still they almost didn't get it through. It doesn't take opposition to kill a bill in Congress—the sheer inertia of the legislative process and the fantastic competition for legislators' time and attention are enough to do in untold numbers of worthy initiatives. Even allies can sometimes be dangerous. Although Hyde, the chairman of the House Judiciary Committee, had expressed his support for the bill, and understood the urgency of it, he had a busy agenda and could find no opportunity to bring it up until April 8. A week later, it passed the House, with Smith sitting in the gallery, and Hyde saluting him from the floor. A frenzy of lobbying in the Senate got the Senate Judiciary Committee to approve a companion bill two days after that, on Thursday, April 17. The Supreme Court had not yet ruled on their petition for *certiorari* in the original case—that is, they hadn't yet said if they would agree to hear the appeal—but enough time had passed that Bruce thought it was imminent. Denials of *certiorari*—the *Smith* team had very little hope it would be granted—often came on Mondays. They held their breath on the 21st but heard nothing. Congress was planning to recess at the end of the month. "The planets are in alignment," Bruce told Rosenthal. "We need this bill signed before next Monday."

It was at that precise moment that the tenacious Len Garment emerged on the scene, spotting an opportunity to help *his* client, Nelson—the American engineer who'd been tortured in Saudi Arabia. A year earlier, Garment had lost his fight over the language of the FSIA amendment when at the last minute Congress adopted the State Department's preferred version, covering only countries on the list of designated state sponsors of terrorism. Garment now began a quiet but urgent campaign to reverse that decision by attaching a new amendment to the bill being sought by Smith. Garment's friend Arlen Specter, the Pennsylvania Republican, put a hold on Smith's bill to keep it from coming to the floor for a vote, while Garment rounded up support—a neat maneuver, if the State and Justice Departments happened to be looking the other way at just the right moment, but a potential disaster for Smith. The stakes had now gotten very high. Zaid and Rutzen been doing much of the lobbying with congressional staffers. But they needed someone who could talk directly to Specter, and luckily Carol Bruce knew the right person—her husband, Jim Bruce, a Washington lawyer and lobbyist whose partner was Fred Fielding, former White House counsel to Ronald Reagan. They told Specter that he was risking years of effort to achieve justice for Smith; that Garment could try for a stand-alone amendment at any time, but that piggybacking a major substantive change onto Smith's technical correction would delay it until it was too late to do any good. Then, independently, under pressure from Sen. Orrin Hatch, Specter relented, and the bill went to the Senate floor, where it passed by unanimous consent at 10:45 on the evening of Thursday, April 24, just before Congress went into recess. But the clock was still ticking on Smith's petition for *certiorari*. Strom Thurmond, the president pro tem of the Senate, and House Speaker Newt Gingrich had to sign a copy of the bill before it went to the president, so congressional staffers had to track them down before they left town. Carol Bruce implored Clinton's White House counsel, Charles Ruff, an old colleague from Covington and Burling, to get the bill to the president the same afternoon. It was signed, all one sentence of it, on Friday, April 25.

And not a moment too soon. As Carol Bruce had predicted, the Supreme Court decided not to hear the final appeal of *Smith v. Libya* on the next business day, Monday, April 28.

14

Constitutional Intervention

After more than three years of effort, they could now begin the work of holding Kaddafi accountable for the murder of Ingrid Smith and 269 others, subject to all the requirements and procedures and safeguards of civil justice. Rosenthal began a fresh analysis of the law of the case, beginning at the most basic level with the question of what specific torts, or wrongs, the complaint was alleging. One, clearly, was the tort of "battery," defined as the wrongful infliction of physical harm, of which the traditional illustrative example is a punch in the nose. This raises, at least in the legal mind, the question of whether physical contact between the defendants and the victims was a necessary element of battery. Aware that it was unlikely that the Libyan agents ever came within 1,000 miles of Pan Am 103, the Sonnenschein lawyers decided it would be prudent to research the question and concluded that indeed there was a precedent for holding someone responsible for battery even though he never touched the victim. Their citation was a case in which a defendant pulled a lawn chair out from under the plaintiff as she was about to sit down. On such humble precedents were all groundbreaking cases constructed.

The complaints would also attempt the relatively untested approach of seeking damages for "intentional infliction of emotional distress," or IIED, known in more poetically inclined jurisdictions as "the tort of outrage." IIED required conduct "so outrageous in character, and so extreme in degree, as to go beyond all possible bounds of decency, and to be regarded as atrocious and utterly intolerable in a civilized community." To show that putting a bomb aboard an airliner met that definition shouldn't be too difficult, they thought. The plaintiffs would also have to demonstrate that the bomb caused them "severe emotional distress," but the lawyers foresaw no difficulty in establishing that, either. And they wouldn't have to rely just on the testimony of the family members, years after the event; their emotions had been captured and documented and preserved for all time by Suse Lowenstein, the sculptor. They fantasized about bringing the jurors to see Lowenstein's sculptures—what would the impact of that be?

There was one complication, though: in order to bring a claim for IIED, courts traditionally required the plaintiff actually to witness the incident in person. The Restatement (Second) of Torts—a codification of statute and case law, with commentary on the underlying principles—justified this limitation by the "practical necessity of drawing the line somewhere, since the number of persons who may suffer emotional distress at the news of an assassination of the President is virtually unlimited." Obviously the family members didn't witness the bombing, the disintegration of the airplane, and its impact on the ground. But the more the lawyers considered this distinction, the less sense it made. The law permitted damages for IIED if, for example, someone called you up as a practical joke and told you your wife had been killed in a car crash. On that analogy, if the terrorists had merely called up the family members and threatened to bomb the airplane, they would have been liable for damages. Should they somehow be exempt for actually carrying out the bombing? In fact, it's hard to imagine a case whose facts seemed to fit the phrase "intentional infliction of emotional distress" more closely than the bombing of Pan Am 103. The aim of terrorism is to inflict emotional distress; its impact derives precisely from the televised scenes of bereaved parents and spouses besieging the airport.

And all this was more than just the necessary formal exercise of fitting together the facts and the law. Rosenthal sought advice from the distinguished tort scholar Professor Marshall Shapo of Northwestern University. "The idea of 'corrective justice' is an important foundational element of the plaintiffs' case," Shapo wrote. He was invoking a concept that goes back to Aristotle, who formulated the notion that the role of justice was to redress an imbalance between two parties caused by the wrongful acts of one of them. "Although it may seem that the enormity of this terrorist act is such that it can be judged only as the crime that it is, there is a crucial symbolic feature in its status as a tort as well as a crime. To view the act as a tort is to provide vindication for individual victims against identified wrongdoers, one on one."

Rosenthal also began reviewing the laws of conspiracy. In the initial complaint, drawn up by Gerson and Zaid, Libya was identified as the author, backer, and prime mover of the plot to bomb the airplane. But life is rarely so simple, and Rosenthal wanted to be sure that Libya would be held accountable even if the facts suggested that it was merely one actor in a broader conspiracy.

The practical necessity Gerson and his colleagues faced involved coming to terms with Lee Kreindler, who was now their ostensible ally in the suit against Libya. In anticipation of a large number of additional suits, Judge Platt had reconstituted the plaintiffs' committee of the Pan Am litigation, with Kreindler continuing as chairman. Gerson and Rosenthal, having already fought and lost one battle to keep the original *Smith* suit in the District of Columbia, accepted the inevitability of their case being consolidated with the others in New York, under Kreindler's direction. No good could come of facing Libya with a divided front, both in the courtroom and in the political fights that lay ahead. Bowing to reality, Rosenthal requested to join the plaintiffs' committee, a request granted by Platt.

But Kreindler resisted dealing with people he considered interlopers in his case, especially Gerson and Zaid. He used his position to press the *Smith* team to yield on the idea of a class-action suit, except as a possible vehicle for a court-approved comprehensive settlement. Kreindler seemed to view it as a threat to his control and a subterfuge for stealing his clients. At least one of Kreindler's original clients had in fact defected to the Gerson/Zaid/Sonnenschein team, which now also included Frank Duggan, the former family liaison for the McLaughlin Commission. For six years Duggan had worked for the families and had earned nothing for it except their trust and gratitude. But those were worth something, now that there was the prospect, however remote, of multi-million-dollar judgments against Libya. Duggan was not a tort lawyer. He brought to the table his lobbying expertise, his government contacts, and his unique insight into what the family members wanted and how they felt. He was especially close to George Williams, the gruff ex-Marine whose only son had been killed in the bombing, and who wielded considerable influence as the president of Victims of Pan Am 103. Williams was the first to ask Duggan and Gerson to represent him against Libya, and others followed, eventually totalling more than fifty, representing the families of more than a dozen victims, besides Smith and Cummock.

Kreindler, who retained the great majority of his clients, appeared to consider this an insult far out of proportion to any possible loss of fees from the defecting clients. It was apparent from the outraged tone of his letters that his pride was at stake. He had long been suspicious of Duggan's role as an unpaid legal adviser to Victims of Pan Am 103. As chairman of the plaintiffs' committee and as the lawyer for the largest number of family members, Kreindler considered the dispensing of advice his prerogative. In March 1997, at Williams's invitation, Duggan attended a meeting of the family group in Massachusetts, and spoke about his efforts to get the Justice Department to assist in the civil suit. This was a step Kreindler opposed, and it infuriated him that someone was talking to *his clients* about it. Duggan had gone to pains to disclaim any interest in soliciting clients at the meeting. On the other hand, if a potential client came to him he had no obligation to turn him or her away. Kreindler announced that he could no longer work with Rosenthal on the plaintiffs' committee and that he would seek to have him removed. Rosenthal vowed to vigorously oppose any effort to oust him, a veiled warning to Kreindler to think twice before trying Platt's patience by forcing the issue. The issue ended up coming before Judge Platt, who advised Kreindler that Rosenthal was to stay on the plaintiffs' committe. In time, the ill feelings were muted, but substantive differences remained.

One of these, of course, was the question of a class-action suit. Rosenthal saw three advantages to filing on behalf of all the relatives as a class: it would preserve the rights of those who for whatever reason delayed filing their own suits but might choose to do so later; it would simplify negotiations with Libya, should they ever reach the point of negotiating a settlement; and it would give the plaintiffs added political clout for what he saw as the next lobbying effort: winning the cooperation of the U.S. Department of Justice in their suit. The evidence behind the indictments of Fhimah and Megrahi would be invaluable in establishing Libya's culpability in the bombing. And putting the evidence on the record now could help the prosecution as well, if there ever was to be a criminal trial. Time was passing, witnesses would eventually die or their memories would fade, but their testimony could be preserved now in the depositions and trial transcript of a civil case. Having the testimony heard in public would also bolster the political case for keeping the sanctions on Libya. Duggan and Trina Vargo of Kennedy's office drafted a letter to Attorney General Janet Reno. The letter, signed by twenty-eight senators, advised the attorney general that

> The families would have preferred a criminal trial involving the two indicted individuals, but almost eight years after the bombing, most have come to the conclusion that there may very well never be a criminal trial. Although the use of the U.S. government's evidence in a civil trial may adversely affect any future criminal trial, the families are asking the U.S. government to provide its evidence and assistance in the civil trial, because this is the only trial they can be certain will occur.

Kreindler, though, opposed seeking the evidence at this stage, and objected to every effort of the Sonnenschein team to get the Justice

Department to join in the civil suit. The prosecutors, he predicted, would never turn over the evidence as long as a criminal trial was still a possibility, and the Scottish prosecutors in particular would be offended even by the effort. He was right, as it turned out, although his own opposition may have made this partly a self-fulfilling prophecy. Even if Reno had been inclined to join the suit, she surely wasn't going to do so over the objections of the head of the plaintiffs' committee. In March 1997 Williams, as president of the Victims of Pan Am 103, wrote to Reno formally requesting her cooperation in the suit. On June 16, she replied:

> I understand your members' frustration with Libyan non-compliance. I can further appreciate that the pending civil action against Libya is a response to the families' yearning for some form of justice. I do not believe, however, that the civil action is the only practicable way to bring Libya and the individual defendants to justice. To the contrary, our experience as prosecutors gives us reason to believe that the Libyan defendants may yet face criminal trial in the U.S. or Scotland. . . . I have, therefore, reluctantly concluded that intervention by the United States as a party plaintiff against Libya, at this time, would imperil a future criminal prosecution.

At the time of Reno's letter, the United States and Libya had been deadlocked for five years over the question of turning over the two suspects for a trial, with no obvious resolution in sight. Yet the issue was far from forgotten. It surfaced periodically at the United Nations, where the Security Council resolutions came up for renewal every 120 days, an occasion invariably marked by a flurry of diplomatic posturing on both sides. Libya would deplore the economic sanctions and propose the latest variation of its long-standing offer to extradite the suspects to a third country. The United States would invariably reply, as Ambassador to the United Nations Madeleine K. Albright did on March 30, 1995, that "a trial of the two Lockerbie suspects in a third country or their trial before a Scottish court sitting in a third country is unacceptable." As it deemed necessary, Washington would take measures to increase the pressure on Libya. A week before Albright's statement, the FBI added Fhimah and Megrahi to its Ten Most Wanted Fugitives list. Their pictures went up in post offices around the country, and anyone with information on their whereabouts was urged to contact the nearest FBI office. Since they were living quite openly in Libya, this had to be regarded as a largely symbolic effort at apprehension. At other times the State Department or the National Security Council would proclaim a new push for an oil embargo, threats that over time began to take on the ineffectual tone of a parent who *has had it up to here, and this time I really mean it.*

What real pressure there was came from Congress, especially from Kennedy and Lautenberg. Lautenberg would regularly attach a rider to the foreign aid appropriations bill, cutting aid to countries that didn't observe the Libyan sanctions, which basically affected a handful of countries in West Africa. The State Department considered this an empty gesture. "It didn't mean anything, because the United States basically doesn't give meaningful aid to most African countries anyway," one mid-level official in the Counter-Terrorism Office said. "We looked at the numbers, there's a pissant little country that gets $100,000 for family planning, so we're going to cut that off? And what good would it do anyway, when Kaddafi is offering half a million directly to the president's Swiss bank account just for showing up to have coffee with him?"

In 1995, largely at the urging of pro-Israeli groups, Sen. D'Amato and Rep. Benjamin A. Gilman of New York introduced bills intended to put additional economic pressure on Iran. Since the United States had long ago severed virtually all its commercial ties to Teheran, there wasn't anything left to cut. The bill was directed instead at foreign corporations doing business there. Companies that sold oil equipment to Iran, or made substantial investments in Iran's oil industry, could be subject to a variety of complex and obscure penalties, including a ban on Export-Import Bank assistance, restrictions on loans by American banks, and prohibitions on the purchase of U.S. technology. Israel was not especially concerned about Kaddafi, but Kennedy, ever on the lookout for ways to help the Pan Am families, tacked on an amendment that would cover Libya as well as Iran. Passage of the Iran-Libya Sanctions Act (ILSA) became the latest of the families' lobbying objectives.

This time the families were fighting alongside the powerful Israeli lobby, but the bill faced opposition from European countries whose commercial interests were at stake, from American business groups, and from the administration itself, which regarded it as another example of Congress's heavy-handed meddling in foreign affairs. The act made slow progress during the winter and spring of 1996, while the families were distracted by simultaneously lobbying for the Anti-Terrorism Act, which passed in April. At hearings before the House Ways and Means Committee in May, George Williams and Rosemary Wolfe—the stepmother of a young woman who was killed on the plane, president of a small breakaway family group called Justice for Pan Am 103—testified in favor of the bill. The opponents would not oppose the Pan Am 103 families directly, of course. Their strategy, rather, was to weaken the bill to the point of uselessness. The *Houston Chronicle* reported in May that "congressional leaders are quietly working to take some of the sting out of an anti-terrorism measure designed to punish foreign companies that sell equipment to Iran or Libya or invest in their oil-field operations. Rep. Bill Archer (R–Houston) chairman of the Ways and Means Committee, is a key player in these talks, which are being closely followed by Houston oil-field equipment suppliers . . ." On June 19, the House passed a significantly weakend version of the bill, deleting the sanctions against companies investing in Libya's oil-field development, without which, Wolfe had told the committee, "the legislation would be meaningless." A stronger version passed the Senate on July 16, and the issue seemed headed for a conference, where industry lobbyists were determined to prevail.

And they might have, but for the intervention of yet another explosion. Congress, as the family members discovered early on, seems to do its most productive work in the aftermath of a highly publicized disaster. On the day after the Senate vote, a TWA jetliner bound for Paris exploded minutes after taking off from New York's John F. Kennedy International Airport, killing all 230 aboard. The investigation into this crash made Pan Am 103 look easy by comparison, since the debris had to be dredged up from the ocean floor. Investigators eventually concluded that the explosion was most likely an accident, the result of a spark igniting fumes in an empty fuel tank. But in the days and weeks after the crash most of the speculation centered on a bomb smuggled aboard the plane, or a surface-to-air missile fired from a small boat (or, among the most conspiracy-minded, an unintended launch of an American military weapon, covered up by horrified bureaucrats).

The possibility that terrorists had blown up an airplane within miles of New York City "made lawmakers want to pass the strongest possible bill," *Congressional Quarterly* reported. Less than a week later the House passed the Senate version of ILSA, which Clinton signed on August 5. "You can't do business with people by day who are killing your people by night," Clinton ringingly declared. Victoria Cummock, Williams, and Rosemary Wolfe were among those invited to the White House for the signing. Susan Cohen, who had lobbied extensively for the bill, demanded to be there as well. In the book she co-authored with her husband, Dan Cohen, she recounts how Clinton "smiled at me and said, 'Glad to have you with us again.'" She glared back, well aware that the act had passed over the administration's opposition. The process bore out Cummock's observation about Congress and public opinion, that you have a six-week window after the bodies are retrieved in a mass disaster to convert the public's outrage into useful political capital.

So, as 1996 ended, eight years after the bombing, the families could look back on a long series of victories: they had forced Bush to create a commission to investigate the disaster, they had helped pass the Aviation Security Act of 1990, added millions of dollars to the reward program to capture terrorists, helped win mandatory Security Council sanctions on Libya, proved Pan Am's "willful misconduct" in letting the bomb on board the plane, erected the cairn, amended the Foreign Sovereign Immunities Act, and helped pass the Iran-Libya Sanctions Act. Yet they couldn't help but feel that despite winning all those battles, they were losing the war. The two suspects remained at large in Libya—closely guarded, according to news reports, against the danger

of kidnapping by American agents. Kaddafi showed no signs of sur-
rendering them for a trial, although he never gave up looking for ways
to wriggle out from the sanctions. His latest offer was a variation on a
scheme proposed in 1993 by Robert Black, a law professor at the University of Edinburgh. Black had become involved in trying to resolve
the deadlock at the behest, he said, of "a group of British businessmen
whose desire to participate in major engineering works in Libya was
being impeded by the UN sanctions." Kaddafi now proposed surren-
dering Fhimah and Megrahi for a trial in the International Court of
Justice at The Hague, under American auspices and with an American
judge and prosecutor, but before a jury consisting of an international
panel of judges. Libya had retained a Miami lawyer named Frank
Rubino to win American support for this idea. Rubino discussed the
plan on *60 Minutes,* but it wasn't a very successful appearance, since
the family members on the show scornfully rejected his proposal—the
Cohens, true to form, refusing to shake his hand and calling for bombing his client, Libya.

On the eighth anniversary of the bombing, about a hundred people,
mostly family members, assembled at the memorial cairn. Jane Schultz
spoke about the cairn, and meeting a soldier there on Memorial Day.
Helen Engelhardt, the editor of *TruthQuest,* the newsletter of Victims
of Pan Am 103, described what happened next:

> We stood in silence and listened to the bells toll for two minutes in
> remembrance of the time it took our loved ones to fall upon the
> border town of Lockerbie, Scotland, and change the world forever.
> The names were read out loud by a group of family members as we
> reflected on all we had lost as individuals, as families, as friends, as
> a nation.

Although they had no way of knowing, events were being set in
motion that for better or worse would break the long deadlock.
Kaddafi was growing more and more restless in the "box" Washington
had put him in, and in 1997 he began to fashion his escape. In 1996
Kaddafi had flown to Cairo, where the Egyptians let him land in defi-

ance of the mandatory air boycott against Libya. Egyptian president Hosni Mubarak, citing this as an example of constructive engagement, told Western reporters that he had persuaded Kaddafi to abandon plans for a poison-gas factory in a tunnel outside of Tripoli. It was impossible, however, to judge the value of Kaddafi's promise, since he had been insisting all along (in the face of American accusations) that the tunnel was actually intended for crop irrigation. In 1997 the twenty-two-nation Arab League made permanent this exception to the UN's mandatory ban on air travel, voting to allow Kaddafi to fly to their countries for state purposes. The Vatican opened diplomatic relations with Libya—a development the State Department protested directly to the Holy See, and Duggan took the matter up with the Roman Catholic Archbishop of Washington, James Cardinal Hickey, whom he knew. "I have spent the last seven years helping the Pan Am families, many of whom are Catholic," Duggan wrote to Hickey. "I cannot tell you how upset they are." Libya hired a London consultant to lure travelers to the country's empty beaches and its spectacular archaeological sites. This was a formidable job, because there was still no commercial air travel to Libya and because Kaddafi made it plain he had no desire to expose his people to masses of foreigners, with their potentially subversive clothes and magazines. The trickle of tourists consisted mostly of wealthy Europeans with a taste for adventure who were willing to endure the long ferry ride from Malta.

It was still virtually impossible for most Americans to visit Libya. In general, you couldn't travel there on an American passport, you couldn't spend U.S. funds in the country, and you couldn't accept money directly from Libya, so most visits had to be at least nominally arranged and paid for by a third country. Nevertheless, Louis Farrakhan, the leader of the Nation of Islam with whom Kaddafi shared some views—about Israel, notably—had managed to visit the leader several times, for which a grateful Kaddafi had bestowed a donation of $1 billion to the Nation of Islam. This was a safe offer, since it was illegal for Farrakhan to accept it. Also in 1997 an American congressman Earl F. Hilliard (D–Ala.) visited Libya. His trip, which was paid for by a Swiss oil company, drew criticism and calls for an investigation by congressional Republicans. Hilliard dismissed these criticisms as racist. "They don't want blacks in power talking to Africa," he told reporters. As for Libya, he said, "We ought to have a relationship with every country that wants to have one."

But those contacts paled before Kaddafi's greatest coup, a triumphal state visit by South African president Nelson Mandela. Most of the bets Kaddafi had placed on third-world insurgencies throughout the 1970s and 1980s had been a bust, but his support for Mandela's African National Congress during the struggle against apartheid paid off handsomely as Mandela called for an end to sanctions against Libya and endorsed the Libyan plan for a trial in a neutral country. Smiling and waving, the two leaders posed before the preserved wreckage of a building damaged in the 1986 American bombing—a picture that ran on the front page of the *Washington Post* under the caption "African Brothers in Spirit." It was of course impossible to criticize Mandela personally, although the State Department managed to express its opposition to the visit. There was at least a grain of truth in the banner that greeted Mandela's fifty-car motorcade on its way in to Tripoli, which read: MANDELA'S VISIT TO LIBYA IS A DEVASTATING BLOW TO AMERICA.

And at the same time Libya renewed its efforts to win over, or at least neutralize, the family members. Abandoning for now its attempts to hire a well-connected American interlocutor, Libya instead addressed the family members directly in a series of letters mailed from Libya's United Nations Mission in New York. It was, of course, horrifying to the relatives to find an envelope from Libya in their mailboxes, addressed "To the Family of" each victim. Just seeing his son's name on a letter bearing the Libyan eagle struck Williams as a desecration. "If they have my address, what's to stop them from knocking on my door next time?" wondered Kathleen Flynn, whose son, John Patrick, died in the bombing. As Rosenthal firmly advised the Mission, it was also a violation of court procedures for one party to a lawsuit to contact the other side except through their respective lawyers. The letters did not convey a financial offer, however, but discussed what Libya had done to accommodate American and British demands. Implicitly acknowledging that "The Great Jamahiriya" had, in fact, supported international terrorism for many years—a charge Kaddafi had long scoffed at—Libya now boasted of "the severance . . . of its relations with all groups and organizations suspected of being involved in terrorist acts . . ." The letter proposed that Fhimah and Megrahi could be tried in The Hague under Scottish law, with a panel of three Scottish judges constituting the jury. It noted that, in seeking a neutral site, it was asking for no more consideration than Timothy McVeigh received when his trial was moved from Oklahoma City to Denver. In a letter sent both to the families and Attorney General Janet Reno, the Libyan ambassador, Abuzed Dorda, wrote: "Why does your government approve to move that trial . . . while refusing the same for citizens of another country? Don't they have the same human rights?"

And for the first time, it seemed, some of the few family members began asking themselves that same question. The movement began with Dr. James Swire, who was a leader among the family members of the English victims. Swire, whose twenty-four-year-old daughter, Flora, was killed in the bombing, was a charismatic figure, lean and white-haired, with a distinguished bearing. He'd been a demolitions expert in the military, and years ago, on his way to the United States for hearings on Pan Am 103, he'd constructed a mock bomb out of marzipan and hidden it, not very thoroughly, in a cassette player. He'd put the cassette player in his suitcase and checked in at the airport, where his luggage was opened, examined, and passed through. When word of this stunt got out a few weeks later, angry British authorities threatened him with arrest, and he became a hero to the American families.

But Swire was also a pacifist, deeply suspicious of American militarism and sympathetic to Kaddafi's protestations of innocence. He had visited the leader in Tripoli, where they exchanged condolences over their dead daughters, and he had announced that if the Americans bombed Libya he would go there himself to treat the wounded. In October, around the time Mandela visited Kaddafi, Swire met with the British foreign secretary, Robin Cook. Afterward Cook said, for the first time, that Britain would consider Libya's proposal to have a trial in a third country.

To most of the American families, including the leaders of the main family groups, the idea of a trial in a third country was still anathema. "There will be no deals with Libya," Williams wrote to the *New York Times*. "If [Kaddafi] offers to have a Scottish trial, with Scottish judges and a Scottish jury, but on neutral territory, then what is wrong with a trial in Scotland, with international observers? What is so sinister about Scotland?" The only organized support came from a splinter family group called Terrorism Watch, which included Bert Ammerman and the Lowensteins—the same families that had boycotted the dedication of the cairn in 1995 to meet with Reno. For them, the important thing was getting the evidence of Libya's culpability out to the public. If this was the only trial they could have, then why not—as the group's chair, Aphrodite Tsairis, wrote in the *Washington Post*— "call [Kaddafi's] bluff"?

Well, why not? There was, first of all, a principle at stake, and to many family members—and government officials, especially in the Department of Justice—it was unacceptable to negotiate with accused murderers over the terms of their trial. McVeigh was granted a change of venue because the courts in their impartial wisdom decided he couldn't get a fair trial in Oklahoma City, not because he refused to show up for one. Second, there were questions about Scottish legal practice. Scottish courts have their own rules of evidence and procedure, which might not be as favorable to the prosecution in this case as those of the United States. Certainly they did not provide for capital punishment, and at least some of the American relatives would be satisfied with nothing less. But the biggest practical objection to the Libyan proposal was that it might, in fact, be a bluff, but one which would never be called—that the political will at the United Nations to keep the sanctions in force, already noticeably weakening, would crumble at the first stroke of a pen on an agreement, after which Kaddafi could stall indefinitely on actually delivering the two suspects.

There was, finally, the sentiment—never quite expressed in public, but strong within certain offices in the State Department and National Security Council—that a trial would only serve to disrupt a policy that had been working well for five years: that it would at best result in the convictions of a couple of mid-level operatives, and at worst their acquittal, and that in either event Kaddafi would be let out of his box, free again to cause mischief in a world that was dangerous enough already.

But that analysis was no longer as powerful as it once was. Albright had taken over as secretary of state, and Sandy Berger was the new national security adviser. On taking office, both had asked their aides to take a fresh look at America's Libyan policy. "I remember one day, probably in the summer of 1997, the secretary had meetings with the Pan Am families, with the widow of a murdered hostage, and with Yasir Arafat," says a former official of the State Department's Office of Counter-terrorism, "and she came back at the end of it and said, my God, isn't there something we can do for *some* of these people?" The impetus may have even come from the president himself. Clinton was close to British's prime minister Tony Blair, and had been urged to settle the Libyan matter by other leaders he respected, including Jordan's late King Hussein. Moreover, it was at least arguable that the policy of containing Kaddafi had served its purpose. The Libyans were telling at least a partial truth in their letters to the families; Libya's direct involvement in international terrorism had mostly ended by the mid-1990s, except for isolated incidents of harassment and assassination directed at Kaddafi's political opponents in exile. The terrorist training camps were being closed, and the arms pipeline to the Irish Republican Army had been shut down. Now the unspoken question became, how should the United States respond? If that represented breaking faith with the family members, it was a betrayal for which the seeds had been sown long ago. No one but the family members (and, probably, the prosecutors in the Justice Department) viewed the question of justice for the 270 victims in the abstract, isolated from America's foreign-policy interests. As long as the broader concern was "how do we contain this madman?" the demands of justice and polity more or less coincided. Now it appeared they might be about to diverge. "Look, Gerry Adams [of the IRA's political wing] has killed more people than you've shaken hands with in your life," said an official who dealt with both the policy questions and with the Pan Am families. "Yitzhak

Shamir was a terrorist, Arafat has blood on his hands. We and our friends deal with terrorists all the time."

He goes on:

Kaddafi is a loathsome guy, but if he's reformed, then he's reformed. What were we supposed to do, keep sanctions on until he surrenders to the U.S. Attorney's office? This is something I could never get from the families. Our discussions became very bitter. They had bad things to say to me, even to my face. But they could not tell me what we were supposed to do, except subordinate every single U.S. foreign-policy interest to the undermining of Kaddafi himself. What can one say? There's just so much that can be reasonably done.

Meanwhile, *Rein v. Libya* and its companion cases were moving slowly through the court—uncommonly slowly, owing to the unique complications of dealing with Libya. American firms, including law firms, weren't allowed to do business with Libya, except under specific licenses issued by the Treasury Department. In order to be paid, therefore, Libya's attorneys—counting only the firms that had appeared in court, they were now on their third set, New York's Mirone & Shields—had to receive clearance from Treasury's Office of Foreign Assets Control. And that office, following bureaucratic procedures to the letter, treated *each plaintiff who joined the complaint as a separate transaction,* approving them one by one, a process that sometimes took as long as two months—at least until an irritated Judge Platt ordered OFAC to show cause why they couldn't issue a blanket license covering all the cases.

Mirone & Shields did exactly as Gerson and his colleagues had predicted: they moved to dismiss the complaint on constitutional grounds—no fewer than six of them, including the one he feared most, that the 1996 amendment violated the separation-of-powers clause. "The original [Foreign Sovereign Immunities] Act made no distinction between foreign states based on the degree of friendliness or hostility that may exist between them and the United States," they wrote. "The Amendment . . . now makes such a distinction and permits civil suits to be brought against what the media calls 'rogue states' . . . By leaving the pivotal jurisdictional finding to the unlimited discretion of an official of the Executive Branch, the Court is transformed into a mere tool of that Branch and loses its constitutionally prescribed independence."

But the plaintiffs had an unexpected but welcome ally in this battle: the United States Department of Justice. A year earlier, in the original *Smith* case, the government had essentially sided with Libya, urging the court to reject Gerson's cherished *jus cogens* argument. Now, though, the government had a stake in supporting the FSIA amendment, which the State Department had helped to draft. And the Justice Department had an obligation—although they had some discretion in whether they chose to carry it out—to defend the constitutionality of the nation's duly passed laws. Or did they want Libya to make them?

Carol Bruce was in close touch with the Justice Department attorney handling the case, Anthony J. Coppolino. In his brief, Coppolino had prepared detailed arguments to rebut each of the constitutional arguments Libya had raised. In oral argument before Judge Platt, his main point was that sovereign immunity is "a matter of grace and comity . . . bestowed by the political branches. It is not a constitutional right." The idea was to deal the other side a knockout punch by arguing that since Libya had no constitutional right to the protections of sovereign immunity, the political branches of government were free to withdraw them. That argument, if it prevailed, would enable the judges to skirt the thicket of constitutional arguments about the separation of powers. But Coppolino was prepared for any eventuality, and in his brief prepared detailed arguments for each of the constitutional arguments Libya had raised.

For this part of the case Libya had hired one of the nation's leading experts on international law, Bruno Ristau, the long-serving chief of the Justice Department's Foreign Litigation Unit, now in private practice in Washington. Ristau had actually written much of the 1976 Foreign Sovereign Immunities Act. Quoting from the preamble, he read: " 'Sovereign immunity is a doctrine of International Law, first recognized in our Courts in the landmark case of *The Schooner Exchange v. McFaddon*'"—decided by Chief Justice Marshall in 1812. He continued:

> Unfortunately, the doctrine has been given currency in recent years in this country that International Law doesn't exist, or to the extent that it exists, Congress can always abrogate it and you as a United States Judge are required to follow the last word from Congress . . . Other countries, civilized countries, since World War II have placed doctrines of International Law in their Constitutions, and they form an element that is above their Parliamentary action . . . One of these days we will become more civilized, perhaps.

Platt was unpersuaded by this plea. On February 26, 1988, he handed down a fifteen-page order affirming his jurisdiction under the FSIA amendment. "Under Article I, Section 8 of the Constitution," Platt wrote,

> Congress has the power "to define and punish Piracies and Felonies committed on the high Seas, and Offenses against the Laws of Nations" . . . Under the law enforcement and treaty powers . . . the President is charged with the duty of enforcing the laws and conducting foreign relations. Hence, it clearly was not a violation of the power of Congress to delegate to the Executive Branch (consistent with its power to conduct foreign relations) the designation of those sovereign nations which may be accorded sovereign immunity by the courts.

"Great news!" Rosenthal wrote in a letter to his clients a few days later. "As you can see, the Court rejected each and every one of Libya's arguments. For example, in rejecting Libya's claim that the Court does not have personal jurisdiction over it, Judge Platt wrote:

> Any foreign state would know that the United States has substantial interests in protecting its flag carriers and its nationals from terrorist activities and should reasonably expect that if these interests

were harmed, it would be subject to a variety of potential responses, including civil actions in United States courts.

It was indeed great news, although tempered by the certainty that Libya would appeal. In the appeal, which was fought over more or less the same constitutional issues, the United States joined the case as an "intervenor," which would accord the government the same rights as a regular party to present evidence, if it chose. Libya brought in its own constitutional expert, David B. Meltz of John Marshall Law School in Atlanta. Oral arguments took place in the U.S. federal courthouse on Foley Square in lower Manhattan, the seat of the Second Circuit Court of Appeals, on November 13, 1998—a date on which Rosenthal and Zaid were busy on other cases. That left Gerson to face the Kreindlers, Lee, and his son, James, on the way into the courtroom. Since they were now on the same side, they shook hands, but coldly. Gerson spotted Baumeister and another member of the plaintiffs' committee who had come from Manhattan for the argument. Frank Duggan, he noticed, was also there, but Gerson chose to sit next to an old Justice Department colleague, Doug Letter. He knew Letter as an expert at appellate argument, and was reassured by his presence.

James Kreindler presented the oral argument for the plaintiffs, which under the questioning of Circuit Court judge Guido Calabresi quickly veered off in a direction none of the lawyers had anticipated. Calabresi, a former dean of Yale Law School, seemed less interested in Kreindler's demonstration that Platt had reached the right conclusion than in plowing unfamiliar ground. When, exactly, did the State Department determine for the first time that Libya belonged on the terrorism list? Shouldn't that be the key to the decision? Did he really need to rule, as Platt had, that the designation as a terrorist state was properly a State Department function, or could he somehow circumvent the issue? Kreindler handled the questions as well as he could— the government lawyer, Letter, seemed better prepared to answer some of them—and afterward, Gerson congratulated him on his performance, but Gerson left the courthouse perplexed. What, he wondered, was Calabresi up to?

When the Appeals Court handed down their opinion, Calabresi's line of inquiry became clear. In a dramatic exercise of a judge's prerogative—some would say his duty—to decide cases on the narrowest possible grounds, he concluded that the FSIA amendment did not represent an unconstitutional transfer of power to the executive branch *insofar as Libya was concerned.* His reasoning was that at the time of the amendment, Libya was *already designated a state sponsor of terrorism,* and therefore Congress obviously intended for it (and the six other states on the list in 1996) to be covered by the amendment. The constitutional question might arise in the future, he conceded, if someone sued a country that was not on the list in 1996 but added later. But as for Libya, Calabresi wrote with an almost palpable sense of relief, "no decision whatsoever of the Secretary of State was needed to create jurisdiction over Libya for its alleged role in the destruction of Pan Am 103. That jurisdiction existed the moment that the [FSIA] amendment became law."

So there it was, that precious and hard-won document authorizing the families to proceed with their efforts to hold Libya accountable for the murder of 270 innocent and unsuspecting civilians. More briefs would be filed, more energy expended on fine points of constitutional law, but there was almost no danger of the Supreme Court reversing both Platt and the Second Circuit judges. The judges had performed their function of narrowing the ground the families stood on until they were almost, although not quite, alone. Now, all the families' lawyers had to do was win the case: to marshal the evidence, serve and complete their interrogatories on a remote and hostile foreign power, and establish Libya's complicity by the facts and the facts alone. It was December 1998, and the victims had been in the ground for ten years. The evidence was growing stale, but the pain of the family members' loss had only grown with each day lived without them.

15

Camp Zeist

In an ordinary trial, the plaintiffs would now quickly proceed to discovery—the process of gathering documents and testimony from the defendants in search of the evidence they would need to prove their case. But this was no ordinary trial. The Justice Department and the Scottish police had gathered a great deal of evidence, but it was locked up in their files for use against Fhimah and Megrahi. The Justice Department had turned down Gerson and his colleagues when they requested access to the evidence, and Kreindler had refused even to ask for it until after a criminal trial. For years, a criminal trial had appeared a distant prospect, but now, in 1998, the time was approaching when a trial might take place after all. It was not, however, the trial that the families had envisioned—the one that had been specified in the UN Security Council resolutions and been declared a bottom-line, non-negotiable demand of the two Western governments for seven years. Dropping their insistence on trying the suspects in the United States or Britain, the two countries were moving toward accepting Kaddafi's offer to surrender Fhimah and Megrahi to the Netherlands. Doug Rosenthal had objected to the idea in a letter to the *New York Times,* which had supported it in an editorial. If the British and American governments capitulated on the demand for a trial in the United States or the United Kingdom, he wrote, world opinion would construe it as an implicit admission that their justice systems couldn't be fair to accused terrorists. He did not want this message to get out as he attempted to push the boulder of the *Smith* case up the mountain of the federal courts.

But events were leading to a trial that neither the Western countries nor, probably, Kaddafi himself ever expected to take place. America's leverage over Libya was declining, along with the support for the sanctions resolutions in the UN Security Council. The two international figures of unquestioned moral stature, Pope John Paul II and Nelson Mandela, had called for lifting the sanctions. In the United States, a consortium of agriculture interests and international corporations had organized under the name USA Engage to lobby against unilateral economic sanctions, such as ILSA. While the United States (and Britain) could veto any attempts to repeal the Security Council resolutions, they could do little to force compliance on the rest of the world.

Then, in February 1998, the International Court of Justice stirred from hibernation, where it had been ruminating since 1992 over Libya's effort to overturn the sanctions. Libya had challenged the authority of the UN Security Council to demand the suspects' extradition, on the grounds that the 1971 Montreal Convention (the Convention for the Suppression of Unlawful Acts Against the Safety of Civil Aviation) gave it the right and duty to try Fhimah and Megrahi in its own courts. This was a plausible, but illogical, argument. As the United States pointed out, the drafters of the convention surely did not anticipate a situation in which the "Unlawful Acts" were perpetrated by agents of the very state to which it granted jurisdiction, which would now essentially be trying itself. The other American argument was that a UN Security Council resolution trumped a multilateral treaty such as the Montreal Convention. The subtext here was America's desire to uphold the primacy of the Security Council, where it held a veto, against the International Court of Justice, on which it had just one of fifteen votes. After six years, the court had ruled that it had jurisdiction to hear Libya's case, and therefore could decide, at some future date, whether Libya was entitled to try Fhimah and Megrahi itself. At that rate, an actual trial on the merits could easily be a decade away. But the vote—thirteen to two, with the United States and Great Britain in the minority—sent an unwelcome message to the State Department. The principle of judicial review over the acts of the other two branches of government has a long tradition in American law, going back to the case every American studies in high school, *Marbury v. Madison*. But the United States did not want this concept to take root in international law, giving the final word to the ICJ judges, not the five major powers at the Security Council. To the State Department, that issue loomed as large as anything having to do directy with Pan Am 103.

At the same time, economic pressures were moving Kaddafi toward a deal. No one really knew just how badly the sanctions had hurt Libya, because both sides had an interest in spreading disinformation on the subject. For domestic consumption in Libya, Kaddafi vowed that his people would never be defeated by sanctions, while American officials assured the families that sanctions were gradually reducing the Libyan economy to rust. "His oil infrastructure is British and American, not metric, and he can't get spare parts for it," one State Department official boasted. "He couldn't pump his full OPEC quota now if he tried." Then, every 120 days when the Security Council sanctions came up for a vote, the two parties would switch sides. The Libyans and their African allies would claim that the Libyan people were suffering intolerable burdens, while the Americans would argue that Libya hadn't suffered enough. Calculating the cost of the sanctions with any precision was impossible, but sources estimated they ranged from $20 billion to $30 billion. During the debate in 1998, the American UN ambassador, Bill Richardson, contended that "Libya remains the wealthiest country in Africa on a per-capita basis . . . Libyan oil production under sanctions remains steady." But even if its oil production remained steady in 1998, its revenues were declining as petroleum prices dropped toward $10 a barrel, threatening the very survival of the regime. A 1999 report from the Washington Institute of Near East Policy by Libya scholar Ray Takeyh noted that:

The government's 1999 austerity budget reduced spending on investment projects by 80 percent . . . [Kaddafi] seems to have opted for an accelerated development of oil and natural gas resources. European oil companies appear ready to oblige the colonel, as a recent survey conducted by the French firm Elf Aquitaine and Spanish energy group Repsol indicated new off-shore sources with enormous capacities. It is here that the Locker-bie issue becomes troublesome, as most firms appear reluctant to sign long-term contracts and exploration agreements at a time when Libya is gripped by international sanctions.

In short, before Kaddafi (now apporaching thirty years in power) could even hope to lead his country into the twenty-first century, he would first have to come to terms with the West. This realization had evidently dawned on him as well.

From the Anglo-American side the breakthrough came in July 1998, when the Clinton administration announced that it would con-sider the deal that Prime Minister Tony Blair had been quietly urging: a trial by a Scottish court sitting in the Netherlands, with Scottish judges standing in for the jury. James P. Rubin, the State Department spokesman, called it a "creative alternative" to the stalemate—a "win-win" proposal that, if successful, would "achieve our fundamental objective, a trial under a Scottish or American court system." The fam-ily members were more skeptical. Several reminded Albright, when she briefed them on the new policy during a conference call, that for nearly seven years a trial *in* Scotland or America had been the govern-ment's "fundamental objective." "Despite all the fancy, frilly talk, this is a collapse in policy," Susan Cohen told the *Times*. "Kaddafi is not being brought to his knees. We're saying, 'You can outlast us.'" But others questioned why the issue had to come down to the geographic location of the courtroom. Weren't the rules and auspices what really mattered? In fact, as the terms of the deal emerged, it could almost be said that the trial actually *would* be in Scotland. Since the International Court of Jus-tice was not involved, the venue would not be The Hague. Partly for security reasons, the governments chose Camp Zeist, an inactive American air base about twenty-five miles from Amsterdam, which would be placed under British sovereignty for the duration of the proceedings. When reporters called Bert Ammerman for a reaction, he told them the administration had adopted "a pragmatic, realistic approach. With the present policy [of insisting on a trial in the United States or Britain] there will never be a trial."

And if it didn't work, Rubin went on—if Kaddafi backed out of a deal he himself had proposed—the United States and Britain would have called his bluff, demonstrating the need to maintain, or even toughen, the Security Council sanctions. And many family members expected precisely that outcome. "We know it's not going to work," Rosemary Wolfe told reporters after meeting with Albright and Berger. "There is no chance Kaddafi is going to turn them over to a Scottish court." Although the British and Americans, once they had drawn up their terms, described them as non-negotiable, Kaddafi tried to negotiate anyway. He moved to substitute an international panel of judges for a Scottish tribunal. He rejected the choice of Camp Zeist, he told CNN, because "America is able, in case the trial is held in an American base, to kidnap the suspects and take them to America." He insisted that the suspects, if convicted, serve their sentences in the Netherlands or in Libya rather than in a Scottish prison. And in case no one was paying attention, he demanded that the sanctions be lifted as soon as an agreement was reached, without actually waiting for Megrahi and Fhimah to be delivered into custody—the equivalent of offering to sell an empty sack for $30 billion.

But under pressure from UN Secretary General Kofi Annan and from his own allies—Hosni Mubarak of Egypt, Nelson Mandela of South Africa—Kaddafi finally took "yes" for an answer. He agreed to a trial in Zeist for the two suspects and, in the event of a guilty verdict, to imprisonment in Scotland under the monitoring of international inspectors. The agreement he reached stipulated that when the two were turned over to Scottish authorities the sanctions would be "suspended." They would remain nominally in place until Libya complied with the other Security Council demands, including accepting responsibility for the bombing and paying compensation. In practical terms,

Kaddafi could be sure that once "suspended," they would almost certainly never be reinstated, unless he blew up another 747. Was Kaddafi backed into a corner by his own rhetoric, compounded by economic desperation? Or did he just accept what he had wanted all along, secure in the belief that after all these years the evidence had grown stale, and the prosecution would never be able to prove its case under the exacting standards of Anglo-Saxon justice? Scotland, although politically a part of the United Kingdom, had a separate judiciary with some features that the Libyans would have found attractive—for example, a requirement that each incriminating fact be supported by at least two independent pieces of evidence. And it offered the judges, in addition to "guilty" and "not guilty," a compromise verdict of "not proven." This would allow the suspects to go free and Kaddafi to claim vindication, without inflicting the embarrassment of an outright acquittal on the American and Scottish prosecutors.

Demonstrating his real concern, Kaddafi demanded and got a letter from Kofi Annan, promising that the trial would not be used to "undermine" the Libyan regime. When the family members heard about this letter, shortly before the trial itself commenced, they naturally demanded to see it. Benjamin Gilman (R–N.Y.), chairman of the House International Relations Committee, formally asked the State Department to turn over the letter, but it demurred on grounds of diplomatic privilege. George Williams, as president of Victims of Pan Am 103, asked also. Sandy Berger, the national security adviser, advised him that "the Secretary General of the UN has not consented" to making it public. Berger assured him, however, that the letter had not "in any way limited the quest for the truth in the Pan Am 103 case . . . As both the Scottish Lord Advocate and the Secretary of State have said, there are no external or negotiated limits to the authority of the Scottish prosecutors in the trial or the lines of inquiry they can pursue. The prosecutors are free to pursue the evidence wherever it may lead them." American and Scottish officials repeated this often during the months leading up to the trial. But what could Annan's promise mean, except that the prosecutors wouldn't try to pin the bombing on Kaddafi himself? In what other way could a criminal trial "undermine" his regime, except by connecting it to the crime at issue? Berger apparently meant to reassure Williams that investigators were free to pursue any independent evidence against Fhimah and Megrahi's higher-ups. But after a decade, the biggest criminal investigation in history hadn't yet found any. "Look, there's no decision memo out there with Kaddafi's initials and the box marked 'bomb' checked off, so we might as well give up looking for it," said one American official familiar with the investigation. Annan's letter had foreclosed the one avenue that might have led investigators up the chain of command, an attempt to get Fhimah and Megrahi to cooperate. The trial would confine itself to the pair whom Bruce Smith referred to as "the least of the Libyans."

On April 5, 1999, an Italian plane with UN markings took Fhimah and Megrahi to a Dutch air base where Dutch officials took them into custody, then "extradited" them a few hours later into the hands of the Scottish authorities at Camp Zeist. A month earlier, a French court had convicted, in absentia, six Libyan intelligence agents, including Kaddafi's brother-in-law, Abdullah Senoussi, of bombing the UTA airliner in Africa in 1989. The three-day trial was mostly symbolic; if the defendants were ever arrested, they would have to be tried again before they could be sentenced. At the same time, the UN Security Council "suspended" its sanctions on Libya, although the United States kept its unilateral ones in force. A few months later, American and Libyan officials met at the United Nations for the first direct talks between the two nations in eighteen years. Within the year, Britain would restore diplomatic relations with Libya, and Libya's airline would resume direct flights between Tripoli and London.

Preparations for the trial were of Olympian magnitude. At a cost of $20 million, the Scots had built a high-security jail on the former air base, plus a courtroom sealed off by soundproof glass from a large visitors' gallery, a press center, offices, conference rooms, and a restaurant. The eventual cost of the trial, including security by 200 well-armed police officers, was estimated at over $70 million, to which Kaddafi did not contribute, although the United States did. Sen. Ted Kennedy had put a bill through Congress authorizing the Justice Department's Office for Victims of Crime to assist the Pan Am relatives; and its deputy director, Kathryn Turman, made elaborate arrangements for relatives who wanted to follow the proceedings. Top officials of the Justice Department and the Scottish Lord Advocate's office briefed the families. Family members (although not the press or even their lawyers) could watch the trial on closed-circuit television monitors in New York and Washington; they had access to a password-protected Web site carrying daily transcripts and commentary; and if they wished to attend in person, the Justice Department would fly them to Zeist and put them up for a week in a pleasant country hotel a few miles away.

Bruce Smith was there when the trial began, after numerous delays, in the first week of May 2000. Daniel and Susan Cohen, who by their own boast never missed a chance to step in front of a camera, were there, too, and so were Bert Ammerman, George Williams, and more than forty others. Smith stood apart in this crowd, avoiding contact with the other family members as much as possible. He had never needed a support group, never sought to ease the pain of his loss by sharing it with others, and now he was dismissive of their desire for companionship. "They make a social occasion out of it," he grumbled.

Jim Swire, the English physician who heads the U.K. family group, was there too, wearing a button that read "Pan Am 103—The Truth Must Be Known." Smith and some of the other Americans wore buttons reading "Pan Am 103—Time for Justice." Asked about this, Swire responded, "Well, it's all the same thing, isn't it?" Smith, however, felt it wasn't the same thing at all. The truth was just a step on the road to justice; otherwise it was meaningless. Yet Smith, while disagreeing profoundly with Swire on the politics of the bombing, felt an affinity with him. The Englishman defended his principles without personally attacking those who disagreed with him, which Smith, who had narrowly escaped physical assault by other family members at meetings, could appreciate. Yet the awful event that had brought them together shadowed their friendship. "Bruce," Swire once told him, "you're a really good friend, but I wish I'd never met you."

The bewigged justices lent the proceedings an air of fusty dignity, although some of the family members noticed that the case was brought simply in the name of "Her Majesty's Advocate." In America, the prosecution represents "The People" or "The United States of America." And since Scottish procedure does not allow opening statements, the trial began quietly, with the matter-of-fact testimony of the ground controller who handled Pan Am 103 as it left Heathrow. Queen's Counsel Alistair Campbell produced a transcript of the radio exchange with the pilot:

" 'Cleared for takeoff'—I take it that means they are now allowed to take off?"

"Absolutely right!"

"The word 'airborne' means it's now in the air, is that right?"

"Absolutely right!"

At this rate, it seemed, the trial could take longer than the predicted year. Because Scottish rules forbade both prosecutors and defense counsel to talk to the press, observers often had to guess at the direction of the questioning. Prosecutors took pains to establish the precise location of the plane when the radar image broke up, apparently to prove that the explosion actually occurred in Scottish airspace and not over England. Defense lawyers questioned the air-traffic controllers closely on the plane's exact altitude when it exploded, presumably to support the defense claim that the bombing was the work of the PFLP–GC, the Palestinian terrorists who had been arrested in Germany. The bombs seized by the German police had barometric triggers, which would detonate at a specific altitude, whereas Libya was known to use timers in its bombs. The lone moment of drama came during the air controller's account of the moment at which the transponder signal from the plane suddenly vanished from his radar screen. One moment it was there; the next it was gone, replaced by a blank box that signified a mute object in the sky, which over the next few seconds broke into three, then five boxes, drifting apart across the screen.

"Was this a matter of concern to you?" the prosecutor asked, in his unvaryingly understated matter.

"Yes, certainly."

"You'd never seen anything like this before?

"Oh, no, nobody had."

Nobody had seen such a thing, nobody could imagine such a thing, nor did anyone on the ground below in Lockerbie realize what was plummeting toward them at 120 miles an hour: the chunks of fuselage, the immense wings with their screaming engines, the flaming kerosene, and the hundreds of bodies that would rain down from the sky. The plane as it fell made a sound "like a train, only it kept getting louder," a policeman testified the next day, and raised "an orange glow like a mushroom cloud" over the town. For the next hour, the clerk read out the roster of the dead: passengers first, then crew, then residents of the town. They were in alphabetical order, with a few exceptions to keep family members consecutive, where they shared a surname with an unrelated victim. In the visitors' gallery, silent but for the sibilant murmur escaping from the headsets, the spectators stiffened or trembled or bowed their heads in turn as certain names were reached. When they came to Geordie Williams, George Williams, who had been waiting a decade to look Kaddafi in the eye and tell him, *you killed the wrong American,* glared straight at the defendants.

Mostly, though, the defendants, who sat impassively in robes and white caps, did not resemble the monsters the relatives were prepared to hate, just two subdued, almost scholarly-looking middle-aged men, nodding occasionally to their own families gathered on the other side of the glass. Halfway through the recitation of the victims' names, they removed their own headsets. To the reporters outside, Bert Ammerman denounced that gesture of seeming indifference. But he overlooked the fact that the defendants' headsets were for the Arabic translation. Inside the glass wall, they could hear the clerk perfectly well, and the list of names were the same in any language.

Only the prosecutors knew the strength of the case, or its weaknesses. After the trial, a Justice Department official admitted to a meeting of the family members that when the indictments were brought in 1991, investigators believed they had "a prosecutable case, but not a strong case." A State Department official had told them not to worry, because they'd never capture the defendants anyway. Now it was nearly a decade later, and cases usually grow weaker over time. They would have to reconstruct the cryptic computer data that traced the path of the suitcase through the Frankfurt airport, from the arriving

Air Malta flight to the first leg of Pan Am 103, establish a chain of custody for each of the hundreds of pieces of evidence from the moment it was scraped from the ground and placed in a plastic bag, and reinterview key witnesses, including the Maltese shopkeeper who had identified Megrahi as the purchaser of the clothing that had been packed with the bomb. He had done this from a photograph; now, relying on his memory of a fleeting encounter thirteen years old, he would have to reidentify Megrahi in person.

And prosecutors would have the dubious honor of for the first time ever putting on the stand a spy for the Central Intelligence Agency. Spectators and journalists had high expectations for the testimony of Abdul Majid Giaka, the pseudonym of a Libyan intelligence agent who had worked alongside the defendants in their cover jobs with Libyan Arab Airways in Malta. Giaka had begun selling information to the CIA in 1988 and defected to the United States three years later. He had spent almost a decade in the U.S. Witness Protection Program, and was brought to court by a squadron of thirty heavily armed U.S. marshals. The security precautions suggested he was about to reveal nothing less than Kaddafi's secret Swiss bank account number. Giaka testified behind a screen, with his video image and voice digitally disguised. Never before had the CIA permitted one of its intelligence sources to testify in open court about his work, and his testimony quickly showed why.

Giaka testified that in December of 1988 he saw Megrahi and Fhimah with a brown Samsonite suitcase, the kind used in the bombing. This helped the prosecution's case but it was far short of conclusive, since he did not see them put a bomb in the suitcase or load the suitcase on a flight. And even that success was short-lived, because the next morning, Megrahi's lawyer, William Taylor, had Giaka for breakfast. The defense lawyers had requested copies of cables between Giaka's CIA handlers and headquarters, which were delivered with whole pages blacked out. The defense demanded to see the excised portions, which left the agency with the choice of risking embarrassment by releasing the cables or handing Libya a ready-made opportunity to charge that Fhimah and Megrahi were being railroaded by a

CIA cover-up. After deliberating for several weeks, the agency did the decent thing and chose embarrassment—which, to be fair, it deserved to share with the FBI. The cables revealed that although Giaka began spying for the CIA several months before the bombing, he never mentioned Pan Am 103 either before December 21 or afterward, when the whole world knew that investigators were trying to trace a brown Samsonite suitcase. Meanwhile he was badgering his handlers for money for various schemes, including a sham surgical operation that he hoped would keep him out of Libyan military service. By 1991 the CIA was ready to get rid of him. His only chance to stay on the American payroll, they told him, was to come forward with information for the FBI about the Lockerbie bombing. Interviewed by FBI agents aboard an American naval vessel off Malta, Giaka suddenly recalled the mysterious suitcase. He recounted a few equivocal conversations with Fhimah and Megrahi, although nothing that actually implicated them in the bombing, and he said he had seen TNT in a desk in the Libyan airline office in Malta—although that didn't prove anything even if it was true; Pan Am 103 had been blown up by Semtex. By the time the judges wrote their opinion, they had discounted virtually everything Giaka said, and long before then, most journalists had concluded that the prosecution's case had fallen apart along with its star witness.

But the few who had been following the trial closely, day by day, weren't so sure. The Scottish prosecutors had essentially reconstructed the case on the bones of the indictment, consistent with the scenario painted by Kreindler and Baumeister in the Pan Am negligence trial. They weren't relying on Heaven dropping a Samsonite suitcase in their laps but on methodically filling the gaps in that case with detailed circumstantial and scientific evidence. And from the time Fhimah and Megrahi were handed over until the trial thirteen months later, they had done just that. Investigators uncovered a crucial new detail in Megrahi's false passport, issued at the request of Libyan intelligence, which he used to travel to and from Malta on December 20–21, and then never used again. Still, Taylor called only three perfunctory witnesses in Megrahi's defense, and Richard Keen, Fhimah's lawyer, called none. As the trial was ending in January 2001, the Libyan ambassador to the Netherlands smugly predicted an acquittal and told a British newspaper, "Without question this trial has significantly improved relations between my country and yours and America. I do not envisage these relations deteriorating again." Robert Black, the University of Edinburgh law professor who had originally proposed a trial in a neutral country, went so far as to tell journalists, "A conviction is—I kid you not—impossible."

16

Civil Trial

On the night before the verdict, January 30, most of the family members slept poorly. The Office for Victims of Crime (OVC) had offered to fly them to one of the closed-circuit video sites, and about fifty had come to Washington and spent the night at the Key Bridge Marriott in Arlington. Their wake-up call came at 2:30 A.M.—8:30 in the Netherlands. Outside, a bus waited to take them to the downtown office building where they would watch the trial's conclusion. Standing in the hotel driveway, Bob Monetti and George Williams stared in amazement at the bus number painted on the side. "Did you see that?" someone whispered. Monetti nodded. The bus company had assigned them bus number 103.

The verdict had brought together family members from all over the East, many of them strangers to Monetti. He was comforted by the presence of an OVC escort on the bus, although after years of coming to Washington on his own it felt odd to have the government take care of him. The mood inside the bus was expectant. They had come so far and waited so long for this moment that it was almost impossible to imagine falling short. But while Monetti chatted with the newcomers, his wife, Eileen, stared silently out at the deserted streets and wondered if anything in life could have prepared her for this moment—a ride across the Potomac and through the eerie predawn darkness of downtown Washington to hear a verdict on the guilt or innocence of the men accused of murdering her son.

The bus stopped outside a building where a block-long line of satellite trucks idled by the curb, their antennas poking through the fog like ships' masts. A crowd of reporters parted to let the family members through—for once, not even bothering to shout questions. Inside, they were brought to a large room filled with family members and Justice Department officials. A table held platters of doughnuts and fruit, and a nurse in a starched white uniform stood ready to revive any family members overcome by emotion. Monetti looked around for a familiar face among the officials gathered there but could only recognize two congressional staffers—Trina Vargo, Senator Kennedy's longtime aide, who had recently left his office, and her successor, Sharon Waxman. Kennedy, having authorized the OVC to look after Pan Am families, had the clout to admit his own staffers to the closed-door gathering.

It was just after 11:00 A.M. in Camp Zeist when the four judges (including one alternate) took their seats in the courtroom. The families fell silent. In a laconic fourteen-minute session, Chief Judge Ranald Sutherland pronounced the court's unanimous decision: guilty on Megrahi, not guilty on Fhimah. "We had all been holding our breath and the oxygen just went out of us all at once with a big whoooosh," said Monetti. "There was clapping and a cheer, but it didn't last long because right away he read the other verdict, 'Fhimah—innocent.'" A Justice Department official tried to explain the evidentiary problems they had faced in making the case against Fhimah, but his explanation bogged down in complex procedural questions and many of the family members drifted away, awaiting the sentencing, which would come later that day.

Word of the verdict crossed the ocean at the speed of light and swept through the crowd on the street outside, just barely beating Susan Cohen as she burst out of the federal building to give her reaction. "When they said, 'guilty,' some people laughed, some people cried," she told reporters. "There was a marked explosion of relief. We would have been devastated beyond belief if it had gone the other way." The verdict, she said, was a great victory; it would allow them to bring to justice the masterminds of the bombing, by means of the civil suit filed in U.S. district court.

Gerson, watching from the fringes of the crowd, nudged Zaid and muttered, "I thought we were only after blood money."

Acting Deputy Attorney General Robert S. Mueller III, who had overseen the American side of the investigation, followed her to the microphone. He was introduced by a Justice Department aide who had taken pains to distribute his resumé to the reporters; Mueller would soon be nominated by President Bush to be director of the FBI. As assistant attorney general in charge of the Criminal Division, Mueller had overseen the American investigation of the Pan Am 103 bombing. With the forceful and reassuring mien of a professional prosecutor he promised that the case would remain open, the investigation would continue, and that no one was immune from justice. It was exactly what everyone wanted to hear, whether they really believed it or not.

Neal Gallagher, deputy director of the FBI, spoke next. He had been with the investigation from the start, and the outcome held mixed emotions for him: the verdict pleased him and he was grateful to every-one, especially the Scottish prosecutors and police, "but," he said, "I was just with the families, and I looked into their eyes and saw their loss."

Other family members followed. Paul Hudson spoke of his "immense joy" at the verdict, and his hope that the civil suit would now proceed with the full cooperation of the government. Rosemary Wolfe spoke of her stepdaughter, Miriam, who wanted to be a writer or an actress. George Williams, who had recently suffered a mild stroke, stood ramrod straight and confidently predicted victory in the civil suit: "Our lawyers, Gerson, Zaid and Doug Rosenthal brought us a miracle before in getting the Foreign Sovereign Immunities Act changed, and if you think we are not capable of doing miracles you are wrong. I am an old man now and don't have that much longer to live, but the important thing is to send a message to Libya that they will have to pay for this."

As he posed for a victory handshake with Williams, Gerson considered the possible consequences had the verdict against Megrahi gone the other way—what an unendurable blow it would have been if both defendants had been acquitted. Duggan had confided that in his never-ending grief, Williams had come close to suicide several times in recent years. Susan Cohen's anger would have been terrifying to behold. Despite the families' half-hearted pledges to press on they would have been at the end of the road. Gerson would, too, for that matter; he had worked on Pan Am 103 for eight and a half years, from the day Bruce Smith had walked into his office at Hughes Hubbard & Reed; he had put his career on the line for it and he had fought his own government in court to get the case before a judge. In principle, the case could have proceeded in the face of an acquittal. As he frequently reminded his clients, the O. J. Simpson verdict had shown that the same facts that fail to prove criminal guilt "beyond a reasonable doubt," may sustain a civil verdict by "a preponderance of the evidence." But with an acquittal, whatever political leverage the United States had over Libya would have disappeared—and with it, Kaddafi's incentive to participate in the trial or to pay compensation. The trial could have gone ahead, but to what end?

Over breakfast, Gerson, Duggan, and Zaid looked back on their efforts. Duggan admitted that he had underestimated the families' staying power; he had thought that the internal politics of the family groups would have long since destroyed their cohesion and with it, their ability to get things done. But somehow through the bickering and bitterness they had managed to unite behind the things that mattered. And the families were coming to a reconciliation with their own government, which had let them down so badly, and which they had fought for so long. For the first time that Duggan could recall, even Susan Cohen couldn't find something to criticize; whatever its short-comings and mistakes, the United States, together with its ally, Great Britain, had investigated the crime, indicted the suspects, brought them to trial, and won a crucial conviction. They could take pride in that.

In the courtroom, the Lord Advocate, Colin Boyd, spoke for a few moments before the judges pronounced sentence:

In an ordinary case, Your Lordships would have heard something of the circumstances of the deceased and the family left behind. In this case it is not possible to do that, and I don't intend to try. I need hardly say to the court that each one left relatives, wives, husbands, parents and children. Something of the scale of the impact can be gleaned from the fact that more than 400 parents lost a son or a daughter; 46 parents lost their only child; 65 women were widowed; and 11 men lost their wives. More than 140 lost a parent, and seven children lost both parents. My Lords, they, together with the other friends and their relatives left behind, are also victims of the Lockerbie bombing.

The mandatory sentence for murder was life. Megrahi's lawyers had nothing to say in mitigation of his guilt, since he maintained his innocence. Three hours later the judges returned to the courtroom and pronounced sentence, recommending that Megrahi serve at least twenty years in a Scottish prison, which would make him sixty-seven years old on his release. His lawyers quickly announced plans to appeal the verdict.

Down in Florida, Victoria Cummock was awakening her children to tell them that Megrahi had been convicted, but was only getting twenty years, or "less than a month per victim." Cummock later told the *Miami Herald*: "My fifteen-year-old daughter, Ashley, burst into tears when I told her. She asked me how this could happen."

In Tripoli, the shock of the verdict appeared to have brought out Kaddafi's most eccentric impulses. Fhimah was immediately released from custody and received a hero's welcome in Libya and an emotional embrace from Kaddafi. Following tribal custom, a camel was slaughtered in Fhimah's honor, "its blood splattered in a thick pool beneath a sculpture of an upraised fist crushing a U.S. plane," reported Howard Schneider in the *Washington Post*. And that wasn't the only blood spilled in Libya over the verdict. Kaddafi, defiant and angry, accused America of pressuring the judges into convicting Megrahi. Libyan officials staged an anti-American rally at which three frenzied demonstrators cut their own throats with razors (although unlike the camel they were believed to have survived). Libya, Kaddafi announced, would never take responsibility or pay compensation for Lockerbie, and he promised to have evidence of Megrahi's innocence that was so powerful the judges would kill themselves in remorse. That naturally created intense interest in his next speech, three days later, but in the end he unleashed merely a two-and-a-quarter-hour table-pounding tirade, long on anti-American rhetoric but devoid of evidence. "Abdel Basset [Megrahi]," he proclaimed, in his familiar vein of bellicose victimization, "can only be viewed in the eyes of international history as a kidnapped hostage."

Yet while in public the leader has always maintained Libya's innocence in the bombing, in a 1999 interview with the journalist Milton Viorst he edged toward a kind of confession. Sitting in a camel-skin tent, with just Viorst and an interpreter present, Kaddafi talked about his nation's reputation for terrorism:

> Whether we were responsible for bringing down the French plane will be decided by a French court. We don't say anything about it. The same is true of Lockerbie. I can't answer as to whether Libya was responsible. Let's let the court decide.

"I was cautiously sipping camel milk in the waiting-tent a few minutes later," Viorst wrote, "when [Yousef Debri, one of Kaddafi's closest aides] returned. In an urgent tone he reported, 'The Leader wants me to remind you that he was not talking officially and that he was not stating policy. . . . He wants you to see the foreign minister for the government's position on Lockerbie.'"

It is tempting, although probably wishful thinking, to believe that Kaddafi might have been suffering from a guilty conscience. Then, just a few months after the verdict, according to a cable leaked to the German press, Kaddafi confessed to Michael Steiner, a top German diplomat, that Libya had been behind both the LaBelle disco and Lockerbie bombings. According to the cable, the Libyan leader stressed to Steiner that he had "abandoned terrorism and seeks the opportunity to make

Libya's new position known." Among those who were told of this remarkable conversation, German newspapers reported, were Chancellor Gerhard Schroder of Germany, President Bush, and Secretary of State Colin Powell.

Was Kaddafi sending a signal, hoping to gauge the reaction to a confession that would clear the way for his long-sought reconciliation with the West? Heads of state never apologize for their countries' crimes before the world. Had the remark not been leaked, it could have been seen as a private *mea culpa*, statesman to statesman, an admission that terrorism was a tactic he had employed in the past—but no longer. Whatever the case, Kaddafi's comments fell well short of what the families were seeking from him—or the United States could publicly accept.

As the families read the judges' long verdict, one finding stood out: that Megrahi, despite his denials, was a member of Libyan intelligence, "occupying posts of fairly high rank." This could prove crucial later in pinning the bombing on the regime, although Libya's lawyers certainly could be expected to argue that nothing conclusive had been shown. They were divided about whether it would have been better to see him executed. Helen Engelhardt later wrote in *TruthQuest,* the newsletter of Victims of Pan Am 103:

Seeing the two of them for the first time in July, separated only by a glass wall, I looked at their faces and felt absolutely nothing. Six months later, persuaded by the testimony that they were indeed responsible for assembling the bomb and starting it on its journey, I looked at them and felt that I could not bear it if they walked out of the courtroom free men. That is, indeed, what Fhimah did, but the pain of that moment was tempered by the satisfaction that Megrahi could not walk out with him.

I am, of course, reliving this today, because Timothy McVeigh was executed by our government this morning. . . . Several Oklahoma family members have commented that the only reason they wanted his life spared . . . was in order to keep alive the possibility of getting at the whole truth. I am relieved on behalf of our families that we will always have the possibility not of Megrahi's remorse (which frankly I don't need or even want) but of Megrahi's knowledge of the conspiracy finally being made public. There is always the chance that he will decide at some point to talk.

If Megrahi does someday break his silence, the families will be listening, and they will make sure the world hears it. And when Megrahi's sentence is up, sometime after April 5, 2019 (twenty years from the day he arrived in the Netherlands), those still alive will remind the world what he did, and on whose orders he did it. They will never give up.

Of course, the rest of the world may not want to know. Even many Americans would be content to relegate the bombing over Lockerbie to a footnote in history—those in government who resist making the connection between individual justice and the national interest, and the oilmen who will tell you, confidentially, that they do business every day with people worse than Kaddafi. In March 2000 the State Department announced it would reconsider the prohibition on Americans traveling to Libya, first imposed in 1981, and portrayed all through the 1990s, in press releases and speeches, as part of the sanctions meant to isolate and punish Kaddafi. Suddenly—less than two months before the trial was to start in Camp Zeist—the rationale for the passport ban shifted, and it was now described as a measure intended to protect American travelers. There was virtually no American tourism to Libya, so the prohibition affected, overwhelmingly, businessmen. Four American consular officials made a one-day trip to Libya to assess whether oil-industry executives would be safe there. The honest answer would undoubtedly be yes, since Libya's government was as eager to have the oil companies back as they were to resume pumping oil. Michael Sheehan, the State Department's counter-terrorism chief, alerted the families to the move in a conference call, after which the family members immediately began phoning newspapers and TV stations. Cummock reached Jim Hoagland of the *Washington Post,* who wrote a particularly scathing column about "the push to close the books on Pan Am 103." The sanctions should be reviewed and debated, he acknowledged;

instead the administration seemed to be pursuing "a stealth policy to bring change but not accept political responsibility for giving up on confronting the dictator who would have had to authorize Libyan participation in the bombing." As of the summer of 2001, fifteen months later, the State Department had taken no action on the travel ban— although it had, in the interim, decided to stop calling Libya, Iran, and their fellow outlaw nations "rogue states." The official State Department term now was "states of concern."

As soon as the trial was over, the families found themselves in a new fight over the Iran-Libya Sanctions Act—the law meant to punish foreign companies who invested in the two countries' oil industries. Business groups opposed to sanctions hoped to defeat it or scale it back when it came up for renewal later in 2001. In April the *Washington Post* reported that a draft of the administration's energy task force report called for "a comprehensive sanctions review," and "a partnership [with Congress] for sanctions reform." Vice President Cheney, who had acknowledged during the campaign that his former company, Halliburton Co., did business with Libya through its foreign subsidiaries, was the head of the task force. The family members (by now no longer a band of innocents camping out in congressional offices with photographs of their children, but a semipermanent presence in Washington, moving easily among the most powerful people in government) sprang into action. In May a delegation of family members met with Attorney General John Ashcroft to discuss future legal action and then headed for the Senate to press for an extension of ILSA. By that time, many of the families' original champions, including Dole, D'Amato, and Lautenberg, were no longer in the Senate. But they found new ones. Sen. Phil Gramm of Texas, chairman of the Senate Banking Committee, would play an important role in the sanctions issue, and as three families' members were leaving a meeting with Ted Kennedy's foreign-policy staff, they saw Gramm striding down a Senate corridor, trailing a camera crew and a pack of aides. In Helen Engelhardt's account in *TruthQuest*,

> George [Williams] recognized him instantly and joined the entourage. I ran after and caught up with them in the next corridor.

Senator Gramm had stopped walking and was listening to George explain how important his vote is for ILSA renewal. The Senator extended his right hand to George and said, "I'm on board," before he continued on his way. George and I just had time to thank him on behalf of Geordie and Tony.

Could the National Rifle Association have done a smoother job? The administration, backtracking, proposed leaving ILSA unchanged but renewing it for just two years instead of five. Congress wasn't interested. Bills for the full five-year extension picked up enough sponsors in both the House and Senate to assure passage. Shortly before the House bill was to come to a vote, Republicans attached an amendment requiring a "review" of the sanctions after eighteen months, but to all intents and purposes, the families had already won. Before the end of the summer, the bill passed in significantly stronger form with the threshold investment that would trigger sanctions substantially lowered.

The families were a new force in the world. To Kaddafi, they must have seemed powerless, virtually invisible—just like all the other grieving mothers and fathers, the sobbing widows left behind by the hooded gunmen of Northern Ireland, by the Serbian militias and the secret police who answered to Pinochet or to Castro. Treatises on international law still referred to them as "subjects." Even the UN Charter, for all its concern for the rights of "peoples," hardly recognized individuals, as Libya's representative reminded the Security Council during a debate over the sanctions. He pointed dramatically to the visitors' gallery and urged the chamber to take no notice of the rabble there. "You shouldn't be listening to those people!" he lectured. "They have no standing!"

But, armored with their invincible grief and outrage, they made their own standing, in defiance of a tradition of sovereign immunity dating back at least to the Treaty of Westphalia in 1648. Hugo Grotius, the Dutch scholar known as the father of international law, considered it a compact among "like-minded states." But that could no longer be said at the end of the twentieth century. With the amendment to the FSIA in 1996, the United States in effect had codified the distinction between two classes of countries: the majority, which retained sovereign immunity under the usual conditions, and a minority of state sponsors of terrorism, *as defined by the U.S. Department of State*, who could be sued for their wrongful acts in the courts of the United States.

In fact, this was a much bigger change than the families had ever sought, or perhaps needed. Early on, Gerson and Zaid had intended merely to carve out the narrowest possible exception to the rule of sovereign immunity, based on violations of *jus cogens*—the most outrageous abuses imaginable, acts falling on a spectrum that begins with bombing civilian airplanes and runs to biological warfare and genocide. They respected the State Department's unfettered right to conduct diplomacy, and the occasional need to deal with unsavory regimes for reasons of security or commerce. They never sought to achieve a new world order based on the rule of law; not only did they consider it futile, they never embraced it as an idea. And so they had drawn their *jus cogens* exception as narrowly as possible, hoping to win the government's support for their case against Libya. As it happened, the government opposed them, even though it would have been in the State Department's interest to help the *jus cogens* argument prevail. Instead the government got the FSIA amendment, which while limiting the number of countries that could be sued, opened the window for individuals to take on foreign governments for a much wider range of offenses, with consequences no one quite anticipated.

The reach of this new doctrine soon became clear. The first beneficiaries of the FSIA amendment weren't the Pan Am 103 families but the families of three of the four Brothers to the Rescue fliers who were shot down by Cuban MIGs in February 1996. This was a crime, certainly, but of a different order than bombing a 747 full of civilians. Brothers to the Rescue had a history of provoking the Cuban defense forces, and on an earlier mission had dropped anti-Castro leaflets from their planes right onto the streets of Havana. This case probably could not have been brought under a *jus cogens* standard. But Cuba is on the terrorism list—as long as Castro remains in power it is unlikely ever to be removed from the list—and so the case fell under the 1996 FSIA amendment. The families sued, and in December 1997, after Cuba failed to respond, a federal court in Miami awarded the relatives a total of $187.6 million.

Even the 1995 murder of Alisa Michelle Flatow might not have risen to the level of a *jus cogens* violation. Flatow, an American college student studying in Israel, had taken a side trip to Gaza and been killed in a suicide bombing of her bus, apparently by terrorists from the Palestinian Islamic Jihad. Her father hired Steven Perles—the lawyer who had represented Princz, the American survivor of Auschwitz—to sue Iran, the alleged government sponsor of Palestinian Islamic Jihad. After Iran failed to answer Flatow's complaint, a federal judge awarded the family a default judgment of $247 million.

The judgment was so high because it included punitive damages, which until then had never been awarded in suits against foreign governments. But Perles had persuaded Congress to pass yet another amendment to the FSIA, greatly expanding the scope of damages available to plaintiffs in terrorism cases. In court—the judge held a two-day trial, even though Iran never appeared—Perles brought in an expert on the Iranian economy to testify that the country spent approximately $75 million a year on terrorism. It even included a line item in its national budget for it. The judge, Royce C. Lamberth of District Court for the District of Columbia, ruled that punitive damages of three times that amount, or $225 million, would "ensure that the Islamic Republic of Iran will refrain from sponsoring such terrorist acts in the future." (The Palestinian Islamic Jihad did not appear to be chastened, however; they responded to the verdict by calling for more attacks on Israelis.)

Other victims of Middle East violence soon filed their own lawsuits—notably Joseph Cicippio, David Jacobsen, and Frank Reed, the Americans held hostage in Beirut by Iranian-backed Hezbollah guerrillas, who with their families were awarded a total of $65 million in compensatory damages. Terry Anderson, the American journalist held hostage by Hezbollah for six years, obtained a judgment of $340 million. In August 2001 Lamberth awarded the estate and family of another Lebanon hostage, the late Rev. Lawrence Jenco, a total of $314.6 million from Iran. Other suits were filed against Syria and Iraq. But then Flatow did something the U.S. government seemingly had not expected: he tried to collect his judgment. Iran, of course, was not about to pay up voluntarily, and it was futile to ask an Iranian court to enforce the judgment. So Flatow turned his attention to Iranian assets in the United States, including those frozen by the government after the Iranian revolution in 1979. But the American government frustrated his efforts to claim—or even to locate—those assets. Diplomatic property was untouchable, under every tenet of international law, and for good reason, as the State Department saw it: the United States has embassies around the world, too. But the government wouldn't even help Flatow claim commercial property. Frozen assets are, after all, assets; they are bargaining chips for the country that holds them. Iran held American assets, too, and the claims and counterclaims between the two countries had kept lawyers busy in The Hague for two decades.

So Flatow sought help from Congress. A bill was introduced to permit terrorism victims to collect against foreign assets held by the United States. Gerson, now Senior Fellow for International Law and Organizations at the Council on Foreign Relations in New York, testified for the bill, despite some reservations about whether the law had been stretched too far to cover some of the claims against Iran and Cuba. The victims had valid judgments which they were entitled to collect, he reminded the Senate Judiciary Committee. "National interests and a sense of national priorities are engaged when countries go to war against American citizens," he testified, and national interests and those of private citizens in such circumstances were intended to be merged, not left at odds with each other. Senior administration witnesses opposed the bill, claiming it would hinder America's ability to negotiate the resumption of normal relations with Cuba and Iran, should that day ever come. Then something interesting happened: the legislation, as it made its way through Congress, was changed to authorize the U.S. Treasury to pay off a portion of the judgments directly to the plaintiffs. The Treasury would then have to collect the money itself from the foreign governments. Only judgments already awarded against Iran and Cuba as of July 2000 were covered. In that form, with the support of the administration, it was passed and signed.

Gerson and his colleagues managed to get a statement into the *Congressional Record* indicating that it was the intent of Congress to cover future judgments against Libya as well—if they ever got one.

The administration portrayed this as a humanitarian gesture toward citizens thwarted in the pursuit of justice. But in fact it was as much a rear-guard action against empowering citizens to seek justice themselves. Even at the cost of hundreds of millions of dollars, the government was determined to keep control of the foreign assets and the bargaining power they represented. The law was painstakingly crafted so that it would not appear as if the taxpayers were actually footing the bill. But plenty of people suspected that would happen anyway—that when the United States and Iran finally normalized relations they would negotiate a settlement of the claims, in which the payment for Alisa Flatow's life and Terry Anderson's lost years would exist only as an accounting fiction. Daniel and Susan Cohen, forever on the alert against compromise, denounced the law in an op-ed article in the *New York Times*. If the government tried to pay them for their claim against Libya under the same terms, they announced, "we will not accept it."

The issue goes to the heart of what the families want, what kind of justice they seek and can realistically expect. Bruce Smith often said that the lawsuit against Pan Am was for money, and the suit against Libya was for justice. Pan Am, however negligent, did not place the bomb on the plane, did not intend for it to crash, and was itself a victim of Libya's criminal intentions. But the Cohens—who sued Pan Am eagerly but joined the suit against Libya only reluctantly, after railing against it for years as "blood money"—seemed to believe the opposite. In their view, Pan Am was a corporation, and money was its lifeblood. That the insurance companies fought so long and hard not to pay them was proof they were being hurt. Libya, on the other hand, was awash in oil money. Even a large punitive damage award would be small compared to the losses already inflicted by the UN Security Council sanctions. Suing Libya means accepting the possibility of settling with it. The judicial system is a forum for resolving disputes, not scoring political points. If you sue for $20 billion and the other side offers it, you have no choice but to accept, and the case is over. If your adversary offers something reasonably close, you are obligated to make a good-faith effort to negotiate a settlement—or run the risk that your suit will be dismissed.

The families are unlikely to ever get what they want most, to put Kaddafi behind bars. The difficulty is not with the evidence. Megrahi, a Libyan intelligence agent, has been convicted of murder, and under the law co-conspirators are equally guilty, as far up the chain of command as prosecutors dare to venture. Rather, the issue is the political will to pursue the evidence wherever it may lead. The record of Western governments on this score is not encouraging. The arrests of Augusto Pinochet of Chile and Slobodan Milosevic of Serbia merely show that sitting heads of state are never indicted, only those that have already been thrown out of power, and then only in the most extraordinary circumstances. The family members can only hope that someday the Libyan people will come to their senses and that Kaddafi will meet the fate of Milosevic. But short of a revolution, it is unrealistic to expect that Kaddafi will ever face justice from the defendants' dock.

That leaves the civil trial as the most promising avenue of justice, as the family members—slowly and grudgingly, in some cases—have come to acknowledge. Kaddafi could drag out the proceedings in the courts, perhaps for years. But if he is waiting for the family members to give up, he is waiting in vain. They will pursue him in the courts of America, and, if successful, around the world if necessary, wherever Libyan assets can be found and seized.

Or Libya could try to settle the case at any time. But Kaddafi will have to offer more than just money. The family members would insist that Libya accept responsibility for the bombing, which is also one of the conditions contained in the UN Security Council resolutions. Of course, any such statement, if it ever appears, would be negotiated word by word, by lawyers and diplomats skilled in the art of creative ambiguity, couched in language that will mean one thing to Americans and something else to Libyans reading it in Arabic.

Is it conceivable Kaddafi could express—or even feel—remorse over the bombing? Someone who could order the bombing of an air-

plane would seem to fit the description of a psychopath, who by definition is incapable of experiencing guilt. Certainly most family members
view him that way. They have said many times they are not interested
in his remorse or apologies, only in having him acknowledge his crimes
so the rest of the world can see him for the criminal he is. Strictly as a
theoretical exercise, though, if one could draft Kaddafi's *mea culpa*,
what might it say? Without implying that any of the family members
would put it this way, here is one possible version:

> *Yes, we bombed the airplane. We considered ourselves at war with the
> United States, a war we could never fight with conventional weapons
> and tactics, so we used what we had available to us. In what I imagined
> was a fight by the oppressed people of the world against the Western
> powers that dominated them, the deaths of a few hundred innocent peo-
> ple seemed acceptable.*
>
> *I was wrong. The evil I have wrought far outweighs any possible
> benefit to the cause I thought I was advancing. I have seen the parents
> whose children will never come home to them, the wives and husbands
> left alone, the children orphaned, and I am horrified and ashamed that I
> was the author of so much misery.*
>
> *I do not presume to ask for your forgiveness. You would never
> give it to me, nor should you. But I acknowledge that your strength,
> drawn from your love for your loved ones, has enabled you to fight
> me to this very day, to win from me this confession, this apology, this
> humiliation, so that others like me might stay their hand and ask
> themselves: Is there anything in the world worth having at the cost of
> so much pain?*

Each year the families gather at the cairn on the anniversary of the
bombing. The toll of time has begun to show. In earlier years, especially
when the president attended, these have been grand and solemn events,
but by the twelfth anniversary, in 2000, it had become a quieter and
more intimate occasion. The U.S. Army chaplain who led the service
counseled them to channel their grief into causes that would make the
world a better place. But, of course, they'd done that already. Since the
bombing, Lockerbie had dominated the family members' lives. George

Williams, retired from the Post Office, devoted himself almost totally to the Victims of Pan Am 103. Paul Hudson became head of ACAP, the aviation-safety organization he had consulted after the bombing; Bob Monetti left his engineering practice to become a consultant on aviation security. Victoria Cummock did her disaster work, gave speeches, sat on commissions. This one day, the anniversary of the bombing, was a time not for the living, but for the dead. Bob Monetti, who had succeeded Williams as head of the family group, addressed his son directly at the end of his talk: We are here for you, Rick, he said, and we will be here next year and every year, for as long as we live. And as the weak sun burnished the cold, rugged stones, they took turns reading out the 270 names of the victims, while a bell tolled with a dull thud, a minute apart, until they finished the roster. Gray clouds covered the face of the sun and the chill wind picked up. The families stood silently for a moment, holding on to the one thing Kaddafi couldn't take from them, their memories. Then they said their good-byes, and dispersed into the gathering dusk of the shortest day of the year.

The verdict in the criminal case revived the civil case from dormancy. Following the Flatow judgment, the plaintiffs had filed a motion with Platt to add punitive damages to their suit. One big advantage of punitive damages was that they would presumably be distributed in equal shares among the plaintiffs—unlike the damages received in the case against Pan Am. Libya deserves no less punishment for killing a college student than a businessman. The inequality of the Pan Am judgments—and the horror of the sessions with the insurance-company lawyers and magistrates—was something no one wanted to see repeated. In July, the plaintiffs' committee lawyers flew to Paris to begin their discovery process, taking depositions from a Libyan national produced by the defendants after Judge Platt threatened to enter a default judgment if they continued stalling discovery. Kaddafi still gave no indication that he was considering a settlement, although news stories from Libya suggested that he had accepted the inevitable and would begin serious negotiations after Megrahi exhausted his appeals. That could take until the end of the year. Spending a few days in Paris was fine with Rosenthal, but it added another sum to the already huge amount Sonnenschein had shelled out on the case. He had, of necessity, been counting the hours he'd spent on it, going back to Smith's original complaint. Gerson had long since lost track of how much of his own time he had invested in the case.

But he wasn't unhappy, and neither was Zaid or Duggan or Rosenthal. Reflecting on the case, he knew that they had accomplished a great deal, that they had in fact helped make history. They had originally sought only to chip a narrow exception into an anachronistic statute, but had been forced by circumstances to rewrite the black letter of the law. In forging a civil action against governments accused of terrorism, they had ushered in a whole new way of thinking about relations between individuals and states so that international justice would no longer be the exclusive province of governments.

And Gerson was proud that he had stuck by his client, Bruce Smith. Smith had had to declare bankruptcy, and when he became too old to pilot on an American carrier he had flown for a regional airline in Africa. When he left Camp Zeist, a few days after the start of the trial, he headed to Florida. His plan was to sail the Caribbean for six months before retiring to Bray, the English village where Ingrid's grave would be only a short walk through the fragrant woods. "The Libyans got the last twelve years of my life," he told Gerson. "I'm not going to give them the rest of it."

He paused.

"But I'm leaving a good suit and a couple of shirts in my son's house. Those are my shore clothes. If you need me for anything, just call."

Appendix

Cast of Characters

Key Family Members

Bert Ammerman—Brother of Thomas J. Ammerman; helped found Victims of Pan Am Flight 103.

Stephanie Bernstein—Wife of Michael, deputy director of Justice Department's Office of Special Investigations; family activist.

Daniel and Susan Cohen—Parents of Theodora and outspoken advocates.

Victoria Cummock—Wife of John Cummock; served as president of Families of Pan Am 103/Lockerbie and established liaison with Oklahoma families.

Helen Engelhardt—Wife of Anthony Hawkins; editor of family newsletter *TruthQuest*.

Paul and Eleanor Hudson—Parents of Melina. Paul was a co-founder of Victims of Pan Am 103/Lockerbie and then co-founded Families of Pan Am Flight 103/Lockerbie.

Peter and Suse Lowenstein—Parents of Alexander. Suse was the sculptor of the *Dark Elegy* figures.

Bob and Eileen Monetti—Parents of Rick. Bob served as president of Victims of Pan Am Flight 103.

Jack and Jane Schultz—Parents of Thomas. Jane was a leader of the effort to build the memorial cairn.

Bruce Smith—Husband of Ingrid; Pan Am captain who was first to initiate lawsuit against Libya.

Dr. James Swire—Father of Flora; head of the U.K. family group.

George and Judy Williams—Parents of George (Geordie). George served as president of Victims of Pan Am Flight 103.

Rosemary Wolfe—Stepmother of Miriam and president of Families of Pan Am 103/Lockerbie.

Lawyers Representing Families or Providing Support

Michel Baumeister—Aviation tort lawyer with Baumeister & Samuels.

Carol Elder Bruce—Represented Smith and others with Sonnenschein, Nath, and Rosenthal; former Justice Department prosecutor.

Frank Duggan—McLaughlin Commission family liaison. Later represented Williams and others.

Richard Emery—Civil rights lawyer who represented Hudson.

Allan Gerson—Attorney for Smith, Cummock, Hudson, and others; first to suggest possibility of successful suit for damages against Libya.

Frank Granito Jr.—Aviation tort lawyer with Speiser, Krause, Madole, Nolan & Granito.

Frank Granito III—Aviation tort lawyer with Speiser, Krause.

James Kreindler—With his father, Lee Kreindler, represented the majority of the Pan Am 103 families.

Lee S. Kreindler—Head of Kreindler & Kreindler, which represented the largest number of families against Pan Am and later against Libya; also served as chairman of the plaintiffs' committee.

Michael Reisman—Prominent international law scholar, Yale Law School, special counsel to Sonnenschein, Nath in briefs on behalf of *Smith et al.*

Doug Rosenthal—Lead lawyer for *Smith et al.* at Sonnenschein, Nath.

Timothy Russell—Attorney with Sonnenschein, Nath who presented oral arguments for *Smith et al.*

Doug Rutzen—Co-counsel with Doug Rosenthal who was active in amending 1976 Foreign Sovereign Immunities Act.

Mark Zaid—Co-counsel with Allan Gerson in initiating Smith suit; played prominent role in amending 1976 Foreign Sovereign Immunities Act.

Lawyers Representing Libya

John R. Bartels Jr.—Attorney, White Plains, New York; was second U.S. lawyer to represent Libya.

Daniel Grove—Partner in Chicago-based Keck, Mahin & Cate, which first represented Libya.

Robert C. Mirone—Attorney, Mirone and Shields, New York, who was third lawyer to represent Libya.

Bruno Ristau—Former head of Justice Department's Foreign Litigation Unit and expert on U.S. foreign sovereign immunities law who joined Libyan defense team.

Other Lawyers

Leonard Garment—Washington lawyer and former counsel to President Richard Nixon who represented Scott Nelson in seeking damages from Saudi Arabia for torture.

Steve Perles—Represented Hugo Princz in claims against Germany and Alisa Flatow family in claims against Iran.

Abraham Sofaer—Former federal judge, legal adviser to the State Department, and senior partner in Hughes Hubbard & Reed Washington office.

Judges and Judiciary

Guido Calabresi—Judge, U.S. Court of Appeals, Second Circuit; wrote opinion upholding constitutionality of the 1996 amendment to the 1976 Foreign Sovereign Immunities Act.

Jon O. Newman—Chief judge, U.S. Court of Appeals, Second Circuit; wrote opinion upholding denial of jurisdiction to sue Libya under the 1976 Foreign Sovereign Immunities Act.

Thomas Platt—Chief judge of the U.S. District Court for the Eastern District of New York in charge of the Libya civil suit.

Stanley Sporkin—Judge, U.S. District Court, District of Columbia, and former general counsel to the Central Intelligence Agency, who presided over the initial Smith complaint.

Ranald Sutherland—Chief judge, Camp Zeist criminal proceedings, who announced guilty verdict against Abdel Basset Ali Al-Megrahi.

Government

Madeleine K. Albright—Ambassador to the United Nations and later secretary of state who dealt with sanctions policy during the Clinton administration.

Robert Baer—Veteran CIA expert on counterterrorism who claimed that the role of Iran and others in the bombing was never fully investigated.

James Baker III—Secretary of state; joined Skinner and Thornburgh in opposing the creation of an independent commission to look into security lapses leading to the bombing of Pan Am 103.

William P. Barr—Acting attorney general at the time of the bombing.

Randy Beers—Senior National Security Council official, Bush and Clinton administrations, dealing with Pan Am 103 matters.

Sandy Berger—National security adviser to President Clinton.

John Bolton—Assistant secretary of state for international organizations, George Bush administration.

Richard Canas—National Security Council, liaison to family members, Clinton administration.

Vincent Cannistraro—CIA deputy chief of operations for Anti-Terrorism, 1988–1989.

Amb. Richard C. Clarke—Director, National Security Council Office on Counter-Terrorism, Bush, Clinton, and George W. Bush administrations.

Michael Kraft—Senior adviser, State Department Office of Counter-Terrorism.

Anthony Lake—National security adviser to President Clinton.

Ann McLaughlin—Former secretary of labor; chaired the McLaughlin Commission.

Amb. Ted McNamara—Coordinator for counterterrorism, State Department, George Bush and Clinton administrations.

John C. Metzler Jr.—Superintendent of Arlington National Cemetery who opposed and then supported construction of cairn at Arlington.

Robert S. Mueller III—Assistant attorney general, Criminal Division, U.S. Department of Justice in George Bush administration, subsequently FBI director designate.

Nicholas Rostow—General counsel to the National Security Council, George Bush administration.

Samuel Skinner—Secretary of transportation, George Bush administration.

Richard Thornburgh—Attorney general, George Bush administration.

Kathryn Turman—Deputy director, U.S. Justice Department Office of Victims of Crime.

Congress

Rep. Dante Fascell (D–Fla.)—Chairman of the House Committee on Foreign Affairs who extended first invitation to Victoria Cummock to testify before Congress.

Rep. Benjamin Gilman (R–N.Y.)—Chairman of the House International Relations Committee, who pressed for release of the Annan letter and later introduced legislation for extension of ILSA.

Rep. Henry Hyde (R–Ill.)—Chairman of the House Judiciary Committee, who oversaw passage of the 1996 Anti-Terrorism and Effective Death Penalty Act.

Senate

Sen. Alfonse D'Amato (R–N.Y.)—Served on President's Commission on Aviation Security and Terrorism.

Sen. Robert Dole (R–Kan.)—Republican leader instrumental in establishing the Aviation Safety Commission and in providing support to the families.

Sen. Orrin Hatch (R–Utah)—Introduced Comprehensive Terrorism Prevention Act of 1995.

Sen. Ted Kennedy (D–Mass.)—Early and sustained supporter of family groups.

Sen. Frank Lautenberg (D–N.J.)—Co-sponsor with Mitchell of bill for nine-member commission to investigate the downing of Pan Am 103.

Sen. George Mitchell (D–Maine)—Majority leader; instrumental in passage of Aviation Safety Commission.

Sen. Frank Murkowski (R–Alaska)—Sponsored bill supporting effort of Bruce Smith to raise the ceiling on federal antiterrorism reward program.

Sen. Arlen Specter (R–Penn.)—Championed torture victims protection in 1996 FSIA amendment.

Congressional Aides

Bob Carolla—Aide to Sen. Mitchell.

Richard A. Hertling—Minority chief counsel to Senate Subcommittee on the Constitution.

Randy Scheunemann—Top foreign policy aide to Sen. Dole.

Trina Vargo—Aide to Sen. Kennedy.

Sharon Waxman—Aide to Sen. Lautenberg and later Sen. Kennedy.

Jim Whittinghill—Aide to Sen. Dole.

Media

Jim Hoagland—Pulitzer Prize–winning *Washington Post* columnist who broke story on Sofaer-Libya retainer.

Middle East Figures Associated with Pan Am 103 Bombing

Al Amin Khalifa Fhimah—Libyan Arab Airways employee who was indicted but not convicted for bombing.

Ahmed Jibril—Head of PFLP–GC, terrorist Palestinian faction implicated in Autumn Leaves Operation.

Muammar Kaddafi—"The Leader," ruler of Libya.

Abdel Basset Ali Al-Megrahi—Libyan intelligence operative convicted of bombing by Scottish court in the Netherlands.

Abdullah Senoussi—Brother-in-law to Kaddafi; indicted by France for 1989 UTA bombing.

Mohamed Abu Talb—PFLP–GC operative who visited Malta prior to bombing.

Oklahoma Families and Supporters

Gerald Adams—Aide to Attorney General Drew Edmondson.

Drew Edmondson—Attorney general of Oklahoma who was key advocate of 1996 Anti-Terrorism and Effective Death Penalty Act.

Diane Leonard—Wife of Donald and leader of Oklahoma families who joined forces with Pan Am 103 families.

Glenn Seidl—Husband of Kathy Lynn, who spurred efforts at *habeas corpus* reform.

Richard Wintory—Aide to Attorney General Drew Edmondson.

Index